George "Mooney" Gibson

10-23
29 30
34-43
45
56
59
67-69
71
77
81
104
112
120
146
150-151
160
162
174
188
191
204
217
220

George "Mooney" Gibson

Canadian Catcher for the Deadball Era Pirates

RICHARD C. ARMSTRONG *and*
MARTIN HEALY, JR.

McFarland & Company, Inc., Publishers
Jefferson, North Carolina

ISBN (print) 978-1-4766-7969-3
ISBN (ebook) 978-1-4766-3858-4

LIBRARY OF CONGRESS AND BRITISH LIBRARY
CATALOGUING DATA ARE AVAILABLE

Library of Congress Control Number 2020008063

Front cover: Pittsburgh catcher George Gibson on a 1911
Turkey Red Cigarettes baseball card (Library of Congress)

Printed in the United States of America

*McFarland & Company, Inc., Publishers
Box 611, Jefferson, North Carolina 28640
www.mcfarlandpub.com*

Table of Contents

Acknowledgments

We had no idea writing a book required so much effort. In the three years it took to research and produce our initial manuscript, we made dozens of trips to libraries and museums, traded hundreds of emails and spent thousands of hours scouring newspapers, books and census information to piece together the story. None of this would have been possible without the support of our families. Thank you for understanding our need to write this book, and for offering ideas, suggestions and encouragement.

Writing this book also presented an opportunity to meet some of George Gibson's family. We owe a huge thank you to Scott Crawford, the Director of Operations at the Canadian Baseball Hall of Fame, for introducing us to David Gibson, George's great-grandson. David introduced us to George's great-niece Julie Anne Baskette, who in turn introduced us to George's granddaughter Bucky Smith. Thank you to all three of you for being so welcoming, and sharing your own personal family stories and mementos.

We would also like to extend a special thanks to Ted Golden. Ted took on the laborious task of performing a complete copy edit of our initial manuscript. A baseball enthusiast himself, Ted ensured content accuracy, highlighted any inconsistencies and called attention to manuscript repetitiveness. He also took great care and attention to our grammar; especially important as we are first-time authors. Ted corrected errors in structure, voice and tense, and also amended general mechanical gaffes. We are extremely grateful for his efforts in assisting us with chronicling George Gibson's story. Thank you, Teditor!

Of course, the manuscript itself would not have been possible without the help of countless others. So many individuals generously contributed their time, knowledge and expertise in helping us bring this story together. We are especially grateful to the following individuals:

Cassidy Lent—Reference Librarian, National Baseball Hall of Fame
Matt Rothenberg—Manager, Giamatti Research Center, National
 Baseball Hall of Fame
Arthur McClelland—London Room, London Public Library
Jeff Causier—London Room, London Public Library
Leslie Thomas-Smith—Archives & Collections, University of
 Western Ontario
Deborah Quaile—Guelph Public Library
Ken Maguire—Camp Zachary Taylor Historical Society
Trey Strecker—SABR Essay Writer
Brian "Chip" Martin—SABR Member, Baseball Historian, Author
Linda Parker—*Pittsburgh Post-Gazette*
Bill Deane—SABR member, Chapter: NY-Cliff Kachline
Sean Lahman—SABR member, Chapter: NY-Luke Easter
Al Arrighi—SABR member, Chapter: MD-Babe Ruth
Brian Hinkley—Artist/Photo Restoration, Brian's Gallery
Chris Wiersbicki—Net54 Baseball, Member
Helena Deng—Manager, Exhibits & Collections, Canadian Sports
 Hall of Fame
Jean Hung—Archives & Collections, University of Western Ontario
Amanda Oliver—Archivist, University of Western Ontario
Carla Reczek—Librarian III Specialist, Digital Lab, Detroit
 Public Library
Tamara Monster—Library Assistant, Mills Library, McMaster
 University
Stephen Harding—London Historian, Friends of Labatt Park
Chris Meiman—Curator/Exhibits Director, Louisville Slugger
 Museum & Factory
Katie Levi—Chicago History Museum
Steve Lansdale—Public Relations, Heritage Auctions
Charlie Pardue—Acquisitions Editor, McFarland & Co., Inc.
Natalie Foreman—Associate Editor, McFarland & Co., Inc.
Lisa Camp—Executive Editor, McFarland & Co., Inc.

Preface

George Gibson was a man of many monikers: Moon or Mooney; Hack or Hackenschmidt; Gib or Gibby. He was also a man of many baseball talents. Throughout his life, George spent time as a baseball player, coach, scout and manager. During the quarter century between 1909 and 1934, Gibby was one of baseball's great minds, and it brought him many accolades. George was named Canada's top baseball player of the first half of the 20th century in 1950, and was inducted into the Canadian Sports Hall of Fame in 1958. He was posthumously inducted into the Canadian Baseball Hall of Fame (1987) and the London Sports Hall of Fame (2002). Despite these honors, the name George Gibson is consistently forgotten among baseball fans. Only some of the most astute proprietors of Canadian baseball history remember his contributions to the game. Ferguson Jenkins, Larry Walker and Joey Votto garner much recognition as Canada's all-time best baseball players, and rightly so, but in error we forget our baseball heroes of years gone by. In this baseball biography, we attempt to remember a Canadian and baseball superstar, champion and luminary.

From the Hand and Mind of Martin Healy, Jr.

Why George Gibson? It was a lifelong journey of baseball fandom that led me to George.

As a youngster, I tried my hand at America's (and for me, Canada's) favorite pastime, but quickly realized I did not possess the tools necessary to be proficient at the sport. I was a skinny kid and had a fairly weak throwing arm, so I attributed my lack of ability to my slight stature and became content to appreciate baseball from a fan's perspective. Now, seeing players such as Randy Johnson or Chris Sale excel at the highest levels despite their rather thin frames, I finally realize and accept the truth of my baseball inefficiencies: I did not put in the effort to perfect the skills which would have kept me in

1

baseball, the game I love most. I have since been able to register that any man, regardless of stature, no matter how fat or thin, short or tall, can excel in baseball, and that's what makes the game relatable and easily enjoyed by many.

I remember visiting Exhibition Stadium as a youth and watching Blue Jay heroes George Bell and Tony Fernandez, and even traveling from Southern Ontario to Montreal to attend an Expos game at the Big O. But I think my favorite part of being a baseball fan as a kid was reading the stats on the back of baseball cards and checking game box scores in my hometown daily paper, *The Hamilton Spectator*. Hamilton baseball was also popular in my youth, and just as I was entering my teenage years and the Blue Jays were in the midst of back-to-back World Series championships, the National League's St. Louis Cardinals relocated their short season A ball team, which played in the New York–Penn League, to less than one mile away from my home. The Hamilton Redbirds would play five seasons in my hometown from 1988 to 1992, and I was sure to be sitting in the grandstand on the Beaver Lumber benches just as often as my dad would take me to Bernie Arbour Memorial Stadium.

Fast-forward almost twenty years, and I found myself with serious health problems after suffering a heart attack. I was a heavy smoker throughout my twenties, and really did not take care of myself in the way a young adult should; I paid for it. So a lifestyle change for the better was in the cards, and I threw away most of my vices, including smoking and drinking alcohol. (Still can't kick the coffee habit, though.) All this took place during my late twenties and early thirties, so luckily, I had no real responsibilities in terms of family or dependents. Not surprisingly, I found myself a lot lonelier as old friends were still in a place I did not want to be. The boredom and loneliness led me back to a place of my youth, Bernie Arbour Stadium, where the Redbirds were long gone, but birds of another feather were ready to give Hamilton baseball fans great entertainment and a hometown team to cheer for.

The Hamilton Cardinals play in the Intercounty Baseball League based in Southern Ontario. The league has an impressive alumnus of Canadian players including the great Fergie Jenkins; two London, Ontario–born greats in Oscar Judd and Frank Colman; and MLB stars of today, moustache aficionado John Axford and Captain Canada, Pete Orr. The Cardinals played most of their home matches on either Friday nights or Sunday afternoons when I first started attending games regularly. Watching the club became a suitable habit and I even began following the team on the road when life would allow. One weekend I decided to follow the club southwest down the 401 highway to a game in London, Ontario, where the Cardinals would face the Majors, a top team in the league. It would be my first time at the historic Labatt Park, and I was amazed at the beauty of the grounds upon my arrival. I was sure to get there early so I could scope out the place and find a good spot to watch the ball game, and really, just soak in the atmosphere. (City of London baseball rooters are "FAN"-tastic!) While I was giving myself a personal tour of the facility, I came across a plaque on the wall commemorating a historic baseball player named George Gibson. Intrigued to the reason this player was awarded a memorial on the wall of the park, I quickly pulled out a pen, jotted his name on my ticket stub and proceeded to watch the game without giving the name George Gibson another thought.

A few days later, I pulled the stub from my pocket before doing laundry and remembered I wanted to throw George Gibson's name into a search engine to see what came up. Of course, Gibson's Wikipedia page was the first web page listed and I thought it as good a place as any to get a quick synopsis on the life of my subject of research. The page stated that Gibson spent a lifetime in baseball, as a player, coach, scout and manager, while also being a World Series champion, a member of the Canadian Sports Hall of Fame and the Canadian Baseball Hall of Fame. He was also named Canada's top baseball player of the first half of the 20th century. Before reading Gibson's Wikipedia page, I knew next to nothing about baseball during the deadball era, in which George played, but I had heard something about the great Ty Cobb, who the Wikipedia write up explained had been held under control on the base paths by Gibson during the 1909 World Series. This had me amazed, and somewhat ashamed to call myself a Canadian baseball fan, not knowing of this man who should be as big of a Canadian sports icon as hockey's Gordie Howe, in my opinion. I decided to do further research on Gibson, who was born just down the road from me in London, Ontario.

I am also a collector. I had always collected Toronto Blue Jay cards, and cards of Canadian-born players, with most being the common Topps-type card that we all collected when we were young. I never even considered vintage baseball cards, as spending hundreds of dollars on a old piece of paper seemed a poor investment. But shortly after I discovered Gibson, I did an eBay search and was surprised with what I found. There were many cards featuring Gibson, which I later learned were used as advertisements for tobacco and candy during the time he played. I never dreamed I would spend a hundred dollars on a single baseball card, but curiosity got the better of me and I purchased Gibson's T206 card from a dealer on eBay. When the card arrived, I was almost dumbfounded how this 100-year-old piece of paper was in such great shape, and perhaps because of my slight OCD, I became obsessed with finding rare George Gibson baseball cards. This obsession led me to a community of like-minded vintage card collectors on an online forum called Net54baseball.com. The forum was a great resource for my collection and put me in contact with many turn of the century baseball card collectors and historians. After a few months of being a member of the forum, I met this fellow, Richard, who coincidentally was also amassing a George Gibson card collection. From there on, Richard and I agreed to share our research and collaborate on accumulating as much information as we could on Gibson, Canada's forgotten baseball icon.

From the Hand and Mind of Richard C. Armstrong

When I was a kid, I hated reading. Just hated it. To me, reading meant sitting there, doing nothing. When faced with the option of reading or being outside, in just about any weather, there really was no question. On the days when being outside wasn't an option, shuffling through baseball cards, or, later, playing video games, was my preference.

But my mom always encouraged reading. As a kid, I always just figured she encouraged it because she enjoyed it. Now that I'm an adult, with a son of my own, I realize she really was trying to stress the importance of literacy. Of course, it's not lost on me that getting us kids to sit down and read also got us to be quiet. When I finally did give in and read, it was always about baseball. Baseball magazines, books of baseball statistics and records and, once in a while, a baseball biography. I didn't read to get lost in a story. I read to learn facts. I wanted to know about the history of baseball. I still do.

The baseball side of my brain, actually my love of sports in general, was fostered by my dad. My earliest memories are of him teaching my brother and me the game in the backyard of our childhood home. It was there that we learned to throw, catch and hit. And despite often working multiple jobs, he always had time for a game of catch. On any given day, you could find us playing some sport, but mostly, it was baseball. Eventually, we outgrew that backyard and took our games elsewhere, and involved kids from the neighborhood. If we had enough guys, we'd venture to a local park or school to play. But most of the time, there were only two or three of us. On those days we'd play on the streets in front of our houses. A game we called "hitting them up the street," because that's literally what we did. The fielders would position themselves a couple hundred feet up the hill, ready to catch a pop fly, and the batter, perched at the bottom of the hill, at a T-intersection, would "monkey hit" a tennis ball. Three outs, and it was the next guy's turn to bat. Hit a house or car, or break a window, and that was game for a few days until we worked up the nerve to return. We played this game every chance we got, and for hours on end.

When I was thirteen, my dad took a new job and the family moved from the city onto a small hobby farm in rural Ontario. Having more room meant more room for me and my brother to play, and less risk of hitting cars or breaking windows. Trust me, we still did both, but with less frequency. Eventually, we outgrew the game, though. As we got bigger and stronger and better at hitting, it became impractical to play with only two people. This happened right about the time high school started, though, and other things took our interests, with baseball falling to the wayside.

Fast-forward to 2002, and I was on a university work term, living alone in the middle of Saskatchewan, in the winter. On the days that it was too cold to go outside, which was most of them that time of year, I still refused to read. It would have been a perfect opportunity to pick up a book, because I needed to get lost in a story. At the time, my mom was battling lung cancer. It was a fight she would lose that Spring, but at only 21 years old, I wasn't ready to come to terms with it. I didn't realize it then, but I can admit it now. I had started following baseball again, about a year earlier, and now that I think about it, that was probably me looking for a distraction. My wife, Sarah (then my girlfriend), clearly had a different perspective; perhaps she could see that I was lost. She sent me a book, out of the blue, thinking I might find it interesting. It wasn't a baseball book. It wasn't even a sports book. It was *The Ingenuity Gap*, by Thomas Homer-Dixon. I have no idea where she found this book, or why she sent it, but it blew my mind. I couldn't put it down. For the first time in my life, I was reading a book because I wanted to, and I enjoyed it. It helped me relax. Eventually, the idea that reading could be enjoyable and baseball got intertwined. I've been reading about the history of baseball—and enjoying it—ever since.

Around 2005, I picked up a copy of *The Glory of Their Times*, by Lawrence Ritter. The book is a fascinating compilation of interviews that Lawrence Ritter conducted with old-time baseball players. The book was originally published in 1966, but as luck would have it, I unknowingly bought the re-released 1984 edition. This is significant, because the 1984 edition contains an additional four interviews not released in 1966. George Gibson was one of those interviews. To read that a Canadian had starred in Pittsburgh in the early part of the 20th century and counted men like Honus Wagner among his friends was intriguing. I set out to find a biography about George Gibson, only to learn that one didn't exist.

In 2011, when my son was born, I found myself awake at night a lot. Not tired enough to sleep, but too tired to do anything overly involved, I decided to try to use that time to start researching to see if there was enough material to write a book on George Gibson. Within a year, I had exhausted every free resource I could access from home. I had a sense that there was enough material to write a book, but I was still lacking a lot. And then Martin came along.

Like Marty, I'm a baseball card collector. I appreciate old and obscure baseball cards from the early 1900s. I focus my collection on George Gibson. It was this mutual interest that made Marty contact me through the forum Net54baseball.com. We'd traded many messages about various baseball card issues and topics, and then one day, Marty asked if I felt there was enough out there to write a book about George Gibson. At this point, my research had gone stagnant, but that message instantly surged it back to life. I couldn't respond fast enough to share that I felt there was, and to ask about collaborating on just such a project. We've been gathering and sharing research ever since, and hope that you get as much enjoyment out of reading about George Gibson as we have out of writing about the Canadian baseball legend.

Introduction

In the late 19th century, the sport of baseball was quickly becoming America's favorite pastime, surpassing the popular English game of cricket as the most enjoyed bat and ball game on this side of the Atlantic Ocean. Crowds gathered at fields to watch young men compete in a game of accuracy and coordination. Everyone wanted to play. Towns, clubs, church groups, schools and families all put together teams to show off their skills.

Larger cities recruited players for traveling teams. The star players hailed from all over the Eastern United States. Hall of Famer Cap Anson was an Iowa boy who played most of his career in Chicago. William "Buck" Ewing was born in Hoagland, Ohio, and made his way to stardom in New York City. Michael "King" Kelly was born in Troy, New York, and later became a hero in both Chicago and Boston. The most traveled of all the stars of the day was Jack Glasscock, who dominated at shortstop for eight different teams. Although most players had their start in the United States, soon Canadian players started to draw the attention of the traveling clubs south of the border.

Bob "The Magnet" Addy, born in Port Hope, Ontario, holds the distinction of being the first Canadian born baseball player to don a major league uniform. On May 6th, 1871, at age 29, Addy took the field at second base for the Rockford Forest Citys of the National Association. The Magnet played parts of six big league seasons and is credited with the invention of the slide into bases. Eight years later, William "Silver Bill" Phillips, born in Saint John, New Brunswick, was the fourth Canadian-born player to suit up in the Major Leagues. In 1879, the Cleveland Blues of the National League were in need of a first baseman and found Bill playing for an independent club in their own city. Silver Bill's career spanned ten seasons, playing six for the Blues before transferring to the American Association in 1885 to play for the Brooklyn Grays.[1] Between 1879 and 1900, a total of 54 Canadian-born players appeared in major-league games. Most had just a touch at the big leagues, lasting from a few games to a couple of years, but there were exceptions. Brothers Arthur and John Irwin of Toronto had careers of fourteen and eight years, respectively. Charles "Pop" Smith of Digby, Nova Scotia, played twelve years, and George Wood of Pownal, Prince Edward Island, kicked around the big leagues for thirteen seasons.[2] The most successful Canadian player of the 19th century, without a doubt, was James "Tip" O'Neill.

James Edward "Tip" O'Neill was born in 1858 in the small Southwestern Ontario town of Springfield. A solid defensive player and even better batsman, O'Neill played ten seasons in the major leagues as an outfielder. While Tip was with the St. Louis Browns, he enjoyed the most success of his career. O'Neill was the American Association batting champion with St. Louis for two consecutive years in 1887 and 1888. In 1887, O'Neill led the league with a .435 batting average, 14 home runs and 123 runs batted in, making him just the second player in history to win the fabled Triple Crown. O'Neill's dominance during this era inspired the migration of Canadians to the major leagues at the turn of the 20th century.[3]

Canadians were anxious to show that they were every bit as capable on the field as their American counterparts. As the 1900s came, more and more of them yearned to prove their abilities south of the border. Just as the call to play professional baseball inspired Americans to relocate and find success hundreds of miles from their homes, so too did it inspire Canadians from nearly every province. Ontario produced the largest number of players, likely because of its population. Some of the best included Jack Graney, Bunk Congalton, Roy "Doc" Miller, Bill O'Hara and Win Kellum. New Brunswickers Art McGovern and Bill O'Neill played on big-league fields along with their Maritime counterparts, Fred Lake and Shorty Dee, who both called Nova Scotia home. Quebec was represented by Ed Wingo and Pete LaPine. Western Canada was producing big-league ball players too. Bert Sincock got his start in British Columbia, and New York Yankee scuff ball pitcher Russ Ford was born in Manitoba. All these men proved that Canadians had the stuff to play baseball in this era where speed, toughness, great pitching and defense were at the forefront. Canadians live in a harsh Northern climate, something their Southern counterparts don't have to deal with. Dealing with nature's unpredictability gives a Canadian player a special type of physical and mental toughness. The kind of toughness which is attributed to an exceptional baseball catcher. In the deadball era (the time between 1900 and 1919, where the games were often low scoring and few home runs were hit), Canadians were ever-present behind major-league plates.

The first Canadian to make the big leagues as a catcher in the deadball era was John "Larry" McLean. McLean was born in Fredericton, New Brunswick, on July 18, 1881. He started his baseball career in the province he was born, having played for the Saint John Roses and the Fredericton Tartars. McLean was an enormous man for the time, standing six foot five inches tall and weighing 230 pounds. Having men that big behind the bat was highly sought after, because they provided large targets for pitchers and could prevent men from scoring. The Boston Red Sox came calling, and on April 26, 1901, McLean made his big-league debut. Although he played decently, there was not enough playing time for him, and he was sent back to the Maritimes to play for the Halifax Resolutes. Over the next few seasons Larry bounced around the baseball world, and, after brief stints in the big leagues with Chicago and St. Louis, he finally got his chance to be a mainstay as catcher when he settled in with the Cincinnati Reds for the 1907 season. McLean played his best years with the Reds. After seven seasons in Cincinnati, Larry caught on with New York Giants. In 1913, he helped them win the National League pennant. The Giants were not so fortunate in the World Series, however, going down at the hands of the Philadelphia Athletics. McLean played with the Giants until the end of the 1915 season, and then left the game for good.[4]

Mclean had problems off the field. He struggled with alcohol abuse throughout his life, and it eventually led to his demise. On March 24, 1921, McLean was drinking heavily at a Boston saloon. He got into an argument with the bartender. Larry attempted to go after the sud slinger but it was a bad mistake. He was shot in the chest and died. Despite his untimely end, Larry McLean's toughness afforded him a lengthy and fruitful career in baseball, and he will always be remembered as the big Canadian who could throw and block with the best of them.[5]

Another Canadian had a lengthy career as a backstop in the deadball era. Tom Daly, a native of St. John, New Brunswick, played until he was 40 years old. Tom made his major-league debut in September of 1913. He served as the backup catcher for the White Sox and Cubs of Chicago between 1913 and 1921. In 1918 Daly helped the Cubs win the National League pennant.[6]

After the 1921 season, Daly headed west to the Pacific Coast League, where he drew more playing time. Daly spent four seasons in the PCL, playing for three different teams: the Los Angeles Angels, the Portland Beavers and the Seattle Indians. For 1926, he trav-

Tom Daly, born December 12, 1891, in Saint John, New Brunswick, Canada, is pictured here circa 1919 while a member of the Chicago Cubs (Healy Collection).

eled back east, signing a contract with the International League team in New Jersey, the Jersey City Skeeters. He spent seven years in the IL, three with the aforementioned Skeeters, two with the Montreal Royals and two with the Toronto Maple Leafs. After the 1932 season, Daly retired from baseball. He wouldn't be out of the game for long.[7]

Daly served as a coach for the Boston Red Sox from 1933 until 1946. Daly's fourteen consecutive seasons coaching for the Red Sox is still a club record. The Boston fans loved Daly as a coach. When he died of cancer in 1946, the Boston papers reported, "No player in the history of Boston baseball was ever held in higher esteem by his associates than Tom Daly, Red Sox coach and scout, who died here today. Where baseball continues, particularly in Boston, the name Tom Daly will be revered not only as a great player, scout and coach, but one whose love of the game was something sacred."[8]

Marines are tough. Jay Justin "Nig" Clarke was a marine. Born in 1882 in Amherstburg, Ontario, Nig Clarke spent his youth on both sides of the border. He migrated between Windsor and Detroit until he made his professional debut with Corsicana of the Texas League in 1902. Clarke quickly moved on to the Southern League and caught for Little Rock in 1903 and Atlanta in 1904. The Cleveland Naps of the American League liked what they saw in Nig and purchased his contract from Atlanta after the 1904 season. Clarke launched his big-league career on April 25, 1905.[9]

Nig paid his dues in the backup role for a few seasons with the Cleveland club. His persistence and patience paid off, and in 1907, he was awarded the starting catcher position. Clarke was a mainstay behind the plate for the next three seasons. By the end of the 1910 season Nig was getting less playing time with Cleveland. It was time to move on.

In 1911 Clarke had a brief stint with the St. Louis Browns before he hooked on with the Indianapolis Indians of the American Association. He played so well there that he garnered interest from the San Francisco Seals of the Pacific Coast League. They worked out a trade and Nig went west. Clarke started behind the plate for the Seals until the end of the 1915 season. He scrambled around the minor leagues for the next few years prior to enlisting in the United States military.

On August 17, 1917, Nig Clarke joined the U.S. Marine Corps. It was nearing the end of World War I. Clarke saw action in France. He was stationed at the city of Brest. Clarke was noted as saying that he wished he had "joined the Marine Corps twelve years ago and never played ball."[10] That may have been his sentiment, but when the war ended, he was discharged and went right back to the diamond.

Upon his return to North America, Clarke had stops in many cities. He protected the plate in Philadelphia, Pittsburgh, Reading and Toledo as well as with many other teams. Even late in his career, Nig was getting accolades. In

1925 *The Sporting News* wrote, "Nig Clarke not only led the league with the bat and the mitt and the arm, he was the very picture of a baseball player."[11] Clarke hung up the big mitt after the 1927 season, ending a twenty-five-year professional baseball career. He rejoined the marines for a while before retiring to his home in Michigan.[12]

There are many different ways to gain toughness. One way is to endure a long working life, as did Tom Daly. Another is to put yourself in the position to become tough like Nig Clarke did when he joined the marines. And some men are just born tough. Larry McLean's natural size made him a force to reckon with. But sometimes, an accident in life makes a man become rugged and resilient. Jimmy Archer had just such an accident.

As a young man, Jimmy Archer was working at a barrel factory in Toronto. While working at the facility, Archer tumbled into a vat of boiling sap. He was hospitalized for many months. Doctors did their best to repair his damaged right arm, but the tendon had shrunk because of severe burns. Archer used his toughness to work his arm back into playing condition. As the arm healed, Jimmy noticed he was left with a unique strength. He stated throughout his career that the way his injury healed gave him the remarkable ability to throw quickly and accurately from a squatting position.[13]

Although born at Dublin, Ireland, in May of 1883, Jimmy Archer was a Canadian through and through. His family moved to Montreal when he was a newborn and then to Toronto by the time he turned three. Jimmy picked up his baseball knowhow playing in the Toronto City League and also for the prestigious St. Michael's College team.

Archer got his first crack at professional baseball in 1903 when a friend asked him to join him in Fargo, North Dakota. His time there was short, because a team stationed in Manitoba offered him more money to return to his home country to play. Jimmy played in Canada for the rest of the 1903 season. In 1904 Archer joined the Boone B.B.C. of the Iowa State League and played very well. Major-league clubs took notice and the Pittsburgh Pirates called him up for a September look. He appeared in seven games with the Bucs.

In 1905, the Pirates sent Archer to Atlanta of the Southern Association to refine his skills. Two seasons later, he left for a second chance at the major leagues with the Detroit Tigers. Manager Hughie Jennings of the Tigers wasn't a fan of Archer's practice of throwing while still squatting, so Jimmy was relegated to third string backstop. He was released at the end of that season.

In 1908, Archer was in Buffalo catching for the Bisons. On an off day, while heading east, the Chicago Cubs stopped to watch a game in Buffalo. Cubs' manager Frank Chance was very impressed with Archer's play and in 1909, when Johnny Kling held out over a contract dispute, Chance signed Archer. Jimmy played eighty games with the Cubs in 1909. Before the 1910 season, Johnny Kling resigned with the Cubs. Frank Chance did not want to lose Archer so he had him split time between first base and handling the catching duties. The great catching tandem of Archer and Kling helped the Cubs win the National League pennant in 1910. Jimmy played so well in the 1910 season that Chicago decided to trade Kling to Boston, and have him take over the starting duties for the following year.

Archer caught for the Cubs until the end of the 1916 season. A contract dispute had him out for most of 1917, and he made just one more attempt at pro ball the following season. He played for Pittsburgh, Brooklyn and Cincinnati in 1918, all in a backup role. When the season ended, Jimmy retired, feeling that his hands could no longer take the beating that a catcher had to take. Making the big league after an accident like what Archer suffered shows great resilience and perseverance, and Jimmy didn't just make it. He excelled at it.[14]

Canadian backstops were at the top of the crop. McLean, Archer, Daly and Clarke all showed the world that Canadians could play the game in the era of defense, speed and toughness. But there was one more, the greatest Canadian backstop ever...

1

Set the Tone

"Yer Out!" ardently proclaimed American League umpire Billy "Big Boy Blue" Evans. Evans, also nicknamed "The Boy Umpire," was overseeing second base in game seven of the 1909 World Series. The series was a battle between the National League pennant–winning Pittsburgh Pirates and the American League flag–capturing Tigers of Detroit. The man out at second was the Tigers fleet of foot shortstop, Donie Bush.

Bush only charitably reached base as a result of being hit with an errant throw by Pirates starting pitcher Charles "Babe" Adams. With two out in the first frame, and very competent batsman Sam Crawford at the plate, Bush took it upon himself to try and set the tone of the game for his Tigers in this series-deciding match. Bush attempted to swipe the midway sack and took off on the next Adams pitch. Pittsburgh second baseman John "Dots" Miller scurried to cover the bag. The Pirates catcher caught and threw the ball down to second without error, and Dots put down an easy tag on the eager Bush. Now, the tone was set. Only not in the way Bush had imagined. He dared to challenge the great pegging arm of the Pirates' backstop George "Mooney" Gibson.

Before the start of the sixth World Series championship, most of the press was fixated on which star player would be the determining factor in his club's chances of winning the title of 1909. Tyrus Cobb of the Detroit club was the champion batter of the American League, and Honus Wagner of the Pirates held that same distinction in the rival National League. Naturally, these future Hall of Fame players were the obvious choice of who would impact the series in the greatest way.

Wagner was by far the Pittsburgh club's leader. Honus had a notable 1909 season. His .339 batting average put him over the .330 mark for the eighth consecutive season. While down from a remarkable .354 the year prior, Wagner still captured the senior circuit batting crown. He made up for the lower batting average by recording an on base percentage of .420, helped by a keen batting eye, as he walked sixty-six times during the season.

Wagner also led the National League in runs batted in with one hundred, showing his elite hitting skills under the pressure of batting with runners on base. Honus was also no slouch on the base paths. He swiped thirty-five bags throughout the 1909 season, which was near the top of the league in the stolen base category. This made him a considerable threat to run at any time in the World Series.

Meanwhile in the Tigers' dugout, Ty Cobb could also handle himself on the base paths. He easily led the American League with seventy-six stolen bases during the 1909 season. He terrorized junior circuit catchers all year long, with only two other American League players even close to Cobb in swiped pillows. Philadelphia Athletics second baseman Eddie Collins confiscated sixty-seven bags for the A's, while Cobb's Tigers teammate Donie Bush stole fifty-three in the year. No other American League player had half of the stolen bases Cobb did in '09. The Tigers as a whole stole 285 bases in the season, dwarfing the Pirates' total of 171. This alone made Detroit the favorite in 1909.

Cobb was also the top batter in both leagues combined. At the age of 22, and in his fourth full season, Cobb destroyed American League pitching to the tune of a .377 batting average. He drove in 107 runs and led the league in home runs with nine, on his way to winning only the second Triple Crown in American League history. Cobb also had a fitting complement of teammates to help him achieve his World Series goal. Along with Crawford and Bush, Cobb shared the field with other Tigers mainstays such as Claude Rossman and Matty McIntyre. All these Detroit dust dwellers were out for redemption after losing the World Series in '07 and '08 to the Chicago Cubs. Because of this experience, the Detroit club had another reason to be called favorites in the build up to baseball's biggest championship.

Detroit manager Hughie Jennings was optimistic about his team's chances prior to the series. He felt the Tigers had a tougher time winning their respective pennant, and in his opinion the American League had better quality teams in 1909. Jennings thought his players were better than, or at least even with, any player Pittsburgh could offer. He noted that Cobb and Wagner would wash each other out, and was sure that Crawford would be offset by either Tommy Leach or Fred Clarke. The only position Jennings felt the Pirates were superior at was backstop with the big Canadian, George Gibson. Jennings wasn't the only one who thought this way.[1]

Back in Gibson's hometown of London, Ontario, the local newspapers were very interested in what their native son was up to in Pittsburgh. They regularly obtained syndicated stories from larger newspapers across the U.S. One article they ran was out of New York, and proved Jennings' concern. The article appeared in the *London Free Press* on October 8, 1909. The day of game one.

Pittsburgh without Clarke or without Wagner would be deprived of a valuable unit, so would it be without Leach or without Miller; yet there is on the team a player, not one of these four, whose absence from the field would make a bigger difference in the season's showing than any of the four stars mentioned. That man is Gibson, the catcher.

He has come to be the most important single cog in the machine, knowing and handling, as he does, all of his pitchers and filling, day after day, as he does, a position in which headwork is a prime requisite. When a catcher is so closely identified with the methods and tactics of a team, catching everyday, there is no place so difficult to duplicate with another man.[2]

Gibson himself agreed with the sentiment the writer proposed in the article. He concurred that he was the man to lead his pitchers. George believed that in all of baseball, he was equaled only by fellow Canadian, and Chicago Cub, Jimmy Archer in the catching department. He did not feel tired, physically or mentally, as a result of all his work during the season. In fact, during the three days off prior to the World Series, Gibson was anxious to get playing. Gibby recalled reporters asking him before the series kicked off if he was nervous. He told them he wasn't nervous, but in those three days, he would anxiously walk around Pittsburgh, back and forth from his apartment to the ballpark, and by the time the games started, he said, "I was ready to play a month." Gibby loved being on the field, and enthusiastically exclaimed: "I was right at home, let's go to it boys."[3] He never wanted to get off the diamond and joked with the press about all his work in 1909, "I am getting warmed up, I intend to catch in California all winter to keep in condition."[4] Gibson had every confidence in his Pittsburgh teammates and his own abilities for the upcoming matchup with the Tigers. Gibby agreed with Hughie Jennings in his thinking that he outclassed the Detroit catchers Boss Schmidt and Oscar Stanage. Gibson also thought Pittsburgh's hurlers bettered the Tigers pitching staff, stating, "The Tigers pitching staff will blow up. They have two good but rather erratic men in Donovan and Mullin. Willis and Camnitz will show them up."[5] Gibby classed Howie Camnitz as the best pitcher in either league, barring Christy Mathewson. Camnitz had arguably his best big-league season in 1909, with 25 wins and a sparkling 1.62 earned run average.

Game one of the World Series took place on October 8 at the newly erected Forbes Field, before a crowd of nearly thirty thousand excited Pirates fans. Rookie pitcher Babe Adams got the start for the Bucs, while George Mullin took the ball for the visiting Tigers. Gibson didn't think Mullin had the endurance for playoff baseball, but it was his own hurler who got off to a rough start. In the first inning, Adams walked two of the first three batters he faced. With men on first and second, Detroit second baseman Jim Delahanty singled, knocking in the game's first run.

Adams got out of the inning on the next batter, when George Moriarty's sure single took a lucky bounce and hit Delahanty on the basepath before he reached second. That out, by interference, kept the Tigers' lead at 1–0. The Pirates tied the game in the fourth on a home run by playing manager Fred Clarke. In the bottom of the fifth, the game fell apart for Detroit. A calamity of errors and timely Pittsburgh hitting led to the Tigers' demise. Pirates Bill Abstein reached on a fielding error by Delahanty, and then advanced to third on a throwing error by Cobb. Next, Gibson ripped a double to center field, easily scoring Abstein. Adams, the next batter, also reached on an error, and then Mullin hit Bobby Byrne to load the bases. Pittsburgh center fielder Tommy Leach smacked a towering shot to left field that was caught, but was hit deep enough to score Gibson on a sacrifice fly. Clarke grounded out to end the inning, but the damage was done: the Pirates were up 3–1.

The battery of Gibson and Adams was brilliant for the remainder of the contest. The game finished in a 4–1 Pirates victory. In all, the duo gave up only six hits over nine innings worked. In the first frame, Adams was surely a bundle of nerves, but Gibson helped him get control, and he ended up dominating the Tigers. Together, they held the Tigers, who led the American League in base stealing, to just one theft on the day: an inconsequential steal of second by Cobb. The steal came with two out in the fifth, and had no impact on the outcome of the game.

After game one, Babe Adams wrote an article that was printed in the *Pittsburgh Press*. He told of how the Tigers had a formidable line up, but also that he was not too nervous in his first postseason start. His excellent showing in this first game had him brimming with confidence leading into the rest of the series. Adams also reported how much he thought the thirty thousand cheering Pirates fans helped in disposing of the Tigers batters. Babe's biggest praise went to the brains behind the plate, George Gibson. Adams wrote: "Much credit, however, for my victory is due to George Gibson. He is the greatest catcher in the game today and it is a wonderful help to have a man like Gibson behind the bat."[6]

In the following day's *Pittsburgh Gazette* there was no shortage of praise for the gem of a start by Adams and the big home run by Clarke. But *Gazette* reporter R.J. Farrel reminded his readers of the great work of unsung hero George Gibson. He wrote:

> And in the giving of glory for the grand result a word is due, after the captain of the crew, to his chief mate, according to yesterday's performance, the good George Gibson, who did things not only in his position behind the bat, but with the stick when the doing of things was most needed. He knocked a pretty two-bagger in the fifth that started things afresh, and was responsible for bringing in two runs and further rattling the bench of the Tigers who, for a time, seemed to do anything but play ball of a championship sort.[7]

Gibson did play chief mate to Manager Clarke's captain, and going into game two it was necessary for Gibby to continue to be as good if the Pirates had any chance of winning the series. The second game took place on October 9, again at Forbes Field. Over thirty thousand fans were on hand. Unlike game one, the Pirates got off to a great start. A walk, combined with doubles by Leach and Miller, had the Bucs up 2–0 after the first inning. That's where anything positive ended for the Pirates. The Tigers registered three hits off of Pirates starter Howie Camnitz in the top of the second, and got both runs back. In the top of the third, Camnitz really began to unravel. Davy Jones bunted and reached on an error, Donie Bush singled and Cobb walked. With the bases loaded, Delahanty hammered a double to center, scoring two and leaving Cobb, who had walked, at third. Manager Clarke had seen enough and replaced Camnitz with Vic Willis. Gibson later stated that Camnitz may have been ill with tonsillitis during this game.[8] George held Howie in high regard, and after such a great season in 1909, there was no reason for him to perform so poorly in the playoffs. Whatever the case, Camnitz couldn't get the job done, so Willis had to try and clean up the mess.

Gibson described the veteran Willis as a big slow fellow,[9] meaning there was a real chance of Cobb attempting to steal home. And that's exactly what happened. Cobb had a favorable lead off third and on the pitch he took off with tremendous speed. Ty arrived at home around the same time as the ball, and umpire Evans called him safe. Over fifty years later, Gibby still contested that Cobb was out on the play. "Ty hadn't touched the plate before I had the tag on him. His spikes hit me on the chest protector, he was out."[10] Gibby also remembered landing on top of Cobb with him short of the plate. Cobb yelled at George in agony, "Gibby, get off my legs. You're breakin' 'em."[11] Gibson insisted he was a few feet down the third base line when he tagged Cobb, making it impossible for Cobb to have touched home. Given that he fell on top of Cobb, as per Ty's shriek of pain toward Gibson, and Gibby being three feet up the baseline, umpire Evans may have had the call wrong. George certainly thought so, and also thought Evans should have had to forfeit his salary for that game because of this perceived error.[12]

The Detroit papers reported the play differently. "While [Willis] was winding up for his first pitch, Cobb dashed for the plate. The ball beat him there a bit, but he slid away from Gibson, who missed the touch and the run counted."[13] The steal of home made the score 5–2 and Tigers pitcher Wild Bill Donovan shut down the Pirates, holding them to just three singles over the last three innings. The Pirates lost 7–2 and the series was tied at a game a piece.

With game two wrapped up, it was off to Detroit. Both teams traveled by train to the new venue. Before the excursion north, reporters were looking for players' comments for the next day's daily. Tigers manager Hughie Jennings was exuding confidence, excited about his team's chances. His confidence was contagious, and his left fielder, Davy Jones, had bold remarks on the series so far: "I can't see anything to it but Detroit. Pittsburgh has only three good men. Gibson is a pretty good catcher, but they have no pitchers."[14] This was in direct contrast to what Gibson had said about his pitchers prior to the start of the series. Before getting on the train for Detroit, Gibby told reporters, with a smile on his face, "They tell me the park over there isn't very big. Oh, well, we'll hit them as far as they do."[15] Gibson and his Pittsburgh teammates felt confident heading to the unfamiliar grounds of Detroit's Bennett Park.

Prior to game three, spectators around Bennett Park tried to estimate how many fans were in attendance. Was it eighteen, twenty, twenty-four thousand? The actual attendance was 18,277, but not all were rooting for the Tigers. Many fans traveled from the Pittsburgh area, and a large contingent from London, Ontario, also made the trip to see their hometown boy play in the World Series championship. London is only 125 miles east of Detroit. A *London Advertiser* reporter estimated that there were just over one thousand fans from London and the rest of Southwestern Ontario in Detroit to see their beloved "Mooney" Gibson. These Gibson groupies followed him around the city, firing questions at him. They caught him just about everywhere: on the street, at his hotel and any appearance he was obliged to make. They shouted to him, "Oh, you, Gibson,"[16] recognizing his great accomplishments and hoping that he remembered that he had honed his baseball skills in London. When he first took the field at Bennett Park, the thousand-strong Canadians sounded off by blowing whistles, shaking rattles, honking horns and creating noise with other sound-making devices. The games in Detroit would be like home games for Gibby.

As for the game itself, the first inning was a statistician's nightmare. The Tigers made three errors and gave up four hits, and the Bucs scored five runs. Pittsburgh tallied another run in the second, while starter Nick Maddox held the Detroit batters to only four hits over the first six innings. Up 6–0, the Pirates seemed to be cruising to a 2–1 series lead. But the Tigers crew came out swinging in the seventh frame, scoring four runs on five hits. When the Tigers came to bat in the bottom of the eighth, the score was 6–4. After a quick first out, George Moriarty took a walk to bring the tying run to the plate. A report in the next day's *Detroit Free Press* told of how the Tigers blew their chance in the critical eighth. "They walked Moriarty with one down. Tom Jones was also on his way to free transportation when Moriarty undertook to steal second. It was an ill advised [*sic*] move, and Gibson trapped him with a good throw. The pitch that Morey [Moriarty] went on was the third ball to Jones, and the next one gave the batter a walk."[17] Moriarty's error in judgment extinguished the Tigers' rally. Instead of having two men on with one out, they had one man on with two out. The threat was ended when Schmidt lifted a lazy fly ball to Fred Clarke. This running mistake was the only steal attempt on Gibby in the game, and it was the most important putout of the contest. The Pirates went on to win 8–6.

Following game three, the Pittsburgh crew went back to their hotel to celebrate. Gibson fans were there in numbers, congratulating him and wishing him luck in the series going forward. A *Detroit Free Press* reporter described the scene in the hotel lobby: "Early in the evening George Gibson, the Pirate backstop, who claims London, Ont., as his home, stationed himself in the Pontchartrain lobby and rivaled Dr. Cook famed as the North Pole discoverer, for handshaking. For an hour it seemed as though every Canuck who could make the landing was on hand to shake hands with their hero."[18]

On a day where temperatures were hovering around the freezing mark, Tigers star pitcher George Mullin came to the park with ice in his veins. In game four, Mullin had his sinker working and retired all three batters he faced in the first inning on ground ball outs. He dominated Pirates hitters, completing the full nine innings and allowing only five hits. Pittsburgh's starting pitcher, Albert "Lefty" Leifield, was not at his best on the afternoon. The game ended in a 5–0 shutout for the Tigers, and could have been worse if not for Pittsburgh's lone bright spot, George Gibson. He threw out Ty Cobb trying to steal second in the first inning, and pegged Davy Jones at second base to end the sixth frame. Even with the loss, the Pirates club was still content with a split in Detroit, and were anxious to return to Forbes Field. After the game, the team rushed back to the Hotel Pontchartrain to pick up their belongings and get to the train station. Their train to Pittsburgh was scheduled to depart at 9 p.m. sharp.[19]

On his way home after watching games three and four of the World Series, James J. McCaffery, president of the Toronto Baseball Club, stopped in at Gibson's hometown. A *London Free Press* reporter asked McCaffery what he thought of Gibson in the two games he watched. "Gibson? I only wish we had two or three like him on the Toronto team. He plays a great game." McCaffery also thought George was a great guy. He was impressed with how Gibby made time for all the fans from London who traveled to Detroit to cheer him on. Prior to the second game in Detroit, some of Gibby's London friends sent a bouquet of flowers down to the field for him. Gibson seemed to not want to accept the gift and fans wondered why. McCaffery explained it as superstition. "Ball players are the most superstitious people of any I know. For instance, I don't care how many games our team might win consecutively, they would never get a telegram from me congratulating them. In this case the flowers were lying on the bench; they were all right, but a policeman with nothing but the kindest of intentions, picked them up and sent them into Gibson."[20] George and his Pirates teammates had won nothing yet, and assumed receiving this gift may be a jinx.

Now back in Pittsburgh, there would be no time for jinxes with the series reduced to a best of three. The Pirates fans were excited their Bucs were back in town. On a cold October afternoon, spectators started arriving at Forbes Field three hours early. They were bundled in blankets, heavy over-coats and other winter gear to keep warm. A coin toss in front of baseball's National Commission had determined that game seven, if necessary, would be played at Bennett Park,[21] making this game the last game of the series to be played in Pittsburgh. Nearly 22,000 battled the bitter cold to observe game five.[22]

Babe Adams got the start for Pittsburgh. After giving up a leadoff home run to Davy Jones, he settled in and continued his excellence from game one. Adams scattered five hits over the remainder of the game. The Pirates were all over the bases and swinging hot at the dish. Gibson had a single in the second, and later gave the Bucs a 2–1 lead, scoring on a wild pitch by Detroit starter, Ed Summers. Each team added runs, and the game was tied at three until the seventh. That's when the Pirates batters really got to work. They scored four runs in the inning on five hits and an error. With a 7–3 lead, Adams made his second mistake of the day and gave up another solo home run, this time to Sam Crawford. Help-ing his pitcher out, Gibson got that run back when he singled in Chief Wilson in the bottom of the eighth. Clearly not content at first, Gibson stole second. Perhaps a bit over-confident, Gibson took a chance at third with two out. Tigers catcher Boss Schmidt threw a great ball to Moriarty and nailed him for the final out of the eighth. The ill-timed steal attempt did not factor into the final score, as Adams retired the Ti-gers in the ninth, securing the 8–4 Pirates win.

With five games completed, the pre-series chatter of Gibson being a determining factor in the result of the series were coming to fruition. The *Pittsburgh Daily Post* reported on baseball observers' earlier predic-tions: "Where the greatest margin in the work of the teams is shown is be-hind the bat. In the five games that

George Gibson taking batting practice during the 1909 season. George batted to a .240 average in the 1909 World Series and registered the game-winning RBI in game one (Healy Collection).

have been played Detroit has but four stolen bases on George Gibson and two of these were made by Cobb, considered by far the best cushion-purloiner in the American League."[23]

Adams and Gibson had another fine match together. Especially against the Tigers leader, Ty Cobb. Before the series, *The Georgia Peach* stated that he would hit Adams harder than he would a high schooler. The three men would banter with each other all series during Cobb's plate appearances. In Cobb's first at bat, he barked at Adams, "Come on, you Babe. I'm Waiting." "You'd better cut out the waiting," answered Adams. "I'm not handing out anything to you fellows these days." "He's Right, Ty," added Gibson. "The young fellow has sworn to strike you out every time you face him in this series."[24] This mild jeering was part of the plan to knock Cobb off of his game. In the first two games that Gibby and Babe formed the battery, Cobb managed only one hit in seven at bats. Cobb's inefficiency versus the duo brought the Pirates within one game of seizing their first World Series championship.

The headline of the October 15 *Pittsburgh Post-Gazette* told the complete story of game six: "Mullin Again Beats the Pittsburgh Team."[25] It was that simple. Tigers pitcher George Mullin allowed three runs in the first inning, and then held the Pirates batters to only four more knocks in the eight remaining frames. The Tigers clawed back to tie the Pirates in the fourth inning and overtook them in the fifth. The Detroit club held a 5–3 lead going into the ninth inning. Only three outs stood between them and extending the series to seven games. The inning started off well for the Pirates, when Miller and Abstein led off with back-to-back singles. The next Pirates batter was fortunate when Tigers first baseman, Tom Jones, committed an error on a bunt attempt. It allowed Chief Wilson, the batter, to reach first base, and let Miller score, bringing the Bucs within one run. With nobody out, and runners on first and third, Manager Jennings pulled Jones from the game, and had Sam Crawford come in from the outfield to take over at first base. The move paid off. The next Pirates batter, George Gibson, hammered a ground ball to Crawford who threw home to retire Abstein, who tried to score on the hit and run. Next up for the Bucs was Ed Abbaticchio. He whiffed and Tigers catcher Boss Schmidt alertly threw down to Charley O'Leary in time to catch Wilson trying to swipe third. Game six ended on a "strike 'em out, throw 'em out" double play. For the first time since adopting a best-of-seven format, the World Series was going to go the distance.

With all the traveling between Detroit and Pittsburgh, the players were excited to have a day off before the deciding game. Manager Clarke wanted to start Babe Adams in the finale, and the extra day gave Babe adequate rest, setting up the possibility for him to make his third start in eight days. The rest of the team were given their freedom. After spending the morning in the Hotel Pontchartrain, many of the players went to the racetrack in Windsor, Ontario.

Others took sightseeing tours of beautiful Detroit.[26] Game seven was pushed up by the National Baseball Commission by one hour, from 2 p.m. to 1 p.m., in order to accommodate the Eastern newspaper reporters.[27]

On the morning of game seven, there was still confusion about which pitchers would start the deciding game for either team. For Jennings, the choice was between Wild Bill Donovan and George Mullin. Donovan hadn't pitched since game two, and was well rested, but Mullin, despite being tired, had dominated the Pirates hitters in games four and six. Manager Clarke was also facing a pitching dilemma. He had been sure of going with Babe Adams, but Adams awoke that morning feeling quite ill. *Pittsburgh Press* sports editor Ralph Davis reported that Deacon Phillippe was Clarke's next choice: "Deacon Phillippe looks like the best bet. The veteran seems to have a lot these days, and cold weather is just to his fancy. George Gibson stopped Phil in the hotel lobby this morning and said to him, 'Deacon, you're a cold weather pitcher, you ought to be able to beat those fellows today.' 'I don't know Gib,' replied Phil, 'but you know that if I pitch I will try my hardest to give them an awful battle.'"[28]

As game time approached, the pitching situation was still up in the air. For the Tigers, both Donovan and Mullin were warming up for a possible start, and on the Pirates' side of the diamond, Manager Clarke had the rookie Babe Adams and the veteran Deacon Phillippe loosening up. Jennings eventually chose Donovan, and Manager Clarke, once he got the thumbs up from the youngster Adams confirming that he was healthy enough to pitch, couldn't deny the duo of Babe and Gibson.[29] Only seventeen and a half thousand fans were on hand to witness the series-deciding game. Frigid temperatures likely kept many away, though as Ralph Davis of the *Pittsburgh Press* noted, many of Gibson's friends from London and Toronto were still in attendance to cheer for him and his Pirates teammates.[30]

The game started with Pittsburgh batting. Wild Bill lived up to his moniker in the first inning when he hit a batter and walked two. The Pirates couldn't capitalize on his mistakes, though, and let the Tigers out of the inning unscathed. The bottom half of the first inning is when Donie Bush's ill-advised steal attempt occurred. Gibson of course threw Bush out, quickly changing the complexion of the contest. In the second inning, Donovan's control issues continued. He walked four batters, leading to two Pirates runs. In the next frame, he allowed two more hits, and although no runs scored, Manager Jennings got out his hook. George Mullin took over in the fourth.

Meanwhile, Adams and Gibson were cruising along. Through four innings, Adams had only allowed four hits and two walks. After Gibson threw out Bush in the first inning, the base-stealing Tigers had yet to try again.

George Mullin didn't fare much better for Detroit. In his first inning of work, he allowed two runs on a pair of walks and a couple hits, pushing the

Bucs' lead to 4–0. In the sixth inning, the Pittsburgh club took the reins and continued their push for the finish. After Mullin got Ham Hyatt to ground out, Tommy Leach punished the baseball, hitting a double to left. Manager Clarke was walked, and the great Honus Wagner socked a ringing triple to left field, scoring Leach and Clarke. A throwing error by Davy Jones allowed Wagner to score on the play, and the Pirates lead swelled to 7–0. In Detroit's half of the sixth, Adams had to face the teeth of the Tigers' line up. Babe induced a ground ball from Ty Cobb, got Crawford to flyout to left field and finished the inning one-two-three when Delahanty popped out to third. The Bucs added another run late and the Adams–Gibson battery continued their fine work, finishing off the Tigers. When the last out was recorded, the Tigers trailed by a score of 8–0. The Pirates of Pittsburgh won their first World Series.

Following the game, back at Hotel Pontchartrain, a mass of Bucco fans had gathered. They were overjoyed with their team's victory. The crowd was so large that Gibby and his teammates literally had to be carried to get through the hotel lobby. The Pirates spent the rest of Sunday in Detroit before journeying back to Pittsburgh on Monday, October 18. They returned home to attend a parade organized by the city of Pittsburgh.

Prior to the parade, Pittsburgh Baseball Club president, Barney Dreyfuss, held a banquet for his team at the prestigious Fort Pitt Hotel. He spoke briefly, and expressed his gratitude toward the players and conveyed his content with their great achievement. He specifically singled out two players for their extraordinary efforts: Manager Clarke and George Gibson. "He closed by presenting to catcher, George H [*sic*] Gibson a beautiful gold watch, which he stated was a token of his appreciation of services rendered by, 'a player who had worked overtime and who might find use for a little timepiece.' Gibbie blushingly accepted the gift, and as soon as the applause subdued, responded with a few remarks that again brought forth cheers. 'I am sure I have not worked harder than a number of my teammates,' modestly said the star backstop, 'but this is indeed a surprise, and I cannot find words to fully express how grateful I am for such a great remembrance. I shall always cherish it, and hope next season to be able to do better work than I have done in the past.'"[31] The Jules Jergensen gold timepiece was engraved, "To George Gibson, In appreciation of faithful efforts. From Barney Dreyfuss, October 16, 1909."[32]

On December 15, 2005, nearly one hundred years after being presented the watch, the Gibson family sent George's treasured memorabilia to auction, which allowed a lucky Pirates fan a chance to carry on the memory of Gibby's great work in 1909 and possess the relic he so cherished. The watch sold for $6,600 USD.[33]

The parade went off without a hitch. Thousands of fans gathered along the route, cheering on their champions. After weaving through the streets

The 1909 Pittsburgh Pirates World Series winning club. George Gibson is pictured in the bottom row, fourth from left (Armstrong Collection).

of Pittsburgh, the parade arrived at Forbes Field, where some of the players made speeches. Gibson spoke first. He shouted through a megaphone that he appreciated the tribute of the crowd more than his words could express. The celebration went on all night. The following morning, the team disbanded, and most of the men departed for home.[34] Gibby stayed in Pittsburgh for another week to attend to business (and likely also to keep the celebration going). His fans seemed willing to accommodate him for as long as he was so obliged. George also participated in exhibition games around the Pittsburgh area, as well as one in Youngstown, Ohio.[35]

Gibson's play during the World Series gained him national attention. Reporters across the country were aware of how important Gibson really was to the Bucco cause. As reported in the October 23 issue of the *Sporting Life*:

> George Gibson not only hit oftener than Detroit's backstop, but, my, how he shone over them in defense. Pittsburg's men had been told that the Tigers would steal cushions on Gibson just as easily as they had purloined on them on the best in the American. Gibson was ready for this band of get-on, dash-and-go gang. He turned them back.[36]

Jack Ryder, a writer for the *Cincinnati Enquirer* and noted baseball authority, also paid high tribute to George. Ryder felt that Gibson thoroughly outclassed the backstops of the Tigers during the World Series, and beyond that, was the best windpaddist in either league across the 1909 season.[37] Other media outlets didn't fully understand, or recognize, Gibson's importance to the Pirates in the World Series until the following season. In September of 1910, Cleveland *Plain Dealer* reporter Sam Cane found himself at the Polo Grounds in New York observing a series between the Pirates and the Giants. It was then that he came to the following conclusion: The actual reason for the Pirates' defeat of the Tigers in the '09 World Series, was the defensive play of George Gibson. Cane stated that Babe Adams was hailed as the only "conquering hero" of the championship series, and while Adams was thrown atop the shoulders of the Pirates fans, Cane felt Gibson's efforts were more or less forgotten. Gibby was not given his due. The Cleveland scribe referred to Gibson as the Pirate club's Gibraltar, as the rock who held the Pirates' ship anchored and who was always at the ready when any opposing player tried to take advantage of his buccaneer moundsman.[38]

Babe Adams was receiving most of the accolades for the Pirates championship, and rightly so, he was the winner in three of the four Pittsburgh victories. But Adams knew that his success had been achieved with help:

> The first thing I found out was that Clarke was the boss, and that he knew more about the game than I ever thought was in it. After a few bumpings I learned that Gibson knew a lot more about what to pitch to batters than I did. I think I began to improve as soon as I found out these two things. At first I thought Gibson made some mistakes in telling me what to pitch. In fact, I was wrong most of the time.[39]

Adams would later look back and laugh at all the mistakes he had made before committing to Gibson's plans. He realized Gibby did more for his pitching career than anyone else. He recalled that during the World Series he made a few mistakes early in the first game. Gibson encouraged Adams and coached him to gain control after the rough start, and came up with a theory on how to retire Tigers batters with a little more ease. Gibson didn't think the Tigers players would be able to hit Adams's low curveball, and that's what they fed them—curveballs on either corner while changing speeds and keeping the ball low in the strike zone. In Adams's opinion, Gibson's plan is what eventually allowed the Pirates to defeat the Tigers for the World Series championship.[40]

Winning the World Series made George a superstar. Not just locally in Pittsburgh, but nationally across the United States. He also became more popular in his native Canada. He traveled home by train via the Pittsburgh-Buffalo-Rochester line, and connected to the Grand Trunk at Niagara Falls. In later years, he told *Pittsburgh Gazette* writer Edward F. Balinger a story about his layover in the Falls following the Pirate World Series victory:

> George Gibson, Pirate Leader, laughingly recalled an incident in which he [was] pronounced a punk ballplayer, but quickly formed a lasting friendship with the man who had expressed his opinion in such an uncomplimentary manner.
> Gibson had just gone through the thrills of the 1909 world series, in which he cov-

ered himself with glory by his brilliant work behind the bat. Along with his fellow stars he had been delayed in returning to his Canadian home by world series banquets and events held in honor of the conquering Corsair heros.

At last he got away and went to Buffalo. With several hours to wait for his train to London he decided to proceed to Niagara Falls and walk across the bridge, for the big Canuck always was fond of exercising his legs. When he touched his feet on native soil he proceeded to the Central Hotel, and put in a long distance call to let the family know he was on his way home.

While waiting for the telephone connection Gibby stepped into the bar room for a couple of sandwiches and a sip of Canadian ale. As he gazed into a large mirror he noticed the reflection of a huge blackboard on which all of the scores of the big Pittsburgh-Detroit series had been displayed. This made him feel he was among the right kind of people.

The barkeeper was a sociable chap and soon they were discussing baseball. The late John Lautenschlager, proprietor of the inn, appeared upon the scene and joined in the conversation. He proved well posted on the national pastime and followed the Pirate-Tiger games closely. The wall of the room was decorated with photographs of all the diamond celebrities of the day. "Do you know that fellow?" inquired Gibby as he pointed to his own picture after they had been fanning for an hour.

"Do I know him?" replied the hotel owner. "Say, that's George Gibson who lives about 100 miles from here, I know him well. He belongs to Pittsburgh, but he's not anything compared to Schmidt or Stanage—in fact I can name a lot of youngsters who could catch the ears off Gibson."

Gibby did not bat an eye, but kept right on with the conversation. Lautenschlager evidently thought he was one of the numerous commercial travellers who used to drop into his hotel. At last he became inquisitive and said: "I certainly have enjoyed talking with somebody who is so well posted about baseball, especially one who attended all the games of the world series. What line of business do you handle?"

The big Buccaneer battery star with a twinkle in his eye, handed his visiting card to the hotel man who glanced at it, took a look at the smiling catcher and then almost toppled from his chair. He started to apologize, but Gibby grasped his hand and remarked, "I am pleased to meet you for I too have enjoyed this talk with a real baseball fan."

"I understand," added the big Canadian. "You are an American League rooter and it's natural that your heart should be with the Tigers even in their defeat. I admire you for your spirit of loyalty."

"You've got the correct dope," replied Lautenschlager. "And what also may have something to do with my feelings, is the fact that your Pirates caused me to lose a lot of wagers, for I banked heavily on Detroit all through the series."

Lautenschlager insisted on having Gibby as his guest at dinner and as train time arrived, the genial hotel man brought his automobile and drove his new acquaintance to the railway station. They met many times thereafter and often laughed about their first meeting just across the northern border.[41]

Although George could go unrecognized while traveling over the Canadian border, that would not be the case where he was going. In his hometown, London, Ontario, everyone recognized the face of the Moon.

2

For He's a Jolly Good Fellow

Before the 1909 World Series even began, top officials in London, Ontario, nicknamed the Forest City, started to plan a dinner and reception for George in honor of his great season in Pittsburgh. Initially, the event was being organized by a few town aldermen and the top brass from the city baseball league, where Gibson was first recognized as a superior baseball talent. By the time the World Series was a few days old, the reception had turned into a full-blown celebration. Alderman Donald Ferguson was elected chairman of the reception, and Dr. A. J. Wyckoff was appointed secretary. The committee concluded that a small reception would not be enough for their local hero, and expanded the plan for the event to be held at the beautiful Victoria Park in London Centre so that Gibby's many admirers could attend. The alderman's idea was to parade Gibson through town, from the London train station to Victoria Park, where presentations would be made.

Meanwhile, West Londoners prepared their own presentation to be included as part of Gibby's reception. The folks of West London held Gibson close to their hearts as it was the area of town where George grew up and learned to play ball. The enthusiastic group raised a large sum of money that went towards creating banners and purchasing fireworks, while the remainder of the proceeds went to the main committee in support of the general reception. West Londoners wanted the reception to be held at Tecumseh Park, which was Gibby's home field as a youngster. They felt it was more suitable because it had stands, which could seat hundreds of people. Another reason they liked this location was the fact that the lighting at Tecumseh Park was far superior to the luminescence of Victoria Park.

The committee decided on Victoria Park because of its central location and proximity to the train station. The plan was to have the parade route start at the London Grand Trunk station, proceed north to Dundas Street, on to Wellington Street and then north again to Victoria Park. Along the route, the

McClary's band would play, followed by the seventh regiment band. Local amateur baseball clubs would also participate in the parade, including some of Gibson's former teams: London West, Struthers, Orients and the McClary's baseball club. Approximately two hundred school boys were on hand to show their appreciation of Mooney. Badges that exhibited an excellent likeness of Gibson where printed for each of the boys in attendance to wear in Gibby's honor.

Gibson was scheduled to arrive in London on Tuesday, October 26, one day after the Canadian Thanksgiving holiday. The town was ready for his arrival. London mayor Samuel Stevely, Alderman Ferguson and Dr. Wyckoff left town early in the afternoon to meet Gibby at Ingersoll, a Grand Trunk junction point approximately 35 miles from London. Gibson's train arrived at 6:00 p.m., as scheduled. Officials from Ingersoll, along with the London delegation, entertained Gibson to dinner. Following dinner, the Ingersolites congratulated Gibson before he and his compadres returned to London.

An hour before the train arrived in London, a crowd started to gather at the station. Enthusiastic fans jockeyed for position to get a touch of Gibson. When the locomotive pulled into London station at 8:30 p.m., the platform was so crowded the reception committee couldn't perform their welcoming duties. Excited fans swooped Gibby off the platform, carried him through the masses and lifted him into an awaiting automobile. The McClary's band was trying to play for him, but the music was drowned out by general excitement and cheers of "Welcome Mooney." The streets were flooded with people. From the confusion and chaotic movement emerged the parade procession. It traveled down the crowd-lined streets of London Centre. Spectators used bells, horns, whistles and, of course, their voices to express their appreciation of

George Gibson circa 1909. After his Pirates won the World Series, George was the talk of the town in London (courtesy Carol Smith).

Gibby.[1] Mooney held a high seat in the automobile he was riding in, allowing everyone along the parade route a glimpse of the star. Gibson's West London friends had, perhaps, the most interesting idea for honoring their hero. They crafted a monster-size baseball that was carried along the parade's path. On one side of the giant ball they painted "Pittsburg 8, Detroit 0," while on the opposite side they inscribed "We like you Pittsburg, but oh, you Mooney."[2]

When Gibson arrived at the ceremony stage, he was handed his son, George Jr., and someone in the crowd said, "Here's your boy."[3] Little George got a hearty kiss from his dad and the fans in the park cheered loudly. Mayor Stevely, Alderman Ferguson and Dr. Wyckoff took the stage along with Gibby and special guest, Hughie Jennings, manager of the Detroit Tigers. An estimated fifteen to twenty thousand people filled the park hoping to get a look at their hometown hero alongside fellow baseball superstar, Jennings. With so many in attendance, it was difficult to hear, even over the loudspeakers. Victoria Park was not designed to hold as many people as had shown up for the celebration. Authorities were worried people would be crushed. Children had to be pulled from the crowd by policemen, but things were eventually brought under control. The police report on the event reported not a single arrest during the festivities. London Police Sergeant Birrell stated, "'Gibson Night' went off without a hitch. It was everybody's night, and we let them have it."[4]

The ceremony began with presentations of trophies and awards for teams and players from the various city leagues. The first delegate to address Gibson was London mayor, the honorable Samuel Stevely. He spoke of Gibson as a compatriot:

> On behalf of the reception committee, I wish to thank the people of London for the manner in which they turned out tonight. Although Mooney Gibson has spent most of his baseball career in the United States, he is still a citizen of Canada and a taxpayer in London. It perhaps would not be fair to say that he was entirely responsible for the victory of the Pirates, but the watch which he now carries, the gift of President Dreyfuss, is sufficient evidence of the club's appreciation. While he has played throughout the States, he is not ashamed to say that he comes from London, Canada.[5]

The London committee also wanted to present Gibby with a gift for his achievements. City residents pooled together money to purchase him a handsome cabinet of silver valued at $250, a hefty cost in 1909. The silver was inscribed to Gibby from the people of London: "Presented by the citizens of the City of London to George 'Mooney' Gibson, catcher of the Pittsburg Baseball Club, World Champions, October 26th, 1909." George was given the case of silver by Alderman Ferguson on behalf of the people of London, and Dr. Wyckoff spoke to the crowd:

> To Mr. George 'Mooney' Gibson, catcher of the Pittsburg Baseball Club, champions of the world, 1909–The citizens of London desire to take this opportunity of express-

ing their cordial congratulations on your signal success in the field of professional baseball. We are proud of the fact that we have as a fellow citizen a man of such high rank in the world of sport and whose character is marked by such sterling integrity. We sincerely hope that you may long retain the unique position that you now occupy in America's national game, and that the close of each succeeding season may be as pleasant and as profitable as the one which has just ended. We ask you to accept this case of silver for Mrs. Gibson and yourself as a token of our esteem and good wishes.[6]

Before the ceremony, London reporters caught up with Hughie Jennings. Reporters and fans alike were in awe that such a superstar came to help in the festivities. Jennings would not allow himself to become the center of attention. "This is not my reception. I came here to help you do honor to a fellow towns-man who has advertised you, and who is a worthy citizen of the town. I was glad to receive the invitation and I am glad to be here. The boy will be proud of his homecoming, I can tell you, and well he should."[7] Jennings was impressed with the turnout by the London people, calling the city a great baseball town. "This is certainly a good turnout to welcome Gibson home, but, nevertheless, Gibson is deserving of it. He has brought great credit to the city.... Gibson as a catcher is the best in the business. There is no better. He can hold his own with any backstop in the world today."[8] When Jennings spoke to the crowd at Victoria Park, he was equally complimentary of George:

> I have not a good voice tonight, so I won't say very much. But I want to tell you and the committee that I appreciate this high honor of being present this evening to attend this grand reception tendered your fellow townsman, Mr. Gibson. I have known the young man for six or seven years, and you have done no more for him than he has done for your city. I say that you ought to be justly proud of him, and I know he is justly proud of this grand reception to him. I speak for the city of Detroit in what I say.[9]

Jennings had equally kind words about the reception committee's idea to have the school boys attend the celebration. He thought there was no better role model for the children of London than George Gibson. He delivered his point to reporters, "There is one thing the reception impressed upon me, and that was the presence of the school boys in the parade. This sort of thing is bound to have a great effect upon the boys, a great moral effect. Here is 'Mooney' who has made a success of his profession. He has done so by hard work and clean living. These boys may not be great ballplayers, but they will have impressed upon them the fact that clean living is the essential thing in success upon the diamond, as well as in other things. I say the reception can-not fail to have a good effect upon the boys. It is an object lesson."[10]

At the celebration, of course, the crowd wanted Mooney. The good-natured fans chanted for Gibby to take his turn in speaking. The mass cheered passionately as their native son took to the front of the stage. He gave a heartfelt speech:

I thank you all for the honor you have bestowed upon me tonight in giving me this grand reception. I do not see that I deserve this, but nevertheless, I appreciate it very much, and I know that Mrs. Gibson does too. In years to come I will look back upon tonight as the happiest of my life, and I may say that I will always be a Canadian.[11]

After Gibson's words, the crowd began a chorus of "For he's a jolly good fellow."

Their jolly good fellow was born 29 years earlier, on July 22, 1880, in what is present-day London, a city located in Southwestern Ontario, just north of Lake Erie and approximately halfway between Detroit, Michigan, and Toronto, Ontario. George was actually born in Petersville, a small village located west of London, that was eventually renamed to London West in 1881, and then amalgamated with the city of London in 1897.

George was the youngest of nine children born to George and Hannah (Southam) Gibson. His father was born in Ireland in 1837, and immigrated to Canada in 1854.[12] His mother, Hannah Southam, was born in Kingsthorpe, Northamptonshire, England, in 1838. Census information shows that the Southam family remained in England until at least 1841. By August 1845,

Gibson Family. George is pictured standing third from left. His father, George Sr., is seated far left while his mother Hannah is seated center (courtesy Julie Anne Baskette).

Hannah, along with her sister and parents, had moved to Lachine, Quebec, Canada. Following a brief stop in Buffalo, New York, the family settled in the London area in November of 1848.[13] The population of London, then, was 4,668, but the town was growing rapidly. "On December 15, 1853, London entered the age of the 'iron horse' when the first railway train chugged into the city."[14] The railway caused London to prosper, attracting more settlers. By 1855, London's population had eclipsed 10,000 and the town was incorporated as a city. Jobs in manufacturing, food processing and brewing were just a few of the reasons to settle in, and around, London. In 1857, oil was discovered in Lambton county, about 50 miles west of London, and that drew even more people to the area.

According to the Canadian Census of 1881, George, Hannah and their children, including a five-month-old George, were living in London West.[15] Located in that same London West was Tecumseh Park, home of the Tecumseh Baseball Club of London, champions of the 1877 International Association.

The Tecumseh Baseball Club of London was formed in 1868, when "the Forest City and London Baseball clubs amalgamated."[16] Among the men involved in the newly formed organization were Harry Gorman, a London newspaperman; Ed Moore, co-manager of the famous Tecumseh House Hotel; Daniel Perrin, a biscuit manufacturer; and *London Free Press* employees Richard and William Southam, Gibson's maternal uncles. Between 1868 and about 1875, the Tecumseh baseball team was playing amateur and professional baseball clubs throughout Ontario and the United States. Many of the teams they played, even those claiming amateur status, retained the services of professional baseball players. Hoping to get an edge on these teams, London began to enlist professional players as well. It is believed that this was largely achieved through the "encouragement and promise of backing"[17] from Jake Englehardt, a Cleveland-born oil refiner who arrived in London in 1868 and would go on to make a name for himself as "a corporate titan, a philanthropist, a rail builder, and a trusted 'rain-maker' for the leader of the province of Ontario."[18] By 1877, George's uncle William Southam had moved to Hamilton, where he bought the *Hamilton Spectator* with a partner and was on his way to building the Southam newspaper empire. Richard Southam remained in London and continued to be involved with the Tecumseh baseball team. Though he wasn't at the same playing level as the American professionals that were on the team, he was still a very talented baseball player, and was named playing manager. Baseball historian Chip Martin believes the appointment was more of a gesture of hometown loyalty, and that "Gorman was the driving force of the club and had some vested interests in promoting the game and his paper at the same time."[19] Following the 1877 championship, the Tecumseh recruited even more American professionals to defend their title. Ross Barnes, a man considered to be one of the best hitters in baseball between 1871 and 1876, joined the London squad and replaced Richard Southam as playing manager for 1878.

Baseball remained popular in London. Undoubtedly, when George and his older brother Robert were old enough to pick up a ball and glove for the first time, their heads had already been filled with history of the London Tecumseh team and baseball stories from their Uncle Richard. The Gibson family supported Robert and George's desire to play baseball as well.

George started playing baseball in West London as a youngster, and claimed many folks called him and his teammates "the forty thieves." Gibby and the West London crew would go out and beat teams that had players two and three years older than themselves. They were denied entry into the actual league because other teams thought they were too small and wouldn't be able to keep up. Gibson remembered his father telling him that those older fellas were scared that the London West crew would "beat their brains out" and "just disgrace them."[20] Gibson recalled his early baseball on "the corner lot," learning how to man the backstop with just a mitt and a birdcage mask. George disliked that mask so much so that many times he would play without it; and, many times he went home with a black eye.[21]

Gibson's dad was a building contractor, and George Jr. assisted him from a young age. Gibson Sr. looked after manufacturing plants around London. If a boiler was down and the men couldn't work, that's when Gibson's dad would get called in. On holidays or during the summer, Mooney would join his father and help out. On holidays, of course, is when George wanted to play baseball, but he was dedicated to his father's business, and promised he would help him even if it meant missing ball games. That said, Gibby's father wasn't against him playing ball—in fact, he enjoyed it. George recalled, "My father was one of the biggest fans that ever you saw, and took more interest in it. Now, he would cuss me and my brother, we were a battery, he was a pitcher and I was a catcher, but he would cuss us. But he'd be the first one over in the gate, to see the game himself." The senior Gibson of course wanted best for his sons, telling them "Play your hardest on the field, or come work for me."[22]

The first time George was mentioned in the local papers was while playing for the Knox Church Baseball Club in 1897.[23] He began gaining local notoriety the following season, at just seventeen years of age, with the same ball club. The Knox Club was not in any specific league in 1898, but would take on any challengers wishing to try their hand at a team of young amateurs. Days after his eighteenth birthday, the local paper noted that Gibson had an excellent game against the more established London Asylum Club when he and his Knox teammates walloped the senior team 9–1. On August 22, Gibby led his team to another surprising win, defeating the senior London Rockets Club 10–7 and bringing their record to an astonishing 16–1.

A week later, the team traveled to Strathroy, Ontario, to take on the

Knox Church Baseball Club circa 1898. Gibson's first star appearance occurred while playing with his youth club. Gibson is pictured third row, center (*London Free Press*, A Division of Postmedia Network, Inc.).

town's club. Strathroy is a town about thirty-five kilometers west of London and had a population of approximately 3,000 people in 1898. The town was a main hub on the Great Western Railroad, which ran from London to Windsor, Ontario. Its location on the Sydenham River made the town a prominent agricultural center at the turn of the 20th century. Although a much smaller town, the proximity to London made for great rivalries. The Strathroy team consisted of men in their mid-to-late twenties, while the Knox players were all under twenty years old. Upon arriving in Strathroy, fans of the hometown side "chaffed" the Knox players, calling them "mere schoolboys." The spectators' opinion of them changed by the ball game's completion, when George and his teammates, the "mere schoolboys," defeated the Strathroy club by a final score of 11–8.[24] At year's end, the *London Free Press* declared the Knox Baseball Club amateur champions of London. The team played the 1898 campaign well above their years and piled up 21 wins on the season.

George played for the Knox Club again in 1899. And again, Gibby and his teammates played well enough to be called London's top amateur club by the local newspapers. In late July, the famous Lucan Irish 9 challenged the Knox Club to an exhibition game in Lucan, a town twenty-two kilometers northwest of London. Many of Lucan's original settlers were Irish Catholic laborers brought in to work on the Grand Trunk railroad, which led to a large Irish population and the ball team's nickname. The late July matchup of Knox versus Lucan proved to be the most prolific game on Gibson's young resume. Knox won the game convincingly, 33–10. Mooney performed well, going 4-for-8 at the plate, with a pair of two-baggers. Defensively, he was also outstanding, recording ten putouts and two assists while committing no errors. The Knox Club, despite their relative youth, started gaining much respect throughout the London area. The game certainly seems to have been notable, as after he passed away, historians erred in saying George had played for the Lucan team; and, although there was a Gibson who played for the Irish 9, his name was Walter.[25] There is no evidence that Gibby ever took the field with the Lucan crew. Whatever the case may have been, Knox had harder competition on the horizon.

On August 2, 1899, the Knox Club played London's semipro team, Gibby's first time suiting up against professionals. The game was played at Tecumseh Park, London's top ball field. The Knox team had played at parks all over London, including the Erie Flats, Springbank Park, Waterloo Commons and the Military Grounds at Wolseley Barracks. But the place that all London ballplayers wanted to play was Tecumseh Park. (As of 2019, Tecumseh Park, now called Labatt Park, is said to be the oldest continually used baseball grounds in North America.) The game was a one-sided affair. The Knox Club showed their nerves in the first few innings and couldn't make up ground, eventually losing the game 13–5. Bert Sheere, London baseball guru and future Gibson manager, pitched for the London's top team that day. George managed two hits, including a double off Sheere, and played really well defensively. He had three putouts and five assists in the game, but where Gibson was especially impressive was the error department. While the amateur Knox team nervously had eleven errors against the pros, Gibson, who caught the whole game, had none. Gibson's great defense, especially against Sheere, really was his coming out party on the London baseball scene.

The 1900 season was George's third consecutive year with the Knox Church Baseball Club. George was joined on the team by his older brother, Robert, a pitcher. The pair formed the team's top battery. Ahead of any baseball being played, tragedy struck the Gibson family. At the end of March, George and Robert's mother, Hannah Southam, passed away at the age of 62.[26] At the time, George Sr. was still active in the construction business. Still living with him in London West, and also active in the construction business, were his sons Edward, Harry, William and Robert, along with his daughter, Matilda.[27]

The Knox ball team's great play made baseball very popular in London. The club received very good crowds all season. Near the end of the summer, Knox was challenged to a match by another out-of-town club. This time it was the City of Woodstock, whose club would eventually be crowned champions of the Canadian Amateur League in 1900. A two-game series was arranged. The first of the two matches was played in Woodstock, a town about forty-five kilometers east of London. Early pioneers settled the area because of its proximity to the head of the Thames River. In 1900, the population of the town was almost 9,000, and it was a main rival for London sporting clubs. The game was a well-played affair. "But for errors in the sixth the home team should have been retired without scoring and the game lost to them."[28] Instead, Woodstock scored five runs, and turned a 3–1 deficit into a 6–3 lead. George had a poor day all around. In addition to going 0-for-4 at the plate, he committed three errors while making his first ever appearance at shortstop, a position he clearly wasn't accustomed to playing. The final score was 7–3 in favor of the home club. The second match was played in London, at Tecumseh Park. Gibby was back to his natural position and the Knox Club fared far better, topping Woodstock 10–6. George made no errors and put out six Woodstockers. He also hit his first recorded home run in the game, a beautiful drive to the fence in left center field. The Knox team was extremely pleased to have turned the tables on the Canadian Amateur League champions and get a split in the two-game series.

Knox again played for the City League championship. This time they went up against a team called the Pastimes, a team they hadn't played all season. Knox was expected to win, and hundreds of fans came out to support them. Despite being favored, the Knox Club was held to only four hits that day by a 17-year-old pitcher by the name of Mr. Early. The Pastimes won in a rout, 10–3. George went 1-for-3 at the dish and scored two of the Knox runs, but the day belonged to the opponents and the 1900 season was over.

The off-season was a busy one for George. He married Margaret McMurphy, of West London, and the couple gave birth to their first child, a son, George Gordon Gibson. At the time of the Canadian Census in 1901,[29] George, Margaret and a very young George Gordon lived in West London. George listed his occupation as bricklayer.

Because of how well the Knox

George Gibson circa 1900 (courtesy Carol Smith).

team played against Woodstock at the end of the previous season, London baseball men decided to put together a traveling amateur baseball team to join the Canadian Amateur League. The cities represented for 1901 were London, Woodstock, Guelph, Waterloo, Galt (now called Cambridge) and Berlin (now called Kitchener). George and Robert both played on the London team. The season began on April 27, 1901, when London hosted Guelph at Tecumseh Park in front of six hundred excited fans, including London mayor Frederick George Rumball. Guelph got off to a hasty start, scoring five runs before the London club even had a chance to bat. London's young southpaw, Kellien, was not on his mark, but their batsmen brought their hitting shoes. By the end of the second frame, London had tied the game 6–6. Over the next six innings, they held Guelph to a single run while scoring seven of their own. With London up 13–7, the game was called after eight innings so Guelph could catch their train. Gibby had a great game. He went 3-for-3 at the plate, with a double and a triple. His day could have been even better if not for the field conditions: "Gibson's drive for three bags would have been a homer but for the hay."[30] The London amateur club got off to a brilliant start for their 1901 season.

The Canadian Amateur League team from London cruised through their first month of existence. George was one of the top performers in the circuit, but in a game on May 24, it was his brother Robert who stole the show. The *London Free Press* reported, "Robert Gibson made his debut on the Tecumseh Park stage, and jumped at once into popularity. Four singles and a hand out were all he allowed to the enemy from Galt, and the result was a shutout."[31] The Gibson brothers had the London fans going nuts, and were said to have, "brought down the house."[32] Beating the team from Galt 3–0 catapulted George and Robert into local stardom.

A few weeks later, London played an exhibition game against the University of Toronto baseball club at Tecumseh Park. Robert was London's starting pitcher. The scholars were no problem for the Gibson brother battery. London won the lopsided affair 14–5. Gibby later recalled about his brother: "He was a pitcher, and hurt his arm … just warming up, he hurt his elbow and … when I looked over my baseball experience, and I've looked at a lot of pitchers … and boy, he had a lot of natural stuff … as a kid."[33]

At the beginning of July, George joined a team including both London teammates and players from other local amateur teams in order to play a doubleheader in Jamestown, New York. Jamestown, located about 75 miles southwest of Buffalo, New York, hosted the London picked nine as part of their Fourth of July celebrations. George caught both games, but Jamestown beat the London squad with relative ease, the scores being 9–0 and 9–6. The series was barely a footnote in local newspapers,[34] but ended up having a profound impact on Gibson's baseball career, though nobody realized it at the time.

By mid–July, perhaps for financial reasons, the London team withdrew from the Canadian Amateur League. London was among the top clubs in the league, so it was not because of poor play. All of the players from the London club went back to their city league teams. George and Robert went to play for the London Drug Store team managed by Bert Sheere. Gibby also played exhibition games for his old neighborhood team, the West London Stars, but with the disbanding of the Canadian Amateur League club, Gibby's 1901 season wound down rather unceremoniously.

With no London team in the Canadian Amateur League for the 1902 season, Gibson played in the city's amateur league. The league consisted of four teams. George and Robert played for a team called the Struthers. The *London Free Press* reported on the proposed roster: "Of these, George Gibson will undoubtedly be at the receiving end of the battery. He is one of the best catchers in the business, and will be a mainstay to the team."[35] The other clubs were the Rockets, the Aberdeens and the Londons, managed by the aforementioned Bert Sheere. Gibby and his Struthers teammates would be rivals to Sheere and his Londons club all season long. The Struthers club recorded their first win on May 24. Gibby and his crew won the hard-fought match, 8–7. George was good defensively, making eight putouts. He went 0-for-2 at the plate, but did take a free pass and managed to swipe two bases.

Struthers and the Londons played brilliantly all season. On August 10 the two teams clashed in what was a notable game for the Gibson brothers. After one inning, Struthers was ahead 5–2. Robert pitched a fine game, and that early lead should have been enough, but nine Struthers errors allowed Sheere and his men to battle back, tying the score in the sixth. The game remained tied until, with two out in the bottom of the ninth, the Struthers pushed a man across the dish to secure the 8–7 victory. George went 2-for-5 at the plate with a two-bagger. By this time in the season, the Struthers and the Londons were easily the top teams, as the Rockets and the Aberdeens were fading from the playoff picture.

A day before helping lead his team to victory over the Londons, George played in an exhibition game that would ultimately have immediate and long-term benefits for his career, the latter of which came to fruition several months down the road. August 9 was the McClary's annual company picnic. McClary's was a prominent employer in the city. At the picnic, a baseball game was played. McClary's had a team in the Manufacturer's League, but had no opponent for this special occasion. The company ended up picking an all-star team from the city league, and Gibson was chosen to catch. In front of 5,000 spectators, Gibby and the city league's picked nine defeated the McClary's club, 7–6. George walked away with a share of the $20 prize that was awarded to the winning team and caught the eye of baseball men outside of the city league at the same time.

A few weeks later, back with the Struthers club, George was handed the ball to take the mound against the lowly Aberdeen club. In his first career start as a pitcher, George turned some heads. The *London Free Press* wrote of his performance: "Mooney Gibson proved to be a stumbling block for his opponents, striking out five of the first ten men up."[36] Gibson ended up striking out ten men, allowing only one run in a 5–1 Struthers win.

The city league season finished near the end of September. The pennant winner went on to play in the city-wide championship, a five-game series against the winner of the Manufacturer's League. Unfortunately, the Struthers fell short, and it was the Londons who advanced to face McClary's, the champions of the rival league. But losing to the Londons wasn't enough to keep Gibson out of the championship. McClary's hadn't forgotten about the young catcher's great performance at their company picnic a few weeks earlier. They offered George a job and a place on their baseball team as the starting backstop. Gibson accepted the offer, and appreciated getting a second chance to defeat his city league rival.

The city-wide championship was decided on a cold mid–October day. With the Londons up 2–1 in the best of five series, the final two games were scheduled on the same day, to be sure to determine a winner before the Canadian weather became too frigid. Bert Sheere did not want to drag the series out any longer, so he took the mound for the Londons, hoping to negate the need for a sudden death game later in the day. Both teams got off to a quick start, scoring runs early. Tied 2–2 in the seventh, the Londons counted a pair to take the lead. McClary's responded immediately, capitalizing on poor fielding and putting up six runs to take an 8–4 lead into the eighth. And then, as described by the *London Free Press*, McClary's brought in their left fielder to pitch "for some unknown reason."[37] He pitched to five batters before being replaced on the mound by George, who managed to get McClary's out of the inning with an 8–7 lead. McClary's hung on to win the game 8–7 and force a fifth and deciding game.

As with the morning game, Bert Sheere insisted on pitching the series finale; a questionable call after such a tough morning. The Londons scored in the first to take an early lead, and increased their lead to 2–0 with another tally in the fourth. In the seventh, just like in the morning game, they clubbed Sheere for seven runs, enough to win the game and the championship. George went 2-for-3, with a triple and a run scored. Perhaps most importantly, it appeared that George had landed himself a pretty good year-round job, and a place to play for 1903.

In the midst of the city championship series, reports came out of Toronto and London that Ed Barrow, manager of the Toronto Club of the Eastern League, had signed George Gibson for his club and would give him a "thorough trial next Spring."[38]

In January of 1903, as Toronto was gearing up for the upcoming season, Gibson was listed among the men on their roster.[39] Whatever chances George had with Toronto ended abruptly once Ed Barrow resigned from Toronto in order to manage the Detroit Tigers. Following that announcement, Gibson's name simply disappeared from the Toronto roster without any mention of him having been released, or of him ever having reported to Toronto for a Spring tryout. George simply remained in London, kept his job with McClary's and maintained his roster spot on their team in the Manufacturer's League.

The McClary's manufacturing company was founded January 1, 1852, by brothers John and Oliver McClary. The central component of their foundry was cast iron stoves, but they also manufactured tin, copper, agricultural implements and machinery. The company encouraged good employee morale, and held picnics and other social events for their workers. Perhaps their most popular morale-boosting activity was sponsoring a baseball club consisting of their own factory employees.

Jos. H. Herrick, president of McClary's baseball program, decided to have two teams from the manufacturing company compete during the 1903 baseball season. One team played in the Wholesale League, and the other played in the City League. George Gibson and brother Richard suited up for the McClary's City League team and acted as the club's top battery. Most City League games were played at Tecumseh Park, where teams competed for the Beck Cup. The six clubs that made up the league were the McClary's, Rockets, Carletons, Anchors, St. John Saints and Londons. Opening day was May 3 and the McClary's were matched up against the Londons. In a 2–1 McClary's victory, George hit an RBI triple, and his brother Robert gave up just two hits while striking out eight. The McClary's club kept winning throughout May, beating all comers and, in some cases, obliterating them. The McClary's nine outscored their opponents, the St. John's Saints and the Anchors, by a combined score of 30–1 during a weekend set of games on May 24 and May 25. These embarrassing games caused the City League to be shut down for a month to deal with a definite competitive imbalance. When the league restarted in late June, the Carletons and Anchors withdrew from the league due to financial issues.

When the McClary's returned to action, they suffered their first lost of the season in a game against the St. John's Saints. They got back to their winning ways a few days later, when George went 3-for-5 and Robert pitched, leading McClary's to a 13–5 win over the Londons. The *London Free Press* said of the ball team's performance: "The factory men seem to have been put on their mettle by Saturday's defeat and went after their old time rivals from the drop of the bat, pounding Sheere without mercy."[40] The McClary's nine knew that Sheere and his Londons were no pushovers and anticipated heated games with them down the stretch.

A week later, the Londons got their revenge. On July 12 they scorched Robert for eighteen hits and twelve runs, handing the McClary's a 12–8 loss. For the remainder of July and August the McClary's played only .500 ball, but owing to their hot start to the season, they still secured a spot in the City League finals.

As the London City League was winding down, a series of events were unfolding in the Eastern League. On August 26, the Eastern League's first place Buffalo Bisons were hosting Rochester. In the top of the first, Buffalo's regular catcher, Al Shaw, "strained his ankle getting after a ball."[41] Shaw remained in the game long enough to finish the inning, but was unable to continue the contest. Bisons manager George Stallings went to his backup catcher, Charley Luskey, and Buffalo still managed to secure a 7–3 victory.

When Buffalo's game on August 28 was rained out, newspaper men filled the extra space by assessing the state of the Bison team. Things looked bleak: "As for the outlook of the team, things seem to remain unchanged and unaltered likewise. Every effort which the management has made to date to secure new players has met with a dearth of results. Buffalo seems utterly forsaken in her time of need. There was never a time when the management was more pressed for players of sound caliber than now."[42]

As it turned out, Buffalo hadn't hit rock bottom yet. The storm that canceled Saturday's game wasn't done wreaking havoc to the ball field. Despite unfavorable conditions, a "holiday crowd"[43] showed up to see the Bisons host the Baltimore Orioles, and the game was played. "Wagon-loads of sawdust were carried to the infield and spread about in great quantities."[44] Efforts to make the playing field usable seemed to have little effect, as both teams repeatedly failed to make routine plays. The game was a high-scoring affair. A major blow was struck in the seventh inning when, "[first baseman Moose] Grimshaw wrenched his lame side in throwing to second base and was obliged to retire."[45] Already short on players, the loss of Grimshaw overshadowed the other loss—Baltimore won the game 11–8. Piling on the disappointment, it seems Luskey wasn't working out as hoped behind the plate: "The position of catcher is lamentably weak. Luskey tries hard, but he is wanting when it comes to headwork."[46]

As Gibson himself would recall years later, a friend of Stallings, a lawyer named Fraser, had witnessed the July 4 games in Jamestown in 1901 and taken notice of Gibson. Fraser went to Stallings, knowing he was in need of catchers, and told him of a catcher he'd seen with an outfit from London. Manager Stallings had exactly one contact in London, and it was precisely the one he needed—Bert Sheere. Upon hearing from Stallings, Sheere headed over to McClary's Manufacturing to see Gibson and told him, "Stallings wants you right away in Buffalo." Gibson "hopped this old electric line down to St. Thomas and then over to Buffalo."[47]

According to newspaper reports out of Buffalo, Gibson was "presented ... to the public" on August 31.[48] Although he didn't play that first day, he did warm up with the team, and the reviews were positive: "Gibson warmed up in practice and he played fast ball. He is a likely-looking youngster and he will undoubtedly make good."[49] News of Gibson joining Buffalo also made it back to Gibson's hometown. Curiously, the topic was not covered in much depth. It was modestly mentioned that "a Londoner" was among "a number of new players to take the place of crippled men of the Buffalo Eastern League team."[50] Included in that group was George "Scoops" Carey, picked up from the Washington Senators to play first base for Stallings. Though the London paper would report the four players as having signed with Buffalo, Gibson explained it differently. He never actually signed a contract for 1903, and instead played for both the Bisons and the McClary's, electing to continue to play for his hometown team in the midst of a pennant race.

In his first game as a professional, Gibson watched Buffalo and Baltimore battle to a 0–0 tie that was called after nine innings on account of darkness. When the two teams met again, Scoops Carey still had not arrived, causing Buffalo to share first base duties among available players. Luskey was once again behind the bat, and Gibson remained out of the lineup. Baltimore won the game, 7–3.

Baltimore and Buffalo met again on Wednesday. Cy Ferry, normally a pitcher, started at first base, and Gibson was not expected to play. However, in the top of the second Ferry failed to make a play that allowed a Baltimore run to score. Seeing this, Stallings walked over to his new catcher: "Did you ever play first base, Gibby?" Gibson responded: "No, I never did Mr. Stallings." Convinced that a defensive switch was still necessary, Stallings ordered Gibson onto the field: "Take your glove and go down and play." Armed with his catcher's mitt, Gibson did as his new boss instructed, and replaced Ferry at first base.[51] In the fourth inning, "Gibson rapped a fast one which Jones impeded."[52] Still, it was not a completely lost turn at the plate as he did advance Charlie Atherton, who had been stationed on second. The next batter, John Shearon, brought Atherton around to score, thus tying the game. Baltimore plated two in the eighth and three in the ninth, putting Buffalo in a deep hole, but there was still more baseball to play. Atherton led off the ninth and managed to gain first base thanks to a Baltimore throwing error. Fred Hartman flew out, and Gibson promptly "poked out a rattling hit,"[53] his first in the Eastern League. Sheared also recorded a hit to load the bases. Shortstop Billy Nattress scored Atherton on a fielder's choice as Shearon was nabbed at second. Nattress and Gibson then worked the double-steal perfectly, and Gibson scored to bring the score to 6–3. That was as close as they got. Charley Luskey batted next and connected on a ball to center field, but it was caught, and the game ended. Despite the loss, Stallings had to be pleased with the young Canadian. The *London Free Press* certainly had some praise for Gibson, noting that "he covered himself with glory. He accepted ten chances and laced out a nice single."[54]

September 4 brought another disappointing outcome for Stallings's men against Toronto. Gibson made his debut at catcher, and "he shaped well behind the bat."[55] Gibson and Carey both handled the bat well, but Toronto simply overmatched the visitors. The final score was 8–3 in favor of Toronto. Following the game, Gibson returned to London, where he joined his McClary's team for the weekend's games. Forming the battery with his brother Robert for both games, the McClary's club lost on Saturday by a score of 6–3, and then bounced back on Sunday to defeat the Rockets 8–0.

Gibson rejoined the Buffalo club in Toronto immediately after the series in London and promptly signed a contract with Stallings to play with Buffalo in 1904. Though Gibson had only played in two games so far, Stallings clearly liked what he saw. The two sides agreed to a $150-per-month contract (equivalent to $4,200 per month in 2019), and $200 if Gibson was still in the league on July 1. Well after his career ended, Gibson explained his thought process in signing that contract: "When you're laying [brick] in the building business, and hard work for nine hours a day, and every day was a holiday to me playing ball."[56]

The three-game losing streak finally stopped for Buffalo on September 11, when the Bisons won the first game of a doubleheader against Providence. George returned to the lineup and caught the entire game, recording three putouts and no errors while contributing a hit in three attempts.

Three days later, against Montreal, Alex Hardy, a Canadian picked up from Toronto a week earlier, formed the battery with his fellow countryman. "Gibson, the young man from Canada, did the backstop work, and he was in no way lacking. He kept busy all the time, and gave Hardy good support."[57] A six-run third powered Buffalo to a 12–3 victory. Stallings marched the exact same lineup back out the next day, save for Louis LaRoy, who pitched instead of Alex Hardy. Gibson played well, and for six innings Buffalo looked great. Bad luck struck in the seventh when "Gibson hurt a finger and went out."[58] McAllister moved behind the plate, Atherton came in from right field to play second and Billy Milligan came off of the bench to play right field. Montreal took the lead in the seventh, before Buffalo tied it again in the eighth and won it in the ninth on a Billy Milligan home run. This would mark the last game George Gibson wore the Bison flannel in in 1903.

The extent of the injury Gibson sustained is unknown. But it wasn't enough to stop him from playing baseball. As had been his routine for September, Gibson returned to London and took the field with the McClary's club. This game was of particular importance, because it was against the Londons. The *London Free Press* predicted it to be "about the most interesting game of the season," adding, "If the Londons win it means that the McClary's have lost their last chance to land the championship. If the factorymen [sic] win they will have a good show to tie with the Londons for first place, or even to win the cup by a narrow margin."[59]

The championship game was played in front of a large crowd at Tecumseh Park in London. Fans were treated to a match that pitted the Gibson brother battery against a London battery featuring Bert Sheere. The Londons got off to a fast start when Bert Stein, after being hit by a pitch, came around to score, staking his team to an early lead. The McClary's answered back immediately, and after one inning the game was tied 1–1. McClary's scored again in the third, and held a 2–1 lead until the Londons tied the game in the seventh inning. With two out in the bottom of the frame, George came to the plate, with runners at second and third. "Never would a clean single have been more opportune, but Geo. Gibson could do no better than put up a short high fly."[60] The Londons threatened in the eighth, but George made a sharp throw to third and "spoiled a bright chance."[61] With two out in the ninth, the Londons plated a pair and took a 4–2 lead into the bottom of the inning. The McClary's never got a man past second, and the Londons won the city championship.

As for Buffalo, after Gibson left, they went 5–6–1 and were never really a threat for the pennant. Buffalo's biggest chance to make a statement came during a three-game series against Jersey City. The Skeeters took all three games, and Buffalo finished the season in second place.

In the off-season, George continued to work at McClary's, anticipating the Spring, which would mark the beginning of his first full season in professional baseball. On a personal note, in early December, he and his wife welcomed the birth of their second child, a daughter they named Marguerite.[62]

3

The Canadian Is a Comer

Preparations for the 1904 season started making news in January. On the 31st of that month, the *Augusta Chronicle* announced, "In all probability the Buffalo team of the Eastern League, will do their spring stunts on the Augusta grounds."[1] In order to arrange the deal, Manager Stallings wired his father, Colonel Stallings, who lived in Augusta, Georgia, and asked that he inquire about the price to rent the baseball grounds in Augusta for the Spring. George Stallings was born in Augusta and had deep baseball roots there, having managed that city's club in the Southern League in the 1890s. He also owned a plantation in Haddock (about 100 miles West of Augusta). It does not appear to have taken long for the two sides to reach a deal. On February 17, the *Buffalo Express* reported that "Manager Stallings has ordered the members of the Buffalo team to report to him at Buffalo on March 12th."[2] Stallings intended to take 18 or 19 men with him, and upon returning north to start the season, would keep any man that made the return trip for at least one month after the opening game of the season.

George Gibson was among the initial congregation of eleven ball players that gathered with Manager Stallings at the Exchange Street Station in Buffalo. The group boarded the Pennsylvania Railroad and left on the evening of March 12. "The probable champions occupied a special car,"[3] which picked up additional players as it headed towards Washington. From Washington, the group traveled to Augusta, where it was expected that more players would arrive later. Per earlier arrangements, the Albion Hotel was ready for Stallings and his team. The men arrived early in the morning, and reported to the hotel. "No time was lost, for Mr. Stallings, after dinner, carried the men to the grounds and started them to limbering up."[4]

Though there was a stiff wind, the weather was warm and ideal for the first practice of the season. Stallings ran his men through a light practice in front of "a good crowd of fans."[5] To get his men in shape, Manager Stallings planned separate morning and afternoon practices and expected to be playing intrasquad games within the first week. Early reports of Gibson's physical condition noted that he was "one of the best built men on the team, and when he works off some of the extra meat that he has distributed over his frame, he will be a fine looking young ball player."[6] Two practices a day certainly helped trim up Gibson and the other players. One early box score reported an intrasquad game between a team of new recruits, referred to as the "Yannigans," and a team of veteran players, referred to as the "Regulars." Gibson caught for the Yannigans and saw his team get thoroughly beaten by the Regulars, 38–2. For about a week, Stallings ran his club through intrasquad matches. It allowed him to get his club into game shape and to test out various roster combinations. For two games, he tried George out as a third baseman.

The end of March marked the end of intrasquad games for the Bisons. With the Eastern League season set to begin April 27, Stallings and his men needed to make the return trip North. Plus, the Augusta Tourists, a team in the South Atlantic League, needed their diamond to prepare for the start of their own season. When Stallings and his men first arrived in Augusta, it was estimated that the cost for the trip was approximately $200 per player. This is a significant amount of money to spend training a minor-league team, especially with Gibson's monthly salary being just $150. Getting the season underway would be the only way to find out the true value of that investment.

Historically speaking, there is some significance to a minor-league team spending such a substantial amount of money to ready their players for the

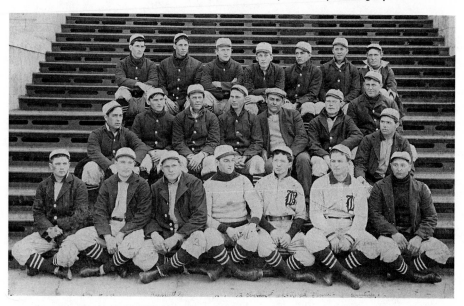

The 1904 Buffalo Bisons, spring training. The year 1904 was Gibson's first professional spring camp. Gibson is pictured second row, far right (courtesy the Ernie Harwell Sports Collection, Detroit Public Library).

season. Spring training certainly wasn't new to baseball, and was becoming commonplace among major-league teams, but with tighter budgets and shorter seasons, it wasn't a common thing for minor-league teams.

Another event took place in Augusta in the spring of 1904 that is perhaps more significant historically. A young man born in Narrows, Georgia, was trying to make his way into professional baseball, and had been invited to try out with Con Strouthers's Augusta Tourists. That young man was a 17-year-old by the name of Tyrus Raymond Cobb. Following his retirement, Gibson would recall meeting Ty Cobb in Augusta that year, playing games against the Tourists and walking back to the team hotel with him.[7] Cobb ended up making the Tourists that Spring, but was cut after only two games.

On April 2, Buffalo hosted the Brooklyn Nationals in Augusta. Ned Hanlon and his men handed Stallings's herd two straight losses. Despite the losses to close out their time in Augusta, the spring training trip was considered a success. The team looked poised to be very competitive in the upcoming season. For their part, Stallings and his men were quite satisfied with the experience. "Stallings said that every one of the boys were stuck on the town, the diamond, the weather, and above all, the girls."[8] Certainly the respect shown by the ball players was reciprocated. "A more gentlemanly set of young ball players have never visited Augusta."[9]

Stallings made the return trip a preseason barnstorming tour. After stops in Tennessee, Kentucky and Ohio, they arrived home to face the World Series champions, the Boston Americans. George did not get much playing time on the trip. Instead, Stallings split catching duties between the men expected to be his two main catchers for the season: Al Shaw and Sport McAllister. On April 23, Buffalo hosted St. Bonaventure College at Buffalo. Al Shaw started behind the plate, but was removed in the later innings and replaced with Gibson. In his only at bat of the game, George "lifted the sphere over the left field fence, accomplishing one of the cleanest four-baggers ever seen on the grounds."[10] That home run counted for three of the six runs plated by Buffalo in the eighth inning, and turned the game into a lopsided affair en route to a 9–1 win. Although this was Gibson's first home run of the season, it was the second one to make the newspapers that Spring. Earlier in March, the *Augusta Chronicle* printed a collection of baseball yarns. Among the stories of home runs being hit through fences and using axe-handles for bats was an anecdote shared by George about a home run he had hit in the previous season:

> Gibson says that once last year he was playing with a country team and the pitcher on the opposing side was a veritable cinch to him as every time he got up to the bat he would paste 'em out for a single or a double. The next time he got up he determined to show the rubes how a ball ought to be hit. The first one that the pitcher floated up was a nice one, right in the groove and Gib let 'er drive. The ball sailed over the fence

and Gibson made an easy home-run. This was the only ball the club had and as several more innings were to be played everybody went over to hunt for the ball. They searched and searched, but the ball failed to make its appearance and it was finally given up. About a month later the man who owned the land adjoining the ball field had a big dinner. 'Punkin' was one of the articles on the menu and when one of these were opened 'the birds began to sing,' but not this time, for inside of it was found the ball that Gib had sent over the fence. When the ball landed it had probably hit the young pumpkin while the skin was soft and went in. The hole finally healed over and the ball was not discovered until the big dinner.[11]

Buffalo played in one final exhibition game before the start of the Eastern League's regular season. Stallings's men hosted Niagara University. The game was never really in question. With nobody available to officiate the game, Gibson and Sport McAllister split catching and umpiring duties, and Buffalo cruised to another 9–1 victory.

Less than a week before the season started, it was announced that the Eastern League's Worcester club was transferred to John Kreitner. John Kreitner was a well-known theatrical man in Buffalo, and a known associate of George Stallings. Kreitner immediately relocated the Worcester franchise to Montreal. While Kreitner controlled the club, the common belief was that it was being treated as an extension of the Buffalo Club. According to newspaper accounts, Stallings gave his captain, Charlie Atherton, among other players, to Montreal.

The Montreal Royals' season got off to a shaky start, and President Kreitner set out to do something about it. He started by acquiring Bill Clancy from California to play first base. Kreitner then purchased the release of catcher Jack Toft from Toronto for $500, but Toft refused to report to Montreal. Still in need of a catcher, Kreitner turned to his friend in Buffalo. Manager Stallings was carrying three catchers, and though he admitted to wanting to get Gibson into games, there simply weren't enough innings to go around. Going from Buffalo to Montreal meant going from a pennant contender to a team yet to record a win. But it also meant going from watching games to actually playing in them. And Gibson wanted to work. Gibson was aware that there was a syndicate between Buffalo and Montreal and was under the impression that Stallings could get him back.[12] The deal Kreitner and Stallings worked out sent George Gibson and third baseman Fred Hartman to the Royals.

Gibson's debut with Montreal came on May 9 in Jersey City. He started as catcher, while manager Charlie Atherton, having already played four different positions so far in the season, "went into the pitcher's box, with the hope of turning the tide in favor of the Royals."[13] The move almost worked. Montreal took a 7–4 lead into the bottom of the ninth, but that's when the Royals' defense let down their pitching manager. Jersey City scored three in the ninth to tie the game, and scored another in the tenth with two out to win it. Despite the loss, Atherton was upbeat, providing the following assessment of the team: "We look like a million dollars now."[14] His assessment of Gibson was also favorable: "He is a fine catcher, and a good hitter."[15]

After going winless in their first 10, the *Gazette* seemed optimistic about the future of the catching situation in Montreal. The club hadn't given up on signing Toft, though he had not yet come to terms with the team and was also trying to negotiate with Jersey City. Despite this news, there must have been some reason to believe that Toft would eventually be seen wearing a Royals uniform when this was published: "A good hitting outfielder would fit on the Montreal team besides a couple of pitchers. Toft and Gibson should make the catching department secure."[16]

On the heels of back-to-back extra inning losses, Montreal was in Providence again on May 12, and finally broke through. Providence's pitcher, Jim Fairbank, struck out eight Royals in the game, but four errors in the top of the fifth allowed Montreal to put up five runs. Montreal won 7–3. Gibson led the offensive charge, registering a 4-for-4 day at the plate to go along with six putouts, an assist and no errors.

Meanwhile, President Kreitner was in New York scouting for players. Additional player acquisitions announced on the 14th were pitcher Billy Milligan from the New York Nationals and catcher Frank McManus from the Detroit Americans. Frank McManus was a significant signing because of the impact he had on Gibson. George later recalled: "I just get to Montreal and here comes an older catcher from Detroit, which I give all the credit in the world. 95% of the credit of my quick advance to the big leagues."[17] Frank McManus was signed by Ed Barrow to play with the Detroit Americans in 1904, but shortly after Detroit's season opened, McManus was sold to Montreal. The move suggests that Kreitner had given up on getting Jack Toft into a Royals uniform.

Immediately upon joining the Royals, McManus took over catching duties. For both games of a weekend series at Providence, George was placed in right field. Montreal won the Saturday game 8–3, but lost on Sunday by a narrow margin of 2–1. For the Royals, the loss marked the end of a fourteen-game road trip, and meant it was time to return to Montreal to play some games at the St. Catherine Street Grounds.

To mark the official start of the season in Montreal, a parade through the city was planned to show off the players in their purple and white home uniforms, led by the Victoria Rifles Band. Optimism was in the air. The *Montreal Gazette* noted, "The home team is in far better condition than they were when they opened with Newark."[18] Manager Atherton went so far as to predict, and offer to bet money, that his club "will be in the first division at the end of the month."[19] With eight teams in the league, a top four finish meant Atherton's club would place in the first division. Before the game could be played, rain fell and the contest was postponed. Team batting averages were published, and Gibson narrowly held the team lead with a .455 average (5-for-11 over three games). Gibson was ninth in team fielding, posting a .929 average (1 error in 14 chances).

By May 17, the weather had cleared, and Montreal and Newark were able to square off. Both bleachers were packed, and a fair crowd was in the covered stands as well. Despite Montreal's poor record so far, the "team received a pleasant welcome from the fans."[20] McManus started behind the plate, but injured his knee on a foul tip in the sixth and had to be removed at the end of the inning. Gibson took over, and turned in a respectable game, including throwing a runner out at third in the seventh inning. Despite Gibson's performance, the Royals were unable to rally back from an early deficit, and Newark went on to win Montreal's home opener 5–1.

Montreal closed out May with a flourish, and made significant improvements to their record. They didn't win enough to get into the first division as Atherton had predicted, but an eight-game winning streak improved their record to 10–13, which placed them in sixth place. A 6–3 loss to Providence on June 2 ended their streak and pushed Montreal back to seventh. Montreal wasn't held down for long. With McManus and Gibson sharing the catching duties, Montreal put together another string of wins and ascended to fifth place with a record of 13–14. On June 7, they faced-off against Toronto, with holdout catcher Jack Toft in attendance. Gibson did not play in this game, but still managed to find his way to the field. "No umpire appeared, and Mills and Gibson umpired half an inning, when Jack Toft took charge."[21] Toronto won the game 9–3. This was as close to taking the field for Montreal as Jack Toft got in 1904. He was eventually sent to Providence, where he finished the season.

As June progressed, the Royals continued to keep things interesting, winning just enough games to keep pace with Newark. By June 16, Montreal was still in fifth place with a record of 16–17, just behind Newark, who were 18–18. Gibson's batting average had dropped to .297, and though it was considerably lower than a month earlier, he still maintained the team lead. He also improved his fielding percentage to 0.946, good enough for second on the squad, just ahead of Frank McManus, who had a fielding percentage of 0.945.

Montreal returned home to start July, and marked Canada's 37th birthday by sweeping a doubleheader against Rochester. Gibson played right field for the first contest and had a forgettable game. Not a single ball made it to right field, and at the plate, Gibson went 0-for-5 with four strikeouts. The second game was a different story. Montreal grabbed a 1–0 lead in the second inning and never looked back. Rochester saved themselves from being shut out by scoring two in the ninth, but it made little difference. The final score was 20–2. Gibson went 4–6 with four hits and four runs.

When the Royals played Toronto on July 12, they had improved their record to 28–28, and were in sole possession of fourth place. After splitting a doubleheader with the Maple Leafs, they slipped back to fifth place. Gibson did not participate in either contest despite McManus injuring himself in a collision with Toronto's catcher, Charles "Nig" Fuller.

On July 13, Frank McManus was held out of the lineup, suggesting that his injury from the previous day was more serious than initially believed. In fact, aside from a pair of appearances pinch-hitting, he did not play again for two full weeks. Over those 14 days, Montreal played 12 games, recording 4 wins against 7 losses, and a 16-inning tie called because of darkness. Despite their record being unimpressive, Montreal managed to remain in the same fifth-place slot they occupied when McManus got injured. This was an opportunity for George to prove that he could play every day in the Eastern League, and in hindsight, he gave a glimpse of the dependable defensive catcher he would become. Over the 12 games of McManus's injury, the Royals played 121 innings of baseball. George caught every single inning; he had one error. On the offensive side of the game, he went 9–46. By the end of the month, Montreal still held the fifth position in the standings, but the gap between them and fourth place Newark had widened considerably. Montreal kicked off August by taking three of four from the league-leading Bisons. Gibson and McManus returned to their routine of sharing catching evenly, and despite winning more than they lost, the team still fell from fifth to sixth, with Toronto ahead of them by 0.001 on August 6.

Perhaps the bigger news on the day, however, was an unconfirmed report out of Toronto that Ed Barrow had been signed to manage the Montreal Royals. Barrow had joined Detroit as their manager in January of 1903, after their previous manager, Win Mercer, died by suicide in a San Francisco hotel. At the time, Barrow was with Toronto of the Eastern League and negotiated his release to join Detroit, though he did maintain a stake in the Toronto club. Barrow's tenure in Detroit ended amidst conflicting rumors of him being fired and having resigned. On the recommendation of George Stallings, Kreitner signed Barrow. Exactly what became of Barrow's shares in the Toronto club is unknown. And for some, why he signed with Montreal instead of returning to Toronto was curious. "Why they have taken this step at this late day is mystifying, unless it is that they did not wish to see an old friend left out in the cold."[22] As Kreitner explained it, "I consider Barrows [sic] one of the superior managers in baseball and secured him immediately the opportunity presented itself. There will be no change with Atherton this season. He is to retain control of the players. Barrow has taken my place as my theatrical interests here prohibit my giving the club the time and attention necessary."[23] Whether Kreitner had put the interests of his club first or was doing a favor for Stallings is hard to say. In signing with Montreal, Barrow turned down offers from at least three other clubs. And despite claims by Kreitner that Atherton would maintain his position with the club, he was traded back to Buffalo nearly as quickly as the ink dried on the Barrow contract. For Stallings, who admitted in June that he missed Atherton, Barrow going to Montreal was convenient, if nothing else. But not everyone was a fan of the move. Catcher McManus and pitchers McCarthy and LeRoy all refused to play for Barrow and left the team. According to the same report, "The going of McManus weakens the team in catching, for young Gibson, an inexperienced backstop, is the only one left."[24]

The departure of McManus presented Gibson with another opportunity to play every day. And it was anything but a weakness for the club. From August 9 until August 18, Gibson backstopped 10 consecutive games for the Royals, and they won 8 of them, including 7 in a row. Though Gibson only batted 5-for-32 during that time, his defense was flawless. Partway through the streak, Montreal found themselves at .500 on the season, at one point getting as high as three games above. Eventually Barrow patched things up with his reluctant players, and Gibson got a rest.

Despite McManus being back with the club, Gibson continued to be the primary catcher. Whether this was Barrow sending McManus a message for abandoning the team or simply getting Gibson experience per his manager's earlier assessment is not known. "Manager Barrows [sic] thinks the Canadian is a comer. Gibson has the goods and is getting the experience."[25] Gibson caught in seven of Montreal's final nine games to end August. The good fortune of the first part of the month had gone, however. When September rolled around, the club had fallen behind Toronto for sixth place, and were six games below .500.

Montreal ended their losing ways on September 2, taking a game from Rochester, 9–2. It improved their record to 49–55, but still left them in sixth place. With the season winding down, talk of players being sold to, or drafted by, major-league teams heated up. Joe Yeager and Frank McManus were sold to the New York Americans just prior to Detroit making draft claims for them. The New York Nationals filed claims for Gibson and pitcher McCarthy. While the major-league draft was happening, Montreal continued to make their push for the first division. Montreal won both ends of a doubleheader on their way to four straight wins. They were going for a fifth against Toronto on September 13, when the game went into extra innings, tied 2–2. Toronto managed to score five runs in the top of the tenth, and Montreal responded by trying to delay the game. Umpire Egan, wise to what was going on, simply called the game and awarded it to Toronto. On September 15, Montreal played another doubleheader. Gibson caught both games as well, and Montreal was successful in sweeping the day from Toronto.

That Friday, Montreal beat fourth-place Newark, and brought their record back to an even .500. They remained in fifth, but were closing in on fourth. On Saturday, McManus made his final appearance of the season for Montreal, when he and Gibson split the work in a doubleheader sweep of Newark. The pair of wins brought Montreal's winning percentage within 0.039 of Newark's, but that was as close as they got the rest of the season. That evening, McManus left for New York. Meanwhile, Gibson remained in Montreal and served as the primary catcher while his draft status was sorted out. On the 27th, the Baseball Commission reported that the claim of Gibson by the New York Nationals had been contested, and not allowed. Montreal closed their season, hosting a doubleheader against second-place Baltimore.

Despite not managing to finish in the first division, the Royals' season closed on a high note as they swept the doubleheader. Gibson caught the first game, and Heinie Beckendorf, making his first and last appearance for Montreal, caught the second. Beckendorf was with Kingston of the Hudson River League, but was secured by Barrow a week earlier to fill the void left by McManus.

Montreal finished in fifth place, with a record of 66–61. Batting in 77 games, Gibson had 54 hits in 265 at bats for an average of .204. His 72 games caught ranked fourth in the Eastern League, and he recorded 316 putouts, 100 assists and 18 errors, for a fielding percentage of 0.959. All of this was good enough to keep Gibson on the Montreal roster for 1905.

To end their 1904 campaign, Montreal played a pair of exhibition games against a college team in Ottawa. Over 2,000 spectators attended each game. The college boys played good ball but were no match for Montreal. The Royals won by scores of 8–2 and 10–3. The second game was described as "the shortest and best game ever seen on the Hull grounds."[26] Following the series, Gibson returned to London for the off-season.

The major baseball storyline in October 1904, of course, was the cancellation of the World Series between the defending champion Boston Americans and the New York Giants. The cancellation was on account of John McGraw and John Brush, the respective manager and owner of the Giants. Though they were staunchly opposed to playing Boston, it seems not everyone in a Giants uniform was happy with that decision.

Giants catcher Jack Warner was among the possible dissenters. Perhaps as a consequence of his pro-Series position, New York sold Warner to St. Louis. Reports suggested that the move was part of an attempt to upgrade their catching, noting that "McGraw is trying to secure Catcher Gibson, of Montreal."[27] Lending even more credence to the reports of a falling out, papers reported a few days later that Roger Bresnahan attempted to buy a controlling interest in a Toledo baseball club. Bresnahan failed and he ultimately played with the Giants through the 1908 season. Despite repeated attempts by the New York Nationals to acquire George, he remained with Montreal.

In early December, Montreal grabbed headlines. First, rumors circulated that Ed Barrow was leaving to manage the Indianapolis Club of the American Association. Then, word spread that John Kreitner wanted to move the Royals to Richmond, Virginia, and sell the team. Eventually, the truth came out (with help from George Stallings, who seemed to go into damage-control mode). Barrow did leave Montreal and eagerly signed a contract with the Indianapolis Indians,[28] but, Kreitner kept the Royals, and they were not relocated.

Once the focus was back on playing baseball, Kreitner set out to find a new manager. Early reports were that first baseman Charlie Carr would secure his release from Cleveland of the American League to succeed Barrow, but that failed to materialize. Midway through the month, Kreitner announced that he had "purchased the release of Jimmy Bannon from the Newark Club. Bannon will manage the Montreal Club this coming season."[29]

With ownership and management figured out, the roster was next. A number of player changes occurred. Notably, the New York Americans decided to send Frank McManus back to Montreal. By March 16, nine men had signed for the 1905 season. Missing among those men was George Gibson. Gibson, it seems, was not interested in taking a pay cut, claiming that he would not play with Montreal for the salary offered by Manager Bannon. At the same time, Toronto's catcher, Tom Raub, was in the midst of his own hold out. To solve that problem, Toronto traded him to Montreal for Jack Toft, who was still controlled by the Royals even though he played with Providence in 1904. This left Montreal with three top-rated catchers, and created an opportunity for the Bisons, who had yet to receive a signed contract from their number one backstop, Al Shaw. Reports surfaced out of Buffalo that the Bisons wanted to deal pitcher Cy Ferry to Montreal in exchange for Gibson. Newspapers in Montreal predicted that Royals fans would not be pleased with the trade, acknowledging that Gibson was a gift from Buffalo while he was still an untried rookie. Kreitner had no interest in that deal, so he bought Gibson's contract and traded McManus for Cy Ferry instead.

With so much going on the business side of the ball club, spring training for the Royals seems to have been an afterthought. Compared to Gibson's experience with Buffalo in 1904, when Stallings announced Spring plans in February, the experience with Montreal in 1905 must have felt unorganized at best. This was understandable as Bannon had only joined the club as manager a few weeks prior. By the end of March, things started to take shape. Bannon arrived in Easton, Pennsylvania, with a small contingent of players and planned to train on the college grounds there until April 12. The team planned to make a circuit of the Tri-State clubs. Those plans were short-lived, however. Within a week of arriving in Easton, Bannon was instructed to cancel his scheduled games with York, Harrisburg and Williamsport on account of the Tri-State League being declared an outlaw league. Montreal quickly filled those open dates with other teams and made their way north for the start of the Eastern League's season.

The earliest recorded Montreal game in 1905 was on April 8, when the Royals hosted Lafayette at Ingersoll Field in Easton: "500 dyed-in-the-wool baseball fans" braved "the icy winds that swept over the town" to witness the afternoon contest. Newly acquired catcher Tom Raub played center field, Gibson was behind the plate and Bannon showed he "was the real stuff"[30] at third base. Still, Lafayette came away with the 7–1 win.

Montreal's next game was against the New York Giants at the Polo Grounds on April 12. The game marked Gibson's first time competing against a major-league club. Frigid weather conditions followed the Royals, and according to the *Evening World*, "this alone favored their escape from entire destruction."[31] George's first at bat of the game came with two out in the second. He singled to right to record the first hit of the game, but was forced out at second by the very next batter. The Giants eventually took a 2–0 lead, but Montreal kept the game close until the seventh inning. Then things turned sour for the Royals. Giants shortstop, Bill Dahlen, earned a leadoff walk and then advanced to third on a single by second baseman Art Devlin. Dahlen scored easily on a wild throw to second by Gibson. The Royals issued a walk to Mike Donlin, and a single by Roger Bresnahan plated another run. A second wild throw by Gibson pushed the score to 5–0. By the time the inning ended, the Giants held a commanding 8–0 lead. Gibson led off the eighth with another single, but three straight strikeouts ended any threat. The final score was 8–0. For his work, Gibson recorded two of the Royals' four hits, but also had two costly errors. Despite the lopsided score, Kreitner was pleased, and was quoted as saying, "The Boys worked out splendidly, and I think they'll do all right."[32]

Montreal was supposed to play in Utica, New York, on April 16 and April 17, but cold weather forced the games to be rescheduled. There is no evidence of the weather letting up enough for any games to actually be played before Montreal headed to Springfield, Massachusetts, to start a series of games against teams in the Connecticut State League. Four wins and one tie later, Montreal concluded their spring training season.

On the eve of the start of the Eastern League, the *Montreal Gazette* took stock of the Royals:

> On paper the Montreal team does not look as strong as the outfit Ed Barrow had in charge when the season closed last year. This seems to be the general opinion of those who follow the game closely, but the work of the team in exhibition games has been encouraging and the critics are prepared for surprises.
>
> The team is especially strong in pitchers, has a high class backstop in Gibson and a good outfield in Bannon, Joyce and Wagner, but a shaky looking infield is at present constituted in Willis, Miller, James and Dyer.[33]

Montreal opened their season with a four-game series in Buffalo against the defending league champions. In the first game, the Royals hung even with the Bisons through seven innings. With the score tied 5–5 in the eighth, Buffalo went on a rampage and scored six runs, and went on to win 11–5. Gibson recorded a single and a triple, six putouts, an assist and no errors in the loss. By the time the Royals departed Buffalo for Rochester, they were 0–4. It would take seven games before Montreal won one, putting them at 1–6 on the season, and planting them firmly in last place. Montreal then secured a second consecutive win with a 4–0 shutout against Rochester.

Despite their 2–6 record, Bannon was pleased with his team. He did admit to having some changes in mind for the club, but felt his pitchers "are as good as any in the league," and, according to the *Montreal Gazette*, "Gibson is said to be playing even better ball than last season."[34]

The Royals' scheduled home opener on May 5 was rained out. When the game did get played, over 6,000 fans crammed themselves into the stadium to watch Buffalo take yet another contest off of Montreal. When the two teams met again on Sunday, the game was far more dramatic. With the game tied 1–1 in the bottom of the eleventh, Gibson strode to the plate with Genser Weidensaul on third with two out. Gibson hit safely to right, and Joe Delahanty, the Buffalo right fielder, unleashed a throw to the plate. If Weidensaul had even a slight lead, and had been running on contact, it seems reasonable to assume he would have scored the winning run, and made Gibson a walk-off hero in the process. Even so, there was a play at the plate, and the catcher Bird applied a tag as Weidensaul slid into home. "Many thought he was safe,"[35] but one opinion matters in these cases—that of umpire Zimmer, and he called Weidensaul out. That ended the inning, and in the top of the twelfth, Buffalo managed to score three runs. Montreal was unable to match those three runs, which resulted in another Royals loss at the hands of Stallings's men.

As of May 9, Montreal was still in last place in the league at 3–8. Having caught in all 11 Royals games to date, Gibson was batting a healthy .270 (9 for 37), good enough for fifth on the team. His fielding average was a decent but far from spectacular .927, as he committed 6 errors in 81 chances. Only Tom Raub had as many chances as George, and nobody else on the team even had 50.

As May wore on, Montreal continued to see mixed results, but Gibson began to demonstrate his ability to swing the bat. When Montreal beat Rochester 3–0 on May 11, "Gibson carried off honors with the stick, knocking out a safe one in each of his four visits to the batter's box. Each was a wallop into right field."[36] The following day, Rochester turned the tables, but "[t]he star performer with the bat was Gibson, whose hitting of late easily brings him to the top of the Montreal lot."[37] In Sunday's match, Gibson "repeated the dose, having two in three appearances."[38] The key hit came in the ninth, when, with one out, Rochester elected to walk two men to face Gibson. "Gibson picked out a straight one, and whacked it off into left center, the ball landing against the short fence, while Weidensaul ambled home with the necessary run to win the game."[39] On May 17 against Jersey City, "Gibson led in useful work,"[40] going 3-for-3 and leading Montreal to the 3–2 victory. However, Gibson's strong play alone wasn't enough to distract fans and newspapermen from the lack of team results. With almost a month of games completed, Montreal found themselves safely at the bottom of the heap with a 9–14 record. A report out of Buffalo noted: "It develops that Mr. Kreitner is far from satisfied with the results that have been attained under Jimmy Bannon, and is seeking a new manager."[41]

Newspapers were quick to defend Bannon, but their argument was hardly convincing. Their claim was that the real responsibility for Montreal's woes rested on the shoulders of John Kreitner as he let Barrow leave for Indianapolis which made it necessary to seek out Bannon in the first place. Even league president Pat Powers wanted Bannon replaced. But Bannon remained with Montreal, and the club continued to play hard-fought baseball. In their final game of May, Montreal scored a run in the top of the ninth to win a see-saw battle with Buffalo, and pushed their record to 11–17. Gibson was effective with his throwing arm while his counterpart in the contest, former teammate and mentor Frank McManus, allowed the Royals to steal five bases.

The arrival of June saw Raub and Gibson begin to share catching responsibilities more evenly, but it did nothing to help the team win. Timely hits still seemed to be in short supply, and their inability to prevent runs in the late innings continued to prove costly. Undeterred by the Royals' poor results, Gibson continued to work hard. His defense continued to shine, and as relayed by the *Montreal Gazette*, "Gibson is the only player hitting the ball."[42] Although he did not know it at the time, he was starting to draw attention from major-league teams. While the Royals were playing in New Jersey, injured Pirates catcher Harry Smith attended as a scout as a favor to Pirates owner Barney Dreyfuss. Smith took notice of Gibson's fine play. But he was not the only one in town to check up on Gibson. When the first game was rained out, John Kreitner took the unplanned free time to meet with Clark Griffith, whose New York Highlanders were also idle due to the weather. Griffith made what Kreitner believed was a pretty good offer for Gibson's services, while Connie Mack, of the Philadelphia Americans, was also in town to size up the Canadian catcher. Kreitner negotiated independently with Griffith, Mack and Dreyfuss over the next week. League president Pat Powers tried to influence Kreitner to make a deal with the New York Americans. How seriously Kreitner considered making a deal with Griffith, or with Mack for that matter, is unknown. What is known is that Smith's advice to Dreyfuss, after seeing Gibson play, was to buy him.[43] When Pirates manager Fred Clarke checked with

Ed Barrow about Gibson, he was told that "Gibson was fast enough for any kind of company."[44] In the end, Dreyfuss purchased Gibson and secured his release from John Kreitner and the Montreal Royals, it is believed, for $2,500.

Gibson caught his last game for Montreal on June 28. The Royals lost 5–2 and the newspapers took note: "As Gibson is a good catcher and was leading the Royals in batting, the fans in that city are naturally dissatisfied with the deal whereby he is torn from them and demand to know how the management expects to strengthen the team by such strategy."[45] Other reports questioned the move in more general terms by pointing out that "it is a bad sign to see a tail-end club selling before the season is half over one of its few real players."[46] Dissatisfaction turned into predictions of lost revenue: "Local fans who have been loyal to the Montreal club despite its poor showing are indignant over the sale of Gibson. The money secured for Gibson will soon be missed at the gate."[47]

The day after Gibson's final game in the Eastern League, Montreal found themselves in an 18-inning marathon with Buffalo. They did sneak away with the win, but Raub was forced to catch all 18 innings. "[Gibson's] loss to the Montreal team was thoroughly appreciated Saturday morning when Tom Raub's finger was split and the team's only catcher was obliged to retire to be

George and his young family. From left to right, his wife Margaret, son George Jr., daughter Marguerite and himself (London Room Photograph Archives–PG E281, Ivey Family London Room, London Public Library, London, Ontario, Canada).

replaced by a slow and uncertain player."[48] That uncertain player was a man by the name of Woelfel. After only four games, a catcher named Buss replaced him,[49] and two days later, the team signed a catcher named George Fox out of the Tri-State League.[50] Before Fox could even get into a game, he was replaced by Tacks Latimer.[51] Clearly, Montreal had a void to fill behind the plate. With so much inexperience in the backup role, Raub, once healthy, was forced to do the bulk of the catching for the rest of the season, and to his credit, he did well. Though they would never truly press for a place in the first division, Montreal was able to improve their rank in the standings, finishing sixth with a 56–80 record. Providence took the pennant by one game over Baltimore.

In 1905, Gibson appeared in 41 games with the Royals, and batted an even .300.

Chapter Note

Modern accounts of Gibson's playing history have him listed as having caught for Kingston in the Hudson River League in 1903. There is no truth to this. In 1903, Gibson was still playing in London, and then Buffalo. When asked, in 1919, how his name came to be associated with the Hudson River circuit in 1903, Gibson said "he could not explain for a certainty, but he understood that somebody got him mixed up with some other player shortly after he broke into the big league, and the erroneous record has been carried on many of the books ever since."[52] A complete review of Kingston's box scores in 1903 show that their primary catcher was Heinie Beckendorf. Gibson did not show up in any box score or article about the team. If, in fact, the mix up was caused by confusion with another player, perhaps Heinie Beckendorf was that player, as he did make an appearance for Montreal in 1905.

4

Here Comes
Hackenschmidt

George admitted he was sorry to leave Montreal, as he had been treated well there. Departing for Pittsburgh, though, meant playing in the fastest company, and he did acknowledge receiving a substantial raise to join the Pirates. Sorry or not, Gibson had no time to waste in getting to Pittsburgh. Accompanied by Kreitner, Gibson grabbed the first train he could get, and made his way to the Steel City. They left on such short notice that George didn't even have time to collect his belongings from the hotel.

The two men arrived in Pittsburgh on June 30. "Gibson, after a brief conference with President Dreyfuss, accepted the terms of the Pittsburg club."[1] When Gibson joined the Pirates, they were third in the National League with a 40–26 record and already had four catchers, making him the fifth. The Pirates catching corps, however, was a banged-up bunch. Only Fred Carisch and the newly acquired Gibson were healthy enough to play. Carisch had his own share of injuries, though, and he too was in need of rest. Fred Clarke planned to test out the newly acquired Canadian at the first chance possible; he scheduled Gibson to play in his first major-league game the day after arriving in Pittsburgh. As fitting as a Canada Day debut would have been, it was not to be. Rain caused the game to be canceled before it ever got started.

With business settled in Pittsburgh, and no baseball to watch, Kreitner returned to Montreal. Gibson, of course, remained in the city. That night, he joined about a dozen of his new teammates and headed to Cincinnati. Less than 24-hours into his major-league career, and yet to play in a single game, reviews of Gibson were favorable. "He has already made a good impression upon his team-mates, and will undoubtedly be popular here. He appears to be a lad full of ginger, and his build indicates plenty of strength."[2] Gibson's large stature is what caused Honus Wagner to shout "Here comes Hackenschmidt" the first time George walked into the Pirates' dressing room.[3] George Hackenschmidt was a famous Russian wrestler at the time. The nickname "Hack" remained with George throughout his time in Pittsburgh.

George made his big-league debut on July 2 against Cincinnati and paired with veteran Deacon Phillippe to form the Pittsburgh battery. Gibson was tested defensively almost immediately. In the bottom of the first and with runners on second and third, Cy Seymour hit a ball on the ground to Wagner, who immediately fired to Gibson to catch Miller Huggins attempting to score from third. Another test came in the bottom of the third. Huggins worked a walk and stole second. Gibson recalled this play years later: "The first man tried to steal on me, I threw a ball over second base. Perfect throw, just knee high. Right over the bag. Honus got within about three steps of it, [Claude] Ritchey got within about two steps of it."[4] Gibson wondered if Wagner and Ritchey were trying to work against him, but in the dugout at the

George Gibson circa 1905 (courtesy Carol Smith).

end of the inning "they both come in and put their arms around my neck … they said: 'Listen. Just keep throwing 'em like that, kid.'"[5] Wagner and Ritchey were used to the throws from their long-time catcher Heinie Peitz, who "used to throw the ball like a rainbow down to second base."[6] It didn't take long for Wagner and Ritchey to learn to be ready for Gibson's strong throws. In the fifth, with Shad Barry on third, Tommy Corcoran hit a grounder to Wagner. Honus immediately relayed the ball to a waiting Gibson and nabbed Barry at the plate. Despite the indications of a Pittsburgh victory, Cincinnati went on to win 4–1.

As far as debuts go, Gibson's was average. From behind the plate, he recorded six putouts and two assists, and caught two would-be base stealers. Unfortunately, three stolen bases against him, an error and his 0–3 batting line easily overshadowed the positives. Writers informed the Pittsburgh fans, "[Gibson] started with the handicap of a badly shattered hand, but performed very well, although his work in the early innings was affected by a show of nervousness, which later wore off. He is apparently strong at blocking runners off the plate. He spoiled two Red attempts to slide to safe territory."[7] Despite the loss, George's toughness made an impression on reporters in

Cincinnati. "In fact, the youngster backstopped well, and showed that he is not afraid of spiked shoes, by blocking off both Huggins and Barry, as they slid for the plate and tabbing them out. His throwing was off-color early in the game, but he improved and he caught the last two men who went down. He is a strong, well-built fellow and looks good."[8] Perhaps most importantly: "President Dreyfuss says the lad is still a little green, but expresses that belief that he will learn quickly, and be a mighty valuable man. He has been playing professional ball but two years."[9]

Ultimately, Gibson's play kept him in a Pirates uniform; however, his injured hand kept him off the field for 11 days. Clarke resorted to a catcher's platoon that consisted of Fred Carisch and Heinie Peitz. It worked out well as the club went 5–1 in their next six games, all of which were away from Pittsburgh. As Gibson's new teammates headed for Pittsburgh, George left for Montreal, having been granted a leave of absence to close up his affairs in that city.

Gibson rejoined the club on July 11 in Brooklyn. Because he was still "nursing a bad hand,"[10] Peitz and Carisch continued to share catching duties. Pittsburgh and Brooklyn split the first two games of the series. In the third game, after Heinie Peitz singled in the third inning, Gibson pinch-hit for the pitcher. Insofar as Gibson needed to advance Peitz, his first career appearance as a pinch hitter proved to be a success. Mind you, that success was in spite of Gibson and not because of him. The pitcher plunked the catcher, and George trotted down to first base. This pushed Peitz to second, one-step closer to his ultimate landing spot at home plate. Peitz's eventual run helped vault the Pirates to a 5–3 victory.

George started on July 18, returning from his injury, and "the battery, Case and Gibson, for the visitors, was the whole works."[11] With the Pirates ahead 1–0 in the fifth, Gibson stepped to the plate to face Christy Mathewson. "The Eastern League recruit clouted the ball away beyond the reach of Mike Donlin in center field for the route. Notwithstanding the intense heat, this wallop chilled the grandstand."[12] Gibson's first career home run put the Pirates ahead 2–0 and they ultimately walked away 2–1 winners.

On July 21, the Pirates played a doubleheader in Philadelphia after the second game of the doubleheader scheduled on July 20 was rained out. Gibson backstopped Pittsburgh to a 7–3 win in the morning game, and Fred Carisch, despite reports of fever symptoms, worked behind the plate in the afternoon game, a 5–1 loss. Carisch caught the entire game, but it was his last for some time, because his fever worsened. Gibson became a more active member of the catching corps. Peitz still handled the bulk of the work, but George appeared in three of Pittsburgh's remaining seven July games, which included an exhibition game in Atlantic City.

Pittsburgh began August in second place with a record of 58–34. New York still had a comfortable lead at 67–25, but the Pirates' surge in July created some doubt in the Giants' ability to win the pennant. The Giants, however, claimed to be even more confident now than in the Spring. Manager McGraw was quoted to have said that he "regards his pennant chances today as just a bit better than at any previous time in this season."[13] Having just won their 12th straight game, McGraw and his Giants headed into Pittsburgh for a 4-game series.

In the first game of the series, the Giants extended their winning streak to 13 games. The Pirates scored a lopsided victory in the second contest and won the third game as well. The excitement of the first three games of the series only served to heighten interest in game four. "The crowd began to arrive early, and although the game was not scheduled to begin until three o'clock, at two o'clock it was impossible to get even a standing room in the grandstand."[14] By the time all 18,383 fans were in Exposition Park—the largest crowd to ever gather to watch a baseball game there—the right and left field bleachers overflowed, and fans were crowded behind ropes on the field. Needing a win to split the series, McGraw chose Christy Mathewson to pitch. Clarke responded with Charles Case.

Pittsburgh drew first blood and scored three runs in the first inning. In the top of the second, Heinie Peitz split his finger on a foul ball. Gibson replaced Peitz when he pinch-hit for his injured teammate in the bottom of the inning. In that appearance, George walked and Claude Ritchey, already on first, scampered down to second. Case advanced both runners with a sacrifice. Ritchey tried to score on an infield hit by Otis Clymer, but was caught at the plate. Clymer reached first base and kept on running. Fortunately for Pittsburgh, Giants catcher Frank Bowerman forgot about Gibson and hurled the ball to second. The throw sailed into center field and Gibson scored. Down four runs in the seventh, the Giants stormed back to tie the game 5–5. Deacon Phillippe entered the game to relieve Case in the eighth and held New York scoreless for two innings.

Still tied in the bottom of the ninth, Ritchey smashed the ball into the crowd in right field and settled for a ground rule double. Gibson batted next.

> Gibson hit a foul, and then a new bat, black and vicious looking, was sent to him. He flung the bat he had been using away from him, gripped the black one tightly and then dumped the ball to the pitcher. The ball went some distance to the side of Matthewson [*sic*], who ran for it like mad, turned around and flung it to Devlin at third to head off Ritchey. Ritchey took a head-first slide, grabbed the bag and swung around. It was no force, and to put him out Devlin must touch him, but he did not do so.[15]

Home plate umpire Bausewine determined that Ritchey was safe. Unhappy with the call, the Giants surrounded the arbiter in search of an explanation. In the absence of a satisfactory reason, they circled second base umpire Bob Emslie. Emslie and Bausewine met to talk it over. The call stood. This brought McGraw out of the dugout, "jumping like a Kangaroo."[16] Before long, several Pirates joined the impromptu infield meeting. After some lively discussion, Bausewine "pulled out his watch, said something that startled the players and walked back to the home plate. When he got there, he studied his timepiece rather curiously for an instant and then shouted: 'The game is forfeited to the Pittsburg club.'"[17]

For the second time in just more than two weeks, Gibson recorded a game-winning hit off of the great Christy Mathewson. The unconventional nature of this one, however, was greatly overshadowed by the reaction of the Exposition Park crowd. In an instant, the fans broke through the ropes and surrounded the entire Giants squad. "The crowd was wild and loud but not pugnacious. It jeered the Giants and gibed them without mercy, but never raised a hand and never intended to. As each Giant walked out of the park guarded by one or more policemen, the crowd taunted and derided them, but the most they did was to yell 'quitters.'"[18]

Following the win, it was revealed that Peitz would be unavailable for at least the next week. Harry Smith was not quite ready to return, so this left George Gibson as the only healthy Pirate catcher. As a result, Fred Clarke telegraphed Fred Carisch, who was recovering in nearby Cambridge Springs, and instructed him to return immediately. Pittsburgh was about to host Boston in a doubleheader and Clarke needed somebody to relieve Gibson. Carisch and Gibson split catching duties as Pittsburgh split the pair of games with the Beaneaters. Pittsburgh won an extra-inning affair the following day, but lost on Thursday in a notable game that saw eight Pirates (including Gibson) swept off of the visiting bench by umpire Klem for allegedly shouting after every pitch thrown by Sam Leever.[19] Pittsburgh lost to Boston once more before they left town for Philadelphia. Gibson backstopped Pittsburgh to three straight wins to start that series, and drew praise as "a wonder at blocking off runners at the plate."[20] He was behind the plate for two more contests before Peitz returned and provided George a five-game rest.

When Gibson returned to the lineup, it was in the second game of a three-game series against the Giants at the Polo Grounds. Gibson ended up going 3–4 in the contest and recorded six putouts, two assists and no errors. The Pirates closed out August reeling off nine straight victories as Gibson stayed behind the plate for each of those games. On August 24, during the second game of a doubleheader in Boston, Gibson relieved Peitz late in the game. When he led off the top of the tenth with a clutch home run, the Pirates took a lead they would never relinquish.

On August 29, the streak continued thanks to Gibson's fortitude. He caught all nine innings during the first game of another doubleheader. Then, Gibby took over for Harry Smith in the ninth inning of the back half of the two-game set. Smith, having just returned from injury, made his first appearance of the season; and, as it turned out, also his last. Due to his nagging injury, he left for Mt. Clemens following the game, where he remained for two months. Clarke went back to rotating catching duties between Gibson and Peitz, and managed to extend the Pirates' winning streak a few days longer. Gibson, for his part, used the extra playing time to prove he belonged in the major leagues. The fans and the newspapers recognized and appreciated his effort. With each game Gibson's popularity rose. The *Pittsburgh Press*'s Ralph Davis clearly saw promise in Gibson and his play on the field. In early September he wrote: "There will no doubt be some changes made in the Pittsburg catching staff before next season dawns, but Gibson is sure to stay."[21] In providing stability for the injury-riddled Pirates catching corp, Gibson helped his team inch their way back into the pennant race.

By September 6, Pittsburgh improved their record to 85–44, good enough for second place in the league. Not surprisingly, John McGraw's Giants juggernaut sat atop the heap. With a month left in the season, Pittsburgh had much ground to make up, but that did not dampen Barney Dreyfuss's optimism. The Pirates president proclaimed that the club would "carry the battle right to the Giants' very door."[22] The Pirates promptly went out and won three of their next four games. When Pittsburgh went to Cincinnati on September 15, the Giants' lead stood at a mere two games. They marked their arrival in the Queen City with an 8–7 victory over the Reds. Unfortunately for the Pirates, the Cincinnati ball club responded with a 6–0 victory the next game. A scheduled three-day break was increased by a day when rain canceled the third game of the series. The Pirates returned to Exposition Park and split a 4-game series with Philadelphia.

Despite their impressive record of 92 wins and 49 losses, the Pirates were still 5½ games behind the Giants. With just 12 games left on the schedule, Pittsburgh needed a near-perfect performance and a complete collapse by New York to win the pennant. As the scheduling gods would have it, the Pirates were afforded the perfect opportunity to make that happen. The Giants arrived at Exposition Park on September 25. The Pirates had three games to make a stand, but fortune favored the team from New York and the Giants swept Pittsburgh without a problem. Pittsburgh's pennant hopes went up in smoke. Losing the series cost the Pirates their last chance to catch the Giants.

On October 2, George demonstrated a level of grit well beyond what anyone could expect of a player—even a rookie with something to prove. During the pre-game warmup, George was "straddling at bat behind the home plate during practice and was paying no attention to the players who were hitting at pitched balls. A foul tip glanced off one of the bats"[23] and struck Gibson in the jaw. The wound required three stitches. While George's injury was being tended to, Pirates manager Fred Clarke started making calls looking for a replacement catcher. "Failing to find one he had about made up his mind to send Hillebrand behind the bat. When he walked out on the field he noticed Gibson, his face covered with court plaster, warming up a pitcher."[24] George refused to remain in the clubhouse and was ready to catch, however, before the first pitch, the rain came, and the game was canceled. Clarke opted to put Peitz behind the plate the following day for both ends of the scheduled doubleheader. After a short rest, George returned to the lineup to play out the remainder of the season. The Pirates finished with a respectable 96–57 record. The Giants, at 105–48, were untouchable, and won the National League pennant. McGraw's men agreed to compete in the World Series, and defeated Connie Mack's American League Athletics in five games.

Before going home for the off-season, George joined a group that included Pirates teammates Honus Wagner, Tommy Leach, Lefty Leifield and Deacon Phillippe. The unofficial consortium barnstormed around Ohio. Though all of their playing contracts extended until October 15, President Dreyfuss allowed them to book exhibition games immediately following the end of the season. Between October 9 and October 18, the team played nine exhibition games. George caught every inning of every game, recorded 11 hits, took a walk and supplemented his fine offense with 61 putouts, six assists and no errors while in the field. Following a win in Steubenville on October 18, the team returned to Pittsburgh with a record of 7–2. Despite invites from many other clubs for more games, some of the players had other commitments, so the team disbanded. George returned to his family in London and

George and his family enjoying a picnic (courtesy Carol Smith).

tended to his contracting company. He kept busy "looking after his brickyard and hunting for game in the Canadian forests."[25]

For George Gibson, his rookie season was a great success. In a season defined by injured catchers, George Gibson proved to be durable, defensively adept and capable of getting a big hit. As Ralph Davis predicted, Gibson did enough to prove that he belonged in fast company. President Dreyfuss affirmed this belief and placed his young catcher on the Pirates' reserve list; Gibby would be back with the club in 1906.

Back in Pittsburgh, Barney Dreyfuss prepared for the 1906 season. In early November, he signed first baseman Joe Nealon away from the San Francisco Seals. A few weeks later Dreyfuss announced that he secured the services of former Princeton infielder Dutch Meier. Amidst these signings, the Pittsburgh papers reported that the Pirates were after St. Louis Nationals' catcher Mike Grady; club officials quickly put that rumor to rest.[26] The Pirates did pick up a catcher, however, when they drafted Irish-born, Canadian-raised Jimmy Archer from Atlanta in the Southern Association. It was not a surprising pick given that Pittsburgh drafted Archer in 1904 while he managed and caught for the Boone team in the Iowa State League. Archer appeared in seven games in 1904, and showed up well, but was released to Atlanta early in the Spring of 1905.[27]

When the winter meetings began in December, Pittsburgh had 34 players on their reserve list for 1906. Nobody expected that all of these players would remain with Pittsburgh. In fact, Dreyfuss himself admitted that within a week "some of the men under reserve will have been disposed of to the advantage of the Pirates."[28] Consistent with these reports, Dreyfuss asked for waivers on fourteen of those players, including four of his five catchers. He refused to release any names, but "when Manager Fred Clarke gave out the names of the men on the squad who were sure of their berths, George Gibson was one of the nine."[29] Consequently, the newspapermen concluded that Peitz, Carisch, Smith and Jimmy Archer were the four catchers on waivers.[30]

As the Spring season approached, the high praise put upon Gibson seemed to support the idea that Pittsburgh did not want to part ways with the Canadian backstop any time soon. According to Dreyfuss, "George Gibson will be one of the finest catchers in the business next season."[31] Heinie Peitz, the veteran catcher who joined Pittsburgh for the 1905 season, also predicted Gibson would be "one of the best catchers in the National league next year."[32] This was high praise, considering Peitz was the club's number one catcher, and had a nice year the previous season, when he played twice as many games as Gibson and batted 45 points higher. Pirates' secretary, William Locke, shared the sentiment with his boss and veteran catcher: "At a time when nearly all the ball teams of the United States are searching for first-class catchers, the Pittsburgh club considers itself lucky in discovering George Gibson."[33] *The*

Scranton Truth declared that George "was the best young catcher who entered the National League in 1905."[34]

When plans were announced for the Pirates' spring training trip Gibson was among the men invited. Expected to round out the catching corps were Heinie Peitz, Fred Carisch and Harry Smith. A group of 25 men were scheduled to depart Pittsburgh on March 12, with ten more joining in St. Louis as they worked themselves down to Hot Springs. Hot Springs is a town located in the Ouachita Mountains of Arkansas. As early as the mid–1880s, baseball teams traveled there before the baseball season to take advantage of its naturally heated springs.[35] After three weeks of training, the team planned to set out on an eight-game exhibition tour culminating in St. Louis on April 11, the eve of their first regular-season tilt.[36]

A week before Dreyfuss's men were set to depart, tragic news poured in to Pirates headquarters. The first reports claimed Heinie Peitz had been stabbed near his heart and was in critical condition.[37] Though the stabbing was a rumor, Peitz did have pleurisy, an inflammation in his lungs, and would not be ready for the start of the Hot Springs trip. The Pirates sent for reserve catcher Jimmy Archer and ordered him to report to Pittsburgh from his Toronto home. Archer, however, was not immediately available, "owing to the sickness of his wife."[38] Already down two catchers, things got worse. Harry Smith, already in Hot Springs, and reporting that his arm was in satisfactory condition, returned to Ohio due to the death of his mother-in-law. This left Carisch and Gibson as the only available catchers on the roster. When Gibson heard the news that neither Peitz, Archer nor Smith were available, he was ready to help: "Never mind, I'll work double turn until the other fellows report."[39]

When the club arrived at the Arkansas resort on the morning of March 14, there to greet them was Manager Clarke. Also there to greet them were rain, wind and freezing temperatures. For the first couple days, Clarke had to decide whether or not to let his team practice. Unable to play actual games, and not wanting to lose too much time, Clarke opted to run his men through throwing, catching and running drills. The Pirates played their first organized game of the season on March 17. The men split into two teams. The Regulars, consisting of Clarke, Wagner, Leach and the other established Pirates faced off against the Yannigans, a squad made up mostly of new recruits. In his first major-league spring training, Gibson was tasked with catching for the Regulars.

For the next two days, poor weather conditions prevented all baseball activities. Those days were not lost, however, as Jimmy Archer arrived at camp, bringing with him news that his wife was recovering, and Harry Smith, much to the delight of his teammates, also appeared. By March 20, the weather improved enough for Clarke to order his men into uniform and over to Whittington Park for drills. By the time the first week of practice ended, Heinie Peitz had also arrived, giving Manager Clarke his full complement of catchers. Having all of his regular catchers present and ready to practice, Clarke needed to make cuts. Jimmy Archer, despite a strong week at camp, was released back to his Atlanta club. Stormy Arkansas weather continued to interfere with the Pirates' on-field training, but let up long enough for Gibson's best game of the Spring. George recorded a single, double and triple to go along with two runs as the Regulars routed the Yannigans 13–2.

While many of the regular pitchers remained at Hot Springs, the rest of the squad headed out on the exhibition tour. George was trying to prove he was the top catcher in camp, so he happily went along on the trip. He and Fred split catching duties. The weather did not cooperate and the team played in just a handful of the games scheduled. Despite the lack of preseason games, Clarke felt his men were ready when they arrived in St. Louis on April 11, the eve of the 1906 campaign. Manager Clarke and President Dreyfuss confirmed they would only carry three catchers for the season. Newspapers speculated that either Peitz or Carisch were on the chopping block,[40] but no one was dropped immediately. Gibson, easily the most practiced catcher of the spring, began the season as the starting catcher.

The season opener was a captivating pitchers duel, as the game remained scoreless through nine innings. It took until the thirteenth frame for a man on either team to cross the plate. Pittsburgh outfielder Otis Clymer led off with a single, and advanced to second on Honus Wagner's stinging single to center. Both Pirates came around to score and Pittsburgh entered the bottom of the thirteenth inning ahead 2–0. St. Louis came out in the bottom half determined to get those runs back as Cardinals third baseman Harry Arndt led off the inning with a hard single. After an out, the Cardinals pitcher rolled over on one right to Wagner, but an error on the double play attempt resulted in both St. Louis men safe on their respective islands. The following batter singled to load the bases for the Cardinals light-hitting outfielder, Spike Shannon. Shannon got a hold of one and smashed a long drive to center, prompting Arndt and Taylor to put on speed and rush for the plate.[41] Arndt scored easily, but Pirates strong-armed outfielder Bob Ganley sent a seed to Gibson, who caught the perfectly thrown ball and put the tag on Taylor before he could score and tie the game. The Bucs won the exciting season opener by a final 2–1.

Following the series in St. Louis, the Pirates returned to Pittsburgh and hosted Cincinnati in their first home series of the season. The day was marked with a parade as fans lined the streets to get a glimpse of their baseball heroes. A band led the two teams onto the field, much to the delight of the thousands of fans in attendance. Fred Clarke was presented a horseshoe of flowers and National League president, Harry Pulliam, threw out the ceremonial first pitch. Following the pageantry, home plate umpire Bill Klem called "Play Ball!" and the game began. The *Pittsburgh Daily Post* captured the moment perfectly:

> Catcher Gibson, of Pittsburgh, put on his cap, with the 'P' toward the grand-stand, donned his chest protector, his mask, spat in the mattress that is termed a glove and then dug in his cleats into the turf behind the batter.
>
> Behind Gibson, to both sides of him, and forming a complete border for the ball field was a solidly woven mass of humanity.[42]

Deacon Phillippe took the mound for the Pirates in their home opener. The battery of he and Gibson were cruising along when Gibson injured his hand in the top of the fourth frame. Fred Carisch was sent in by Clarke to replace George and he filled in admirably, including a game-saving defensive play in the tenth inning. The Pirates won 3–2 over Cincinnati in twelve innings and improved to 3–0 on the season.

George sat out the next four games, and the Pirates were forced to rely on their catching depth to get by without him. Things did not go according to plan. On April 19, Harry Smith made his first start of the season, but after only two frames, Fred Carisch replaced him behind the plate. An injury Smith sustained two seasons earlier had done him in and he requested his release from Pittsburgh so that he could return to his old trade. The Pirates granted Smith his release, but after a short reprieve from the game, he was back with the Pirates in 1907.

George briefly returned to the lineup near the end of April. After he appeared in a game on April 25, Gibson was forced to take his second leave of the season from the club. This time, he had to attend the funeral of his brother Henry, who, at 36, had passed away suddenly, back in London. This left Heinie Peitz to do all of the backstop work until George returned in early May. The Pirates were in the midst of a 4-game losing streak. The streak lasted until May 8, when George returned. He went behind the bat and helped win the fifth and final game of a series with Chicago. Gibson was described as "death to would-be base stealers."[43]

The Pirates were in fourth place and their tumble in the standings was blamed on poor hitting by the entire club. Fans began to question the batting order and suggested changes were necessary. Despite being hitless through eight games, Gibson was spared when the papers called out individual players. In his short time with the Pirates, George had not established himself as a hitter, but rather as a defensive specialist, and a month into his sophomore campaign he was performing well behind the plate. The Pirates did figure out their hitting woes much to the relief of their die-hard rooters. The club went on a five-game winning streak with Gibson and the veteran Heinie Peitz sharing the catching duties. During the streak, Pittsburgh released Fred Carisch to Rochester of the Eastern League and signed former Pirate Eddie Phelps, who had been released by the Cincinnati club. "With Peitz and Gibson going at their present speed, there is not much need for an extra catcher, but in the event of an accident to either man Phelps would come in handy."[44] Phelps jumped right in to another five-game winning streak that vaulted Pittsburgh into third place. Phelps was also used off the bench as a pinch hitter for George Gibson when Manager Clarke needed an offensive boost. Gibby was slumping with the bat as the *Sporting Life* noted: "One man on the Pittsburgh team who promised so well in 1905 is not keeping up the pace predicted. George 'Hackenschmidt' Gibson is not there with the stick."[45]

Eventually, Gibson started to hit the ball, and his batting average climbed. But he was never seen as an offensive threat, so Fred Clarke continued to turn to pinch hitters for George in the late innings of tight games. As May rolled into June, the Pirates put together a third five-game winning streak. That streak ended on June 3, and the following day they started another. Between May 14 and June 15, the Pirates went 23–5 before rain put them on the sidelines for four straight days. The Pirates ended June with a record of 42–20, good enough for second place, four games back of Chicago.

While Chicago slowly ran away with the pennant, Pittsburgh and New York slugged it out for second place. In the middle of July, Ed Barrow, now managing Toronto of the Eastern League, wired President Dreyfuss "for his lowest cash price on Catcher Gibson."[46] Manager Barrow was in the process of making "wholesale changes" to his club and was "bringing in a host of new players."[47] Dreyfuss responded, "I'm not selling players, but there is only one price for players these days, and that is $10,000."[48] Gibson later recalled that price tag "broke off the deal."[49] After the Barrow deal fell through, Gibson recorded hits in four out of five games, all Pirates wins. By the end of July, New York and Pittsburgh shared second place with a record of 58–32. Chicago was comfortably out front with a record of 66–28.

Pittsburgh started August with four wins against three defeats. Gibson caught five of the seven games, recording hits in four of them. During the Pirates' August 8 tilt against Boston, George took home plate on a squeeze play in the eighth-inning. The insurance run put the Pirates ahead 2–0 and helped seal the victory, the Pirates' fourth straight win over the Beaneaters. The second-place Pirates faced the third-place Giants in the subsequent series. New York took Pittsburgh to the woodshed with five victories in just four days. The swing vaulted New York ahead of Pittsburgh in the standings and Gibson was unfortunately in the thick of things. George caught three of the games, and went hitless in all of them. Gibson's woes at the plate subsided after the New York series and Clarke rewarded his catcher with increased playing time. It seems Clarke had moved Gibson to the top of his catchers' depth chart. On August 28, George caught both ends of a doubleheader for the fifth time in his career. The Pirates won their last six games in August, and for the third consecutive month were at second place in the standings. George caught 21 games in August, while Peitz and Phelps combined to catch eight, further suggesting that Clarke favored his second-year catcher.

The Pirates carried that momentum into September, with four wins in five games. Regrettably, Pittsburgh ran into a hot Chicago team and lost four straight, which dropped them back into third place. With the season winding down, the losing streak essentially ended their aspirations for second in the National League. Gibson's campaign ended in much the same way his team's did. On October 2, George caught for Vic Willis in a game against Brooklyn. In the sixth inning, he took a foul tip off of his finger, which not only ended his game but also his season. The Pirates went 2–2 in October and finished with a record of 93–60. While the Giants came to the finish line just ahead with a 96–56 record, the Chicago Cubs dusted them both with 116 wins against 36 loses. The heavily favored Cubs went on to the World Series, and were swept in four games by the Chicago Americans, a team dubbed "The Hitless Wonders."

It is safe to say that George did not live up to expectations in his first full season in the major leagues. While there were some bright spots, his hitting was his most glaring deficiency. He appeared in 81 games and recorded 42 hits for an abysmal batting average of .184. Ultimately, Gibson's durability was the real story. George suffered a pair of minor injuries, but just like in 1905, he demonstrated his toughness. Time and again, George held his ground by making plays at the plate, and holding would-be base stealers at bay. More importantly, when George caught, the Pirates won. Gibson demonstrated enough stamina to last a full season, and with him behind the plate, the Pirates went 51–29.

Following the Pirates final game of the season, George joined a group of barnstormers led by Tommy Leach and toured around Ohio, Pennsylvania and West Virginia. Much like the regular season, Gibson played a lot, but did not hit very well. When the exhibition tour ended on October 24, Gibson departed for his home in London.

As he prepared for his winter job "slinging beer kegs,"[50] sportswriters back in Pittsburgh started to look forward to 1907. To help improve the team, the papers first suggested that Pittsburgh needed new catchers. Peitz, they said, was "too old and too slow," Phelps was rated as "a good mechanical catcher" but "of practically no help to young pitchers" and George "proved an utter failure as a batsman."[51] Pittsburgh reporters could not deny the strength of Gibson's defense, but felt the Pirates needed a better bat at the catcher position. "The records show that the Pittsburg pitchers did their full duty, but the catchers were not so good, and it would not be a bad move for the local management to make some trades in backstops, or else buy a good man for this position outright, if such a thing could be accomplished."[52]

Dreyfuss and Clarke must have agreed that their club needed catching help because in early December rumors suggested that Pittsburgh had signed a sixth catcher. At different points during the winter meetings, the Pirates were rumored to be after St. Louis catcher Mike Grady, Philadelphia catcher Red Dooin and Cincinnati catcher George "Admiral" Schlei. According to the *Pittsburgh Press*, "The indications are that if Clarke gets the catcher he is after, few other changes will be made in the local team."[53] The winter meetings ended without any announcements of new catchers being signed, but shortly after the meeting ended, one was traded away. Veteran catcher Heinie Peitz was traded to the Louisville Colonels for outfielder Billy Hallman. In spite of all the rumors, no other moves were made and Peitz's departure left Gibson as the Pirates' primary catcher heading into 1907.

5

Nearly as Good
as They Come

As 1907 approached, the Pirates needed to settle on their catchers for the upcoming season. After the team cut ties with Heinie Peitz, only Gibson and Ed Phelps remained on the roster. It is unclear how the Pirates hoped to fill out their depth chart, but, based on a letter from Fred Clarke to Barney Dreyfuss, it appears they looked outside the organization for additional options.

In that letter, Clarke made position-by-position suggestions for the coming season's lineup. Clarke inserted a name at each non-pitching spot on the diamond. Conspicuously, the manager left the catcher's spot blank. A report in late January printed in the *Pittsburgh Press* explained that the "team has not the catchers that it might desire, but it is likely that Clarke will hold on to Phelps and Gibson until he is sure that one of the newer backstops is good enough to keep for regular work."[1]

On February 3, the Pirates announced their full preseason plans. Dreyfuss scheduled the Pirate batteries to leave on March 10 for West Baden Springs, Indiana. The group planned to work out there before heading to Hot Springs on March 18. In Arkansas, they intended to "get right down to work."[2] Finally, the Pirates scheduled a series of exhibition games between April 3 and April 9.

As March drew nearer, these plans evolved. Under Clarke's direction, the team released many of the men on the Pirates' reserve list. However, they retained extra catchers for the spring season. Gibson had to battle Ed Phelps, Harry Huston and Harry Smith for a spot on the club. On March 4, Fred Clarke sent a congregation of pitchers and catchers to West Baden Springs ahead of the everyday players. Pitchers Sam Leever, Lefty Leifield, Deacon Phillippe and Vic Willis joined catchers Phelps and Gibson. While Gibson claimed to arrive in top shape thanks to an active off-season, reporters noticed he arrived in Pittsburgh a little heavy and stated that he "bore every indication of having been well fed at his home in London, Ont."[3] Having lost 13 pounds in the months leading up to spring training, Gibson felt he could quickly drop an additional 15 pounds in order to reach his ideal paying weight of 175 pounds. The group arrived at West Baden on the afternoon of March 5 and immediately got to work. Since the weather prevented any outside activities, the Pirates exercised on a diamond constructed inside an enclosed bicycle track. In the evenings the players attended social events such as dances. On one such occasion, "George Gibson made a striking appearance."[4]

Fred Clarke arrived on March 11, intent on settling in West Baden for a bit. However, it rained heavily and Clarke grew impatient while confined indoors. He decided to depart West Baden Springs early. On March 18, now in Hot Springs, Clarke split the men into two teams, the Regulars and the Yannigans. Harry Smith caught for the Regulars while Gibson took his position for the Yannigans, a likely indication of his standing with the Pirates brass. However, when Harry Smith injured his foot, Gibby took full advantage of the opportunity. George moved to the regular squad after helping the Yannigans to three consecutive wins. Gibby's youthful exuberance inspired the veterans to play better ball and the Regulars snapped their three-game slide against the upstarts. In that Friday's game, Gibson returned to the Yannigans; however, he took the field at first base. For the first time, George's team lost, but not before he recorded a pair of singles, a sacrifice hit and a remarkable nine putouts. Clarke continued to rotate his catchers through both teams in order to give each a good look. Clarke eventually reorganized the Regulars to be "the players who will hold permanent berths under the Pittsburgh banner during the summer campaign."[5]

On the morning of April 3, the Pirates embarked on an exhibition tour through Arkansas, Tennessee, Kentucky and Indiana. On April 6, they arrived in Louisville, and the blustery and unfavorable weather went with them. "After breakfast the players went to the local bat factory, where they inspected half of the sticks in stock and made selections to the number of about two dozen."[6] Although there is no record that Gibson signed a promotional contract with Hillerich & Bradsby Company, maker of the famed Louisville Slugger, he did have a relationship with them throughout his career. In the afternoon, Clarke had his men get into their uniforms and head out to the ballpark. After "a conference with the local manager it was decided to call the contest off."[7] The Pirates, dressed in heavy sweaters, spent two hours working out instead.

The poor weather settled in for the duration of the team's time in both Louisville and Indianapolis. As opening day approached, the unfavorable weather forced Dreyfuss and Clarke to issue final cuts without seeing the men take the field. Dreyfuss seemed suspect when it came to his prospective catchers. The Pirates president wired Charles Murphy, the Chicago Cubs owner. He wanted Cubs backstop Johnny Kling to don the grey, blue and red threads of the Pirates. In response to Dreyfuss's inquiry, Murphy fired back: "You can have [Kling] for $1,000,000 in real money" or in exchange for "Hans Wagner and $80,000."[8] In the end, Dreyfuss stuck with Smith, Phelps and Gibson as his catchers. While their pecking order on the depth chart remained undecided, reporters narrowed the choice down to either Harry Smith or George Gibson for top spot:

> There is also some doubt as to who will do the backstop work in the opening game, but all the arguments and all the indications are for Harry Smith. He is unquestionably in his old-time form. He is as good as he was in the days when his clever throwing, united with his genial personality, won for him a warm spot in the hearts of Pittsburgh patrons of the game. His enforced retirement has improved him, if it has had any effect at all. Hackenschmidt Gibson, the iron man, also gives promise of playing the most brilliant game of his baseball career. He has accomplished wonders during the training season in the way of reducing flesh and limbering up his muscles after a winter of hard work in a Canadian brewery. A marked improvement in his batting may be expected. If it is not Smith behind the bat in the opening game it will be Gibson.[9]

Gibson caught a break when Harry Smith complained of abdominal pains. The illness left Clarke with little choice and Gibson started behind the plate to open the season.[10] With Deacon Phillippe on the mound, the Pirates held a 2–0 lead until the sixth inning, and went into the eighth inning tied. Clarke resorted to pinch-hitting for Gibson in the late innings of the game, just as he had done in 1906. The Pirates failed to score, though, and Cincinnati put a pair of runs across in the bottom of the ninth and won the game. Over the next few days, "large flakes of snow falling in goodly numbers prevented the second game"[11] of the season. The cold spell continued and prevented any baseball activities for another two days. The Pirates returned home to Pittsburgh a day early and used that Tuesday to practice in anticipation of their home opener, to be held the following day.

The day's festivities kicked off with a parade that started at the Fort Pitt Hotel. Led by the Grand Army Band, a procession of automobiles drove the Pirates and visiting Cubs through town to Exposition Park. Even with the temperature hovering around freezing, over 8,000 teeth-chattering fans greeted the teams. The cold prompted Gibson and his Pirates teammates to dance and hold hands in an attempt to defeat Jack Frost. National League president, Harry Pulliam, threw out the ceremonial first pitch from the press box. At three o'clock, umpire Hank O'Day called things to order and the game got underway. George Gibson and Victor Willis formed the battery for the Pirates, and Jack Taylor and Pat Moran countered for the Cubs. "George Gibson was the only local player to secure more than one bingle in the opening game."[12] George, all too familiar with Canadian winters, remained unaffected by the adverse weather. He went 2-for-3, with six putouts and no errors; however, Chicago walked off with the 6–3 victory.

Then, for the second series in a row, snow interfered. When the snow finally dissipated, George caught an errorless game, but the Pirates as a team recorded six misplays, affording Chicago an easy 5–1 win. Clarke's men headed to St. Louis following the Chicago series. In the first game against the Redbirds, Phelps paired with Phillippe and they gave up 13 hard hits. The Pirates won in spite of the batterymen's poor performance. Clarke opted to use Gibson in game two of the series. He paired up with Vic Willis to dominate the Cardinal hitters. Willis surrendered only one extra-base hit and two runs. The Pirates managed to take four straight games from the Cardinals before two days of rain gave the men from Missouri some reprieve. The Pirates helped themselves to another pair of victories when the two teams returned to the diamond. The Pirates ended April with a record of 7–3, good enough for third place behind Chicago and New York. George played in seven of the Pirates' first ten games during the first two weeks of the season.

To begin May, the Pirates won two more games over the Cardinals and continued their dominance over the Missouri-based club. Fans numbering 3,160 at Exposition Park witnessed Clarke's men win their eighth straight contest highlighted by watching "George Hackenschmidt Gibson deliberately accomplish the first home run made by a local player on the Pittsburgh grounds this season."[13] Gibson's home run led off the bottom of the seventh. Cardinal outfielders "Kelly and O'Hara raced it almost to the flagstaff, but Hackenschmidt flew home, and thereby won enough prizes, offered by local firms, to fill a moving van."[14] Community businesses ran promotions at Pirates games as a way to gain publicity.

On May 8, the Pirates visited New York to face the Giants for the first time that season. The series provided Clarke and his men with their first chance to see how they measured up against John McGraw and his crew. The series also provided George his first chance to see Roger Bresnahan and his new catching equipment. On opening day, "Bresnahan created somewhat of a sensation when he appeared behind the bat for the start of play, by donning cricket leg guards. As he displayed himself, togged in mask, protector, and guards, he presented no vulnerable surface for a wild ball to strike."[15] According to baseball historian Peter Morris, "Several earlier catchers and infielders had experimented with added protection for their shins but had done so by wearing inconspicuous pads under their uniforms."[16] Bresnahan wearing shin guards wasn't unique, but openly wearing them was.

New York won both games against Pittsburgh, although the Pittsburgh papers did not mention Bresnahan's extra shielding. Following the series, Fred Clarke "protested to President Pulliam, of the National League, against the shin guards worn by Catcher Bresnahan, contending that with this armor a player can easily block a baserunner without danger of being injured."[17] Eventually, President Pulliam decided in favor of the Giants, citing that "there is no rule in the National league to cover the point, which leaves him powerless to act."[18] In response, Clarke declared "that he will have his catchers as well as his first and second basemen wearing shin guards,"[19] noting that he had placed an order "and within a few days the Pittsburgs will be on equal footing with New York, at least, as far as shin guards are concerned."[20] Gibson, void of any shin guards, continued to take his turn behind the plate. He appeared in 10 of Pittsburgh's final 18 contests in May and batted .342 (12-for-35) to go along with 37 defensive putouts. The Pirates ended the month in fourth place with a record of 19–15.

June began with a four-game series in Chicago; however, the squads only managed to play two games on account of constant downpours. The Pirates dropped both games and then made a beeline home to host the Boston Doves at Exposition Park. The Pirates easily won the first game 6–0 thanks in large part to Gibson. The catcher clubbed a two-run homer—his second of the season—in the bottom of the second to get the offensive assault started. George repeated the feat three days later when he hit his third home run of the season in a 14–3 rout of Brooklyn. Gibson's three home runs to date tied him with the American League's Harry Davis for tops in all of baseball.

George caught eight of the next ten games and recorded 10 hits in 27 plate appearances. His eight-game offensive onslaught pushed his batting average to an impressive .294. On June 20, the Pirates hosted the Philadelphia Quakers, the forefathers to the Phillies, at Exposition Park. In the fifth inning, Philadelphia shortstop Mickey Doolin "came into the plate feet-first, but Gibson never budged an inch. He put the ball on Doolin quickly and neatly, and then stepped out of the way of Michael's sharp spikes." George made this type of play time and again without being injured, but the play reignited the conversation about the use of shin guards. Giving in to pressure from Clarke, Gibson had tried to wear shin guards, but when he "strapped the ungainly things to his shanks, and then tried to move about in them. He said that it felt as if his legs were encased in plaster of paris, and promptly tossed them to one side." When asked about his decision to wear the armor, Gibson opined: "If I can't catch without those things, I guess I'll go back to Ontario and quit the game for good."[21] George maintained that the shin guards limited his mobility. He openly accepted the risk of injury and pointed to his years of experience catching without any serious injuries as reason enough not to wear protection. Coincidentally, George was injured two days later, when hit by a pitch while batting. No shin guard could have prevented the injury. When the club left for a doubleheader in Cincinnati following the game, Harry Smith and Eddie Phelps went on the trip and George stayed behind in Pittsburgh.[22]

When the Pirates returned to Exposition Park, Clarke thrust Gibson back in the lineup for seven of the final eight games of the month. On June 25, he and Phelps split a doubleheader against Cincinnati. Five days later, Gibson caught both games of a doubleheader in Chicago without any help. George's play at the end of June moved him near, if not to, the top of the depth chart. At the end of the month, the Pirates sat in third place with a record of 34–25.

While Gibson's play in June suggested he belonged at the top of the catcher's order, his play in July cemented his place atop the bill. George caught 23 of the 29 contests the Pirates played. After losing the first game of the month to Chicago, the Bucs put together an eight-game winning streak that allowed them to catch New York and take second place in the standings. Pittsburgh continued to play good baseball and ended the month with a record of 55–33. Chicago still led the National League with a record of 66–24 and that ten-game spread in the standings suggested the Pirates could do no better than second place.

As July rolled into August, Gibson's bat went cold. In the first 10 days of the month, he made 18 plate appearances and didn't register a single hit. His defense remained steady and error free, but Pittsburgh needed George to improve his offense to give the team a fighting chance to track down Chicago. Clarke started to weave his other backstops, and their hotter bats, into games to try and get offensive production from the catcher's spot. When Gibson returned to the lineup on August 22, the Giants and Pirates started a six-game series and he broke out of his slump in a big way. He hit a double, a triple and two singles on his way to a 4-for-5 performance. The Pirates posted 20 runs to the Giants' 5, and took 4 of the 6 games. The Pirates played .500 ball the rest of the month and entered September in third place, with a record of 69–49.

An eventful September reaffirmed Gibson's rank among the Bucs' catching corps. From September 1 to September 8, he appeared in all 11 Pirates games. On September 5, Gibson paired with Howie Camnitz and held the Chicago Cubs to a single hit against just 28 batters. On the eighth, he caught the first game of a doubleheader and started behind the plate in the second game. He was moved to first base after Alan Storke departed while Smith took over for Gibby behind the plate. Over the 11 games, the club went 7–3 with a tie. On September 9, the Pirates sat in second place with a two-game lead over New York.

On September 9, Pittsburgh traveled to Cincinnati for a series of field events scheduled for the following day. Players from both the major and minor leagues competed in a skills competition for medals and prize money.[23] Pirates players participated in events such as timed races around the bases, fungo hitting and throwing accuracy. Although it rained heavily the night before the competition, and some entrants withdrew from the contest, the pool of competitors remained strong. Even so, the Reds rescheduled the competition for the 11th. Of the five events held, an established major-league player won just a single one: the throwing contest. "Five well-known and reliable catchers each threw three balls from home at a target over second base, and George Gibson, of Pittsburgh, alone hit once, while McLean, familiar with the grounds, only grazed the 14-inch disc."[24] Chicago's Johnny Kling finished third.

Following the competition, Gibby and his Pirates returned to work with a newly acquired pitching prospect, Nick Maddox. Less than a month earlier, on August 22, Maddox tossed a no-hitter for the Wheeling Stogies in the Central League. The notable performance caught Dreyfuss's attention and Maddox signed within the month.[25] On September 13, George went behind the plate to guide Nick Maddox through his major-league debut. He fanned 11 batsmen, gave up just five hits and allowed only two men to reach third base. His 5–0 shutout was deemed "one of the best games ever pitched at Exposition Park."[26] Needless to say, Maddox's career got off to a promising start. On September 20, while the Pirates were in the midst of a five-game winning streak, Gibson and Maddox joined forces again. In his second big-league start, Maddox outdid himself. The *Pittsburgh Daily Post* called it "the most remarkable contest seen at Exposition Park this year."[27] Maddox twirled a complete game, and achieved something no other Pittsburgh Pirate had. "For the first time in the annals of the Pittsburgh baseball club, one of the members of the Pirate pitching staff yesterday performed the rare feat of letting an opposing team down without a hit."[28] Maddox wasn't the first rookie to throw a no-hitter, but his first two major-league starts proved he was primed for the show. Gibson called two straight gems for Maddox, which was an early sign of his talent for handling young and inexperienced pitchers.

It is fair to call the Maddox–Gibson no-hitter the high point of the Pirates' season. The team played hard for the remainder of the season, but never really threatened the Cubs. Their 91–63 record put them 16 wins behind Chicago, who finished 107–45. The Cubs went on to play the Detroit Tigers in the World Series, and won the title in five games.

George continued to ascend in 1907, his most successful season to date. He set career highs in every offensive category. He played in 113 games, batted .219, hit 3 home runs and tallied 84 total hits. Gibson appeared in 110 games, including one at first base. In 956 innings behind the plate, he recorded 499 putouts and 125 assists against 642 total chances. His fielding percentage was .972 thanks to 18 errors.

The Pirates hosted a skills competition at Exposition Park a day after the regular season finished. The six-event extravaganza celebrated the team's second-place finish. The Pirates squared off in an intrasquad game before the field events began. George competed against Eddie Phelps and Harry Smith in the accurate throw contest. Surprisingly, George failed to hit the target. Smith also failed to hit the target, but Phelps hit the target squarely on his fifth attempt. Gibby also competed in a race circling the bases with slides at second and third base. Tommy Leach won that event in a time of 16.2 seconds, while George fell on his attempt and came in last with a time of 25 seconds.

George joined Tommy Leach and a team of barnstormers after the field day events. They traveled to Alliance, Ohio, for the first of a series of exhibition games. Gibson and the barnstormers made 14 stops before returning to Pittsburgh. "From every standpoint, it was the best trip ever taken by a Pirate barnstorming aggregation. In every town the financial result was good and the players will thus have a little 'extra' for the winter months."[29]

On October 21, George departed Pittsburgh for his hometown of London. Just like the year prior, barely a week after Gibson departed, the local papers rated his performance on the completed season. Unlike 1906, however, newspapermen did not call for his release, and instead acknowledged the "almost supreme value of a great catcher to a baseball team."[30] The scribes pointed out the contributions of Johnny Kling to the Cubs' success, Roger Bresnahan to the Giants' success and George Gibson to the Pirates' success. "The Canadian is nearly as good as they come, and is constantly improving, but the local team would be far better fortified if it had another man of the same caliber to help him out. Gibson was called upon to do practically all of the catching during the past season, owing to the doubt about Harry Smith's condition, and the inability of Eddie Phelps to show more than fine mechanical ability. However, good catchers are hard to secure, and the Pirates will be fortunate indeed to land another Gibson."[31] Even in December, when recent memories of season past started to fade, the young Canadian continued to draw praise, especially from Pittsburgh reporters.

> Pittsburgers fail to see where the Giants possess any class over the Pirates. In the catching department George Gibson is as good a man as McGraw has on his staff now. He is a young, aggressive backstop, and the contests held last summer proved him to be the most accurate thrower in the business. He is a good hitter, and when he lands on the ball, he lands hard. Not so much can be said of the other Pittsburg catchers, but Phelps and Smith are both good men to have around. Gibson will be depended upon again, however, to do the majority of the backstopping, and he can fill the bill to the queen's taste.[32]

What a difference a year makes.

President Dreyfuss and manager Fred Clarke devised a preseason plan for 1908 comparable to the plan they ran in 1907. They intended to include more exhibition games but at the same time minimize travel. Clarke objected "to spending valuable spring days on the railroads," and argued that "it is more important to get work and plenty of it than to make long jumps with the hope of picking up a few dollars at the gate."[33] On March 14, a group of Pittsburgh players would leave Pittsburgh and arrive at West Baden Springs on the 15th. After a week in Indiana, they would depart for Hot Springs and practice at Whittington Park. From April 3 to April 13, a series of exhibition games were scheduled to begin at Little Rock, Arkansas, and end at Kansas City, Missouri. The preseason exhibition tour would end just in time for the

Gibson leaning on his teammates in 1908. From left to right: Paddy O'Connor, Chief Wilson, Howie Camnitz, George Gibson, Harry Swacina, Ed Abbaticchio and Tommy Leach (SDN-006900, *Chicago Daily News* negatives collection, Chicago History Museum).

season to open in St. Louis. "The novel feature of the spring practice of the Pittsburgh team will be the visit to Fred Clarke's big farm on April 8, the day after an exhibition game at Winfield, which is Fred's nearest town. There will not be any baseball played at the farm, but Clarke believes that the Pirates will get all the exercise they need if they inspect the place under his direction."[34]

In late January, Dreyfuss and his staff mailed out all the players' contracts. Gibson and Smith seemed to be locks for the roster. Signed contracts started to stream into Pittsburgh and one-by-one, most players fell in line. As February came and went, four key Pirates still had not yet inked their names to contracts. Honus Wagner hadn't returned his contract yet, because he was contemplating retiring from baseball to pursue other business ventures. Tommy Leach did not affix his name to a contract for 1908, and his reasons were well documented. During the off-season, Clarke negotiated with Cincinnati owner Garry Herrmann over Leach's services. The deal, which would have made Leach the Reds' manager, ultimately fell through. It left Pittsburgh fans joyous that Leach was staying in the Steel City for another season, but upset Tommy, and he held out "as a direct result of his failure to land the Cincinnati management."[35] Meanwhile, Harry Smith remained unsigned. Unsure of the condition of his throwing arm, he made a deal with Dreyfuss to join the club on their training trip without a signed contract. The collective waited to see how his arm held up before the backstop inked his contract. That left George Gibson as the final player yet to send Dreyfuss a signed contract. In 1907, Gibson returned his signed contract "without a murmur and unequivocally admitted that he didn't deserve an increase."[36] In 1908 he sent his contract back unsigned because he felt he was owed a raise based on his performance in 1907. As quickly as Barney Dreyfuss confirmed that his catcher was holding out for more money, newspapermen speculated what made him feel he deserved more. The *Montreal Gazette* printed that "some of the Pittsburg players have combined to hold the club up for higher salaries. Geo. Gibson, the London catcher, formerly of Montreal, is one of the gang" and that Gibson's "head has become swelled through winning a prize for accurate throwing at the bowlers' day field sports in Cincinnati."[37]

When the Pirates began their voyage to West Baden Springs, Leach was signed, Wagner still considered retirement, Smith's status remained up in the air and Gibson kept off the radar. A report out of Chicago claimed that George "decided to go into the contracting business in the Windy City with his cousin," having "signed to catch for the Pastimes on Saturday and Sunday."[38] Officially, the Pirates had "no intention of making any advances"[39] to Gibson. George had not signed after two weeks of training camp. Pittsburgh reporters hadn't given up, though, and figured Gibson would come along "sooner or later."[40] Reporters from *Sporting Life* magazine did not feel the same way. They printed a story out of the Windy City that stated, "George Gibson, the Pittsburg catcher, is coming here to accept a position in his brother's firm and will play semi-pro ball Saturdays and Sundays."[41] When Barney Dreyfuss heard that Gibson accepted a position with the Chicago Semaphores he remarked: "They will have to pay him $62.50 per game to equal his salary here." This led the paper to speculate that his salary in 1907 was $3,000.[42] And then, something changed.

On April 3, Gibson traveled from his home in London to Pittsburgh. He registered at the Fort Pitt Hotel and held a pair of conferences with Barney Dreyfuss. "During their second session all differences were adjusted"[43] and George finally accepted terms for 1908 and signed a contract. The next day, Gibson and Dreyfuss boarded a train for Wichita, Kansas. Harry Smith and Honus Wagner, who had still not signed, joined Gibson and Dreyfuss on their journey. Dreyfuss wired ahead to Pirates' team secretary, William H. Locke, to let him know that he boarded a train for Wichita and brought along Wagner, Gibson and Smith. "The news quickly spread through the air and there was joy among the Buccaneers."[44] The foursome arrived in Wichita and met up with the rest of the Buccaneers prior to their nine o'clock practice. "Nobody was happier over the return of George Gibson than Tommy Leach. The wee one and the big fellow were roommates all last season, and are thick as two peas in a pod."[45] The group planned to watch the Pirates play the Wichita squad and then tag along as the Bucs were "escorted to the 'Little Pirate' ranch, where they will be guests of Manager Clarke."[46] Gibson and Smith were in uniform when the Pirates squared off against Wichita, but did not participate in the game. Despite Wagner's claim that "he had not given up his original idea of resting from the game all season,"[47] many fans were confident that this was a sign that he would be back in the game.

When Wichita and Pittsburgh dueled again the following day, reporters described George, who passed most of the winter at home in London, as "fit to don a uniform and play ball at once in his old time form."[48] He split catching duties with Paddy O'Connor, a rookie trying to make the squad. Gibson recorded a pair of singles in two plate appearances. Behind the plate, he recorded three putouts, an assist and an error. The Pirates won the contest 15–3. The following day, the people of Winfield proclaimed April 7 a general holiday in honor of Fred Clarke. The Regulars battled the Yannigans and the fans in attendance witnessed a game that "was well played throughout."[49] George caught for the Regulars, who won 4–3.

George and his teammates spent the following day at Little Pirate Ranch. "Clarke's program embraced hunting, rabbit chasing, broncho busting, lassoing and rope manipulation, rough-riding and a fight between a dog and a coyote."[50] Wagner and Smith returned to Winfield with the Pirates after the day at Clarke's ranch. When they arrived at the small Kansas town, their teammates were disheartened to learn the unsigned Wagner and Smith were leaving camp for Pittsburgh. The Pirates traveled directly to Kansas City after two days of rain prevented exhibition games in Coffeyville, Kansas, and in Joplin, Missouri. On the 11th, the Pirates played the Kansas City Blues. "George Hackenschmidt Gibson was the stellar performer with the willow, cracking out two doubles and a single in three times up."[51] Despite the offensive outpouring from the big Canadian, the Pirates still lost 6–5. The Pirates avenged their loss the following day by securing an 8–3 victory in their final tune-up before the season began.

On April 15, the Pirates opened their season in St. Louis against the Cardinals. Despite spending just a week at spring training, George started and formed the battery with Howie Camnitz. The Pirates won the game 3–1 and continued their winning ways as they swept the Cardinals in three straight. When the Pirates arrived in Cincinnati for their next series, they found Honus Wagner waiting for them. He had changed his mind about retiring and signed a contract with Barney Dreyfuss for the 1908 season. On April 19, Honus made his season debut. Camnitz and Gibson formed the Pirates battery against Bob Ewing and Canadian Larry McLean. Despite the return of their all-time great, the Redlegs handed Pittsburgh their first loss of the season.

On April 22, the Pirates returned to Pittsburgh to play their home opener at Exposition Park. Clarke gave Gibson the start, and when he walked out onto the field in his new uniform, the crowd greeted him with a warm ovation. The Pirates defeated St. Louis 5–1, which pleased the home crowd. On April 25, in the fourth game of the series with the Cardinals, George led off the eighth inning with "a cannon-ball smash which made Higgins duck his head, and it bounded safely over the central lawn."[52] Gibson's hit started a rally that resulted in two runs and pushed the Pirates' lead to 3–0. The Bucs ultimately won the game 3–2 and took the series three games to one. Then the rain and cold weather returned and kept the Pirates idle for three days. When they finally returned to the field, they beat the Cubs 7–4. By the end of April, the Pirates found themselves in second place at 7–4. At 8–3, Chicago sat atop the National League, and New York, at 8–6, rounded out the top three.

Poor weather followed the Pirates around through the first week of May. By May 8, they had only managed to play two games, and though they won both, they remained in second place. The Pirates hosted the Chicago Cubs when the rain finally let up enough to allow a game. George's defense was one of the features of the game. In the sixth inning, Gibson tossed to Wagner to catch a would-be base stealer. Later, he picked Frank Chance off of first base with "a scorching play … and the park resounded with cries of joy."[53] In the seventh inning Cubs catcher Johnny Kling batted with third baseman Harry Steinfeldt on third base. The *Pittsburgh Daily Post* described what unfolded:

> Kling smashed a long fly nearly to the flagstaff and both Clarke and Wilson got under it. Fred, however, stepped aside and determined to test the young Westerner's wonderful wing. Wilson was equal to the emergency, for he caught the ball and instantly heaved it homeward. He purposely threw it toward the north side of the plate and thereby displayed rare judgement for the strong breeze bent it in and Gibson got it at the gum just in time to kill the hopes of Steinfeldt. It was one of the prettiest double-plays seen in many a day and the fans stood up and howled long and loud.[54]

Despite the play, the Pirates failed to score against the Cubs and lost the game 1–0.

On May 15, after catching 11 straight contests dating back to April 24, George finally got some rest thanks to Philadelphia pitcher George McQuillan. The Phillies pitcher simply outclassed the Pirates hitters. Gibson started the game for the Pirates and through two innings nothing was out of the ordinary. By the fourth inning, however, the Phillies had figured out Vic Willis. Down by a score of 7–0, Clarke raised the white flag. He replaced Willis with Phillippe and Gibson with O'Connor to give his overworked battery a much-needed break. The Pirates were held to four hits and handed an embarrassing 11–0 defeat. Gibson's break was short-lived. He played 11 of the final

13 Pirates games in May, but the club remained ice cold. Their record dipped as low as 15–15 before they started to recover. On the last day of the month the Pirates split a doubleheader with Chicago. At 18–16, the Pirates were in fifth place.

At this point in the season, only five wins separated the top five teams. On June 3, in the midst of this battle, George made life miserable for Chicago's pitchers. His three hits helped chase both Carl Lundgren and Three Finger Brown en route to a 12–6 victory. A second win against Chicago catapulted Clarke's men ahead of New York and into second place. Then, Pittsburgh won three out of four against Chicago, and repeated the feat in Philadelphia and again in New York. A day of deep sea fishing in Beachmont, a shore suburb of Boston, allowed George, an avid fisherman, a day of relaxation with his comrades. When they returned to land, they handed a series of beatings to the Boston club and left town with a four-game winning streak.

On June 27 in St. Louis, Gibson played masterfully. He threw out five base stealers, and the Pirates secured a 4–1 victory. On June 28, George played the second half of a twin bill, and made his 52nd start of the season. At this point, Barney Dreyfuss recognized that his team possessed a glut of catchers. He released Harry Smith from his Pirates contract. This allowed Smith to join the Boston Doves, where he remained for three seasons. On June 30, the Pirates played an exhibition game in Bicknell, Indiana. Paddy O'Connor caught for Pittsburgh, and Gibson got to rest while his Pirates teammates put on a pitching and hitting clinic. Deacon Phillippe pitched for Pittsburgh, and only gave up three hits on the way to an 18–0 victory. While the Pirates showed the amateurs how pro ball was played, the Cubs lost to the Reds, which gave the Bucs first place in the National League for the first time in 1908.

In July, the weather, and the intense rivalries between the Pirates and their National League foes, heated up. Despite the rivalry, there was some civility between the clubs as evidenced by the Pirates and Cubs before the early game of a twin bill on Independence Day. "Gibson and Moran wore the same windpad yesterday morning, and it was 'on the bum' at that. They took turns at inflating it between half innings."[55] Unfortunately for Gibson and his Buc teammates, they lost both games. On July 24, Pittsburgh arrived in New York, still holding on to first place. The Pirates and Giants split the first two games of the series. Pittsburgh won again on July 27, but not without some controversy. The Pirates, never fans of their New York counterparts, called out the Giants for using rowdy tactics. The *Pittsburgh Press* explained: "George Gibson seldom complains, and when he protested against the bases on balls handed to Bresnahan by Umpire Klem, the other Pirates heeded him. Gibson declares that three of the so-called balls while Bresnahan was at bat were in reality perfect strikes. Bresnahan violated the rules by running out of the box at every pitch, but the umpire did not even caution him."[56] Bresnahan's attempted trickery failed to tip the scales in the Giants' favor, and the "Pirates took a tighter hold on first place in the big union race ... by upsetting the New Yorks 4–3...."[57] On July 31, the Pirates got a scare in Brooklyn. "During the battle Rucker hit Gibson on the arm that he uses so well behind the bat. Gibson is as plucky as they make players but even he danced from pain. He would not retire, but the bruise on his arm got sorer the longer he remained on duty."[58] The Pirates came away with the win over the Superbas, which soothed Gibson's pain.

Pittsburgh entered August in first place with a record of 56–36. New York trailed by a half game, and the Cubs sat close behind in third. George started the month with a three-game hitting streak, highlighted by his first home run of the season. Between August 11 and August 22, George appeared in 10 straight games and recorded 8 hits in 33 at bats (an average of .242). On August 24, the Pirates sailed into New York City where they planned to remain a thorn in the side of McGraw's Giants. The first day, the teams played a double-header. Gibson caught the morning game, which was his 37th consecutive start. Clarke rested George in the afternoon and allowed Phelps to don his mask for the first time since early July. The Pirates lost both games of the twin bill by a combined score of 9–2. They also lost the third game of the series, which suggested to the *Pittsburgh Press* that Gibson looked tired and overworked. The Giants completed the sweep with a 4–3 victory in the final game of the series. The Giants scored the winning run at least in part to a miscue by Gibson. "Wilson made a perfect throw to the plate in the ninth inning, after catching a long fly, but 'Hack' let the ball get away."[59] The *Pittsburgh Press* doubled down on their hypothesis. Clearly, a catcher as defensively sound as Gibson would not perform so poorly unless his team taxed him unnecessarily.

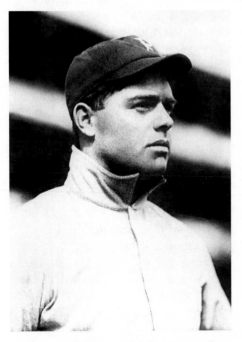

George Gibson standing with focus in 1908 at the West Side Grounds in Chicago. George would later tell journalist Lawrence Ritter, "Thinking had to be my specialty" (SDN-006905 *Chicago Daily News* negatives collection, Chicago History Museum).

Despite the paper's perspective, Clarke continued to go with his number one catcher. As the catcher's inning count continued to climb, people, especially the newspaper folks, took notice: "'Good Old Gib' is just about as popular with the fans as any player who ever donned the Buccaneer uniform, and well he may be, for no man has ever given the club more valiant returns for the salary paid him."[60]

The Giants used the three-game whipping to vault over the Pirates into first place. All the while, the Cubs stood in third, clawing at the Pirates' backs. Pittsburgh then took 3-of-4 from Philadelphia, which helped stymie the Cubs' push. In the first game, George again proved his grit when he served up the game-winning hit. The series concluded on August 29 when the third and fourth games were played as a double bill. The Pirates took a 1–0 lead into the top of the ninth in the morning game. In the bottom half of the inning, Philadelphia right fielder John Titus led off with a double and advanced to third on a sacrifice. Then Kitty Bransfield came to bat. "Bransfield's duster was deftly gobbled by Abby, who shot the leather home and Gibson tagged Titus before he could tally, and by a quick heave to Wagner, doubled Bransfield up on the way to second."[61] The 3–2–6 double play ended the game and secured the Pirates' victory. George sat out the afternoon contest, just his second game off in August. Without their key cog, the Pirates lost 5–1 and missed out on an opportunity to further distance themselves from the third-place Cubs. The loss proved extra costly as the Cubs won on August 30 and overtook the Pirates for second place. The National League standings on September 1 were as follows:

Team	W	L	Pct.	GB
New York	69	45	.603	--
Chicago	71	47	.602	--
Pittsburgh	70	47	.598	½

By the time September started, it seemed as if Dreyfuss decided to double back after selling Harry Smith. Dreyfuss thought Gibson could not keep up his pace, so he purchased John Sullivan from Kansas City to spell their mainstay backstop. Clarke disagreed. The *Pittsburgh Press* noted that "Sullivan is said to be quite a catcher, but Gibson never was better in his life and Clarke will keep him behind the bat as long as possible."[62] On September 4, the Cubs were in Pittsburgh with second place on the line and Gibson behind the plate. The Pirates loaded the bases with two out in the bottom of the tenth inning. With Pirates rookie Warren Gill on first base, outfielder Owen Wilson laced a walk-off single and Fred Clarke scored the game-winning run. Gill stopped running to second when Clarke crossed home plate. Instead he turned and headed for the clubhouse to avoid fans running on the field. Johnny Evers, the veteran second baseman, called for the ball and immediately stepped on second base to record a force out, which ended the inning and negated Clarke's run. "As soon as Clarke crossed the home plate, Umpire Hank O'Day turned and walked to the players' bench to get a drink of water."[63] Once the Cubs got the umpire's attention, his reported reaction was to merely remark: "Clarke has crossed the plate."[64] The Pirates recorded the win and retained second place. Cubs president Charles Murphy protested the loss to National League president Harry C. Pulliam. Pulliam eventually ruled that the Pirates had won the game not because Gill didn't need to touch second base, but rather because umpire O'Day had not witnessed that he hadn't.[65] The next day, the Cubs blew out the Pirates 11–0. Gibson left the ball game after five innings, and gave way to the newly acquired catcher John Sullivan. Sullivan caught four innings, but was otherwise ordinary. Dreyfuss and Sullivan failed to agree to terms, because "Catcher Sullivan thought he was worth more than $250 and refused to sign."[66] On September 12, Sullivan was returned to the Kansas City Blues. Dreyfuss and Clarke must have agreed that Gibson didn't need help after all.

On September 18, the Pirates stood tied with the Cubs for second place, three games back of the Giants. The Bucs embarked on a critical four-game series in New York against the G-Men. Ahead of the series, George showed confidence in his team: "I have not given up hope of beating New York and won't until the season is over. We still have a good chance and intend to fight it out."[67] The Pirates failed to capitalize on their opportunity and only managed a split with the well-prepared Giants. The Pirates, however, continued to battle the rest of September and closed the month with eight wins against one loss. Despite their great play down the stretch, the Bucs finished September looking up in the standings at both Chicago and New York. The National League standings on September 30 were as follows:

Team	W	L	Pct.	GB
Chicago	94	54	.635	--
New York	92	53	.634	½
Pittsburgh	94	55	.631	1

With just five games left in their season, Pittsburgh had no room for error. On October 2, the Pirates took a five-game winning streak into a doubleheader against the St. Louis Cardinals. They won the first game easily and then ran into some luck in the second game. As their season hung in the balance, George stepped to the plate with two men down in the seventh inning and St. Louis leading 1–0. He ripped a drive to the right pasture and the ball whizzed past Cardinals fielder Al Shaw. "By the time it was recovered, Gibson was on his way to third. Then he took a long chance and got away with it. When he set sail for home it was apparent that nothing but a wild throw or an error would save him." Shaw relayed the ball to second baseman Chappy Charles and he delivered the ball to catcher Jack Bliss. When Bliss attempted to tag Gibson, he dropped the ball and George scored. Gibson's second home run of the season tied the game, and in the ninth, Wagner also hit a home run that the press described as "the hardest hit ball of the season."[68] The Pirates won the game 2–1.

With victories in their next two contests, the Pirates catapulted into first place. Although the Pirates won again the following day, the Cubs and Giants remained right on their heels. On October 4, the *Pittsburgh Post-Gazette*'s front page headline declared "If The Pirates Beat The Cubs Today The Pennant Is Ours."[69] Manager Clarke predicted victory for the Pirates on the final day of the season in a must-win match. The Pirates brimmed with confidence walking into Chicago's West Side Park on account of their 12–9 record against the Cubs in '08. The Cubs wasted no time putting a run on the board. Up 1–0 in the bottom of the first inning, they proceeded to load the bases. With two out, Gibson caught a Joe Tinker foul ball to end the threat. Gibson had Tinker's number again in the fourth inning, when he threw him out at second after a Johnny Kling strikeout. In the top of the sixth inning, Pittsburgh battled for two runs and tied the game. However, in the bottom of the inning, the Cubs recaptured the lead and held on to win the game, 5–2. The Cubs' hero of the day was pitcher Mordecai Brown, who only allowed seven Buc hits. On the other hand, the goat for the Pirates, according the *Pittsburgh Daily Post*, was Hans Wagner, who "played the field all afternoon much like a cheese sandwich without mustard."[70] The Flying Dutchman made two errors in the pivotal game. The Bucs' season was over. They finished with a record of 98–56, one game behind the Cubs, who ended tied with the Giants at 98–55.

While Pittsburgh and the rest of Major League Baseball tallied 154 games that season, the Cubs and Giants reached the finish line with only 153. The pennant contenders finished one game short thanks to their match on September 23. On that day, Giants rookie Fred Merkle committed a base-running blunder later labeled as "Merkle's Boner."

In that controversial game, the Giants and Cubs kicked off the ninth inning all tied up. With two outs in the bottom half of the frame, Giants shortstop Al Bridwell stepped into the batter's box. Moose McCormick stood on third, and Fred Merkle on first. Bridwell drove a pitch to center field for what should have been a game-ending single. Unfortunately, when McCormick crossed the plate, Merkle stopped running and headed for the clubhouse. Thinking the game over, he felt it prudent to get off the bases in order to avoid the mass of fans that already started to storm the field. As this happened, Cubs second baseman Johnny Evers, just as he had a few weeks earlier against the Pirates, noticed that Merkle failed to touch second base. Knowing that he could nullify the run if he collected the ball and touched second base, Evers called for the ball.

After that, all hell broke loose and in the absence of video evidence, a lot of circumstantial facts came to pass. Evers tried to retrieve the game ball, his teammates tried to assist him, Giants players tried to stop him and fans ran rampant. Eventually, Evers obtained the ball, and proceeded to step on second base. Hank O'Day, the home plate umpire, dutifully administered his decision: Merkle was out, the run did not count and the game needed to continue. Unable to restore order before darkness fell, O'Day declared the game over and National League president Harry Pulliam determined the game a tie.

Had the Pirates taken care of the Cubs in that last game of their season, they would have advanced to the World Series and Merkle's mistake might well have settled in as a footnote of baseball history. As it happened, the loss put the Cubs and Giants in a dead heat with 98 wins against 55 losses, half a game better in the standings than the Pirates. Pulliam issued an edict and required the "missing" game, in its entirety, needed to be replayed. The Cubs prevailed, took the pennant and eventually the World Series and spent the off-season as baseball's first back-to-back champions.

While the Cubs and Giants went on to stamp their names in the book of baseball lore, Pittsburgh returned from Chicago defeated but not dejected. Masses of fans waited for them at Union Station and Gibson, being one of the clear cut leaders in the clubhouse, addressed the crowd: "The players will not soon forget the treatment accorded them on their return home today. We did the best we could, but as a rule the loser does not receive much consideration, no matter how game a fight he may put up, and it was a pleasant surprise to find the people with us this morning. Those of us who were with the team next year will take pleasure in remembering the cordial reception."[71]

It seemed a rather innocent speech at the time. A speech often given in lip service to the usual chatter required from players after a disappointing defeat. However, Gibson's speech may have been sincere. Perhaps he realized the Pirates were on the cusp of greatness, and the city of Pittsburgh would soon have their champion.

6

Iron Man

Despite the heartbreaking end to the 1908 season, George had to be pleased with his individual performance. He appeared in a staggering 143 contests and played more games as catcher than anyone in all of the majors. George improved on nearly every career best that he had set in 1907 and headed off into the off-season content to keep things simple.

He joined a group of his teammates on a barnstorming tour just like after the previous season. When that ended abruptly on account of poor weather conditions, Gibson departed for London to spend the winter with his family.

George hunted in the off-season both for pleasure and cardiovascular conditioning. He chased jack rabbits ten miles a day in the cold Canadian winter, which in turn helped with his endurance. Although he was no "Buffalo Bill" Cody, Gibby's years of shooting made him proficient with a rifle. In the winter of 1909, Gibson engaged in an epic battle with an undercover jack rabbit in the Southern Ontario grasslands. Reports of his clashes with the elusive varmint stole headlines across the Eastern United States and Canada. His hometown paper, the *London Free Press*, picked up a dispatch from a New York dateline that told of Gibby's hunting frustrations in a humorous way: "George Gibson, premier catcher of the National League, is bending his hand to literature. He is writing a yarn called, 'The Phantom Jack Rabbit,' based on a remarkable adventure. It seems that for two winters Gibson has been chasing a mighty animal in the wilds near his London, Ont, home. The last time Gibson saw the thing it loomed up fully three feet high. Just as Gibson was about to pull the trigger the animal disappeared into ether. Only its tracks convinced Gibson he was not dreaming."[1] In January, Gibby sent a telegram to Barney Dreyfuss, telling him of his adventure with "the Phantom Rabbit." When the Pittsburgh newspaper men caught wind of Gibby's chase of the deceptive hare, they recounted his efforts with a cheerful limerick:

> George Gibson was chasing a rabbit;
> Way out in Ontario's plains;
> Old Gib has the marathon habit

Yet bunny was making some gains;
His ball with a vim,
He threw and soaked him,
'Twas not but a second base throw.[2]

Gibson cordially accepted the wisecracks and banter from friends and reporters, but of the deceptive cottontail, there's no word on if Gibby ever made the catch!

Still, when it was time to return to the Pirates, Gibson put down his rifle and picked up his mitt. As in previous seasons, the Pirates' battery crew began training 10 days before the team's position players started. Manager Fred Clarke appointed ten-year veteran Tommy Leach as acting manager, to lead the pitchers and catchers in the Indiana resort town of West Baden Springs. In addition to Gibson, catchers Paddy O'Connor and Caleb "Pop" Shriver joined the pitchers at the early camp. Leach planned to engage the batterymen in light practices before the group rendezvoused with Clarke and the other Buccos on March 21 in Hot Springs.

On the first day in West Baden Springs, heavy rain flooded the grounds and limited the players to nothing more than a long walk. The Pirates were forced to continue to stay indoors because of the inclement weather, where all they could do was challenge each other in billiard matches. The chance of getting in any real baseball work looked uncertain, because the ball field was under five feet of water. Program leader Leach remained hopeful that his players would get some work in over the next few days. That did not happen as the fields in West Baden Springs were so waterlogged that the groundskeeper announced that they would be unplayable for at least two weeks. Leach called off training activities at West Baden Springs and ordered his troops to Arkansas.

On March 13, the advance Pirates crew arrived in Hot Springs, a week earlier than expected. Gibson, the incumbent catcher, was thought to have the starting job in hand, which left the other three men to battle it out for two back-up spots. Shriver and O'Connor were joined by rookie Mike Simon, who was attending his first spring training with the Pirates. Because the advanced group arrived early in Arkansas, no official schedule was prepared. Acting manager Leach requested George lead a group of a dozen men on a hike. Gibson did, with pleasure. He gave them a hard walk of about seven miles through the Ouachita mountain trails near the Hot Springs lodge where the club was stationed. Gibson, already in condition from trekking through the Canadian wilderness all winter, happily continued to lead groups through the trails in an effort to get his teammates in shape before serious baseball activities began. On March 18, Manager Clarke arrived in Arkansas and brought with him the club's uniforms. It was noted by the press that George went above and beyond to help team trainer Ed Laforce measure up the players for their 1909 season rags.

The Pirates, all suited up in their new duds, started their spring with an intrasquad game. After a couple weeks of scrimmages, Clarke took his club on a road trip to Little Rock, Arkansas, and Memphis, Tennessee. Gibson and Mike Simon served as catchers on the journey. After a pair of poor performances against the Southern League clubs, Clarke escorted his Pittsburgh team back to Hot Springs to work on fundamentals and to prepare for opening day.

On April 14, the Pirate crew opened the 1909 season in Cincinnati. The early spring weather brought ideal conditions for baseball and despite re-

Pirates catchers at 1909 spring training at Hot Springs, Arkansas. Standing, left to right: Gibson and Mike Simon. Sitting, left to right: Paddy O'Connor and Caleb Shriver (Wiersbicki Collection).

cent rains throughout the Midwest, League Park in the Queen City was in fine condition. As expected, Gibson started as catcher while Howie Camnitz twirled pitches from the mound. On the Redlegs side, another Canadian, Larry McLean, caught Cincinnati ace, Arthur Fromme. Many of the 22,000 excited fans who showed up in Redsland went home disappointed. The Camnitz–Gibson battery put the kibosh on the buckeye hitters and allowed only six hits in a 3–0 Bucs victory. Unfortunately, the team performed poorly on the remainder of the season's opening road trip. The Bucs lost their next three games in Cincinnati before traveling to Chicago. In the Windy City, Camnitz and Gibson dominated again in a 1–0 Pirates win. The lone run came in the twelfth frame perhaps in spite of, and not because of, Gibson's ability at the plate. After Chicago pitcher, and future Hall of Famer, Mordecai "Three Finger" Brown allowed Pirates first baseman Bill Abstein to reach third, Gibson came to bat looking to hit a sacrifice fly. Gibby took a huge cut at the ball, halved it and grounded it directly to Cubs shortstop Joe Tinker. The usually sure-handed Tinker had plenty of time to throw Abstein out at home, but he fumbled the ball and the Bucs first baseman scored the winning run.

Despite the rocky start to the season, Pirates fans knew they had a pennant contender and enthusiastically awaited their team's home opener at Exposition Park. The year 1909 was the last time the Pirates began their season campaign at the historic Exposition Park. The park hosted its first baseball game in 1882, when the Alleghenys' of the American Association called the grounds home. In 1890, the next occupants of the park were the Pittsburgh Burghers, of the Players League. When the Players League folded following its only season, the Burghers consolidated their assets with the Pittsburgh Nationals, who played at Recreation Park, and the new club made Exposition Park their home. On April 22, 1891, the first Pirates game to took place at Exposition Park and the grounds on the North side of the Allegheny River hosted every Pirates opening day up to and including 1909. The celebration for the park's final home opener started at one o'clock, with a concert featuring the Grand Army Band. Fans were allowed to enter the park early to watch the players warm up, and the game was scheduled to start at 3pm. Many City of Pittsburgh dignitaries were on hand, including Mayor William A. Magee, who threw out the ceremonial first pitch. Right-handed pitcher Chick Brandom got the start on the mound, in front of what turned out to be a surprisingly low number of fans. Just 9,024 paid patrons showed up at the stadium, which is just as well considering the outcome. Brandom pitched well as Gibson guided him through five innings of work. Chick surrendered just three runs before Lefty Leifield came on in relief. The Bucs went into the ninth inning ahead 4–3, but the Reds spoiled the game for the home team and won 7–4. The Pirates' faithful, who braved the cold and overcast conditions, went home unsatisfied. Gibson played his typical stellar defense, but struggled with the bat in the final Exposition Park opener. The Pirates played fine during their first twelve games and ended the month with a 6–6 record. Though George finished April with only 8 hits in 37 at bats, the *Sporting News* still saw improvements in Gibson's all-around play:

> With the race for 1909 well started, it is entertaining to look over the initial frays and note the active figures. Usually one or two men will cut a bigger dash than others. For instance in the Pittsburg's starting series Gibson and Wagner shone far above the rest in brilliancy, while Abby was the slumper. Gibson began to bat grandly as soon as the championship bell rang. He also cut a splash in active fielding, so much so that a Redtown observer commented as follows: 'Gibson is a better catcher than imagined.' It has taken a long time for circuit men to discern this fact. 'Hack' has been showing ability as a backstop for moons, but was unable to arouse words of praise. Might be well to mention here that Gibson is a 40 per cent better batsman than in 1907. Originally weak in meeting a high ball, striking down on it with his bat, the big catcher was fed high ones by ninety-nine twirlers out of the century. No longer do the lofty tosses fool. They are met with snappiness and go screaming to the outfield. Took a long time to break the man of his old habit of meeting them. Seems to have mastered a high ball nowadays.[3]

In May, Gibson and his Pirates teammates showed marked improvement at the plate. The club began the month on the road with a four-game sweep of Chicago. In the final game of the series, Gibson collided with future Hall of Famer Frank Chance at the plate. The following day, when the Pirates played the Cardinals at Exposition Park, Clarke rested Gibson on account of the catcher's now stiff neck. His replacement, Paddy O'Connor, played a "classy game"[4] in his stead, going 3-for-4, in a 6–5 Bucs win. O'Connor commented after the game, "I'm sorry Gibson was hurt, but I am certainly glad to get a chance to get off that bench."[5] Even with O'Connor's strong game, Clarke did not rely on him much that season. In turn, Gibson rarely relinquished the big mitt in 1909. Be that as it may, the win over the Cardinals contributed to a seven-game winning streak that kicked off the month. The Pirates kept their foot on the gas and won 19 of their 25 contests that May.

Gibson and the Pirates continued to gather momentum throughout June. They closed out May with four straight wins and then used June to extend their winning streak to fourteen consecutive games. In those fourteen games, Gibson contributed twelve hits in forty-eight at bats. While he also recorded his first defensive faux pas of the year, which ended his 42-game errorless streak, Gibby played extremely well behind the plate. Still, the papers took notice of his blunder: "George Gibson spoiled his fielding record when he made a wild throw to second to catch a Quaker napping."[6]

On June 16, the win streak ended when the Pirates hosted John McGraw and his New York Giants at Exposition Park. Future Hall of Famer Christy Mathewson started on the hill to thwart the home team. Matty, as he was known, wasn't dominant, but he led the Gothamites to an 8–2 victory. In

Gibson leading off third base at the West Side Grounds in Chicago (SDN-054854 *Chicago Daily News* **negatives collection, Chicago History Museum).**

spite of the loss, Gibson tagged Mathewson for three hits. While Pirates fans were certainly disappointed in the loss, they had no problem overlooking the performance given the Bucs' dominance since the beginning of May.

On June 23, Gibson called a great game for starting pitcher Vic Willis in a 3–1 win over the St. Louis Cardinals. The Pirates battery gave up just four hits and George made a putout that modern baseball fans might consider "Jeter-esque." The circus catch was reported by the *Pittsburgh Daily Post*: "In the fifth inning Gibson ran back to the grandstand and picked a foul off the crowd with his gloved hand. He had to stick his mitt over the railing to get the ball, but he got it and a good hand as well."[7] The Pirates closed out June with three momentous games that resonated throughout the organization and with the fan base.

On June 28, following a five-game series in St. Louis, the Pirates made a quick one-game stop in Cincinnati. The following day's *Pittsburgh Daily Post* bluntly stated: "Gibson's Bat Baffles Reds." The Pirates defeated the Reds 3–2 thanks in large part to Gibson, who was perfect at the plate for the only game in 1909, when he went 4-for-4 in the Queen City. A *Daily Post* reporter penned: "Gibson cuts wide swath. The star of the contest was a husky Canadian from London, Ont., who officiates behind the bat, by the name of George Gibson. He was personally responsible for two of the Pirates runs, one on his triple and another in the eighth inning that proved to be the winning tally on a single that scored Wagner after two men had been retired. Gibson faced Ewing three times and Dubuc once and on every occasion he succeed in clouting the ball where the Cincinnati fielders weren't." The paper also remarked on Gibby's lumber: "George Hitemhard Gibson was there yesterday with his magic wand—the mighty willow." No other note was ever made of whether Gibson called his bat the "Mighty Willow," but in June, his willow surely had some magic in it.[8] *Pittsburgh Post-Gazette* writer C. B. Power, also praised Gibson after that game. "Gracious, goodness, how that old Hackenschmidt Gibson is pasting the pulsating pill. Four more yesterday. Say, George, I have always held you in high esteem as a catcher—no, not merely a backstop—but really, I did not think you would be so coarse and vulgar enough to even make an attempt to wrest the batting honors from our dear old Honus. Say, Mr. Gibson, we are all very much to the tickled and the wish from the whole push is that you may be able to keep right on banging the ball with great force and precision."[9] Gibson's great day served as the perfect lead-in to the final two days of June. George played an instrumental part in the Pirates' move from Exposition Park to their new home, Forbes Field.

On June 29, 1909, the Pirates' time at the historic ball ground at Exposition Park came to an end. The Pirates opposed their pennant-seeking rivals, and the defending world champion, the Chicago Cubs. Exposition Park had a capacity of approximately 16,000, but only 5,545 fans showed up to say farewell. Clearly the hot ticket was the opening of Forbes Field and not the closing of Exposition Park. The hometown club treated those who turned up to a commanding performance. The Pirates scored four runs in the first inning off of "Three Finger" Brown, and never relented. The Leifield–Gibson battery executed brilliantly and only allowed seven scattered hits on their way to an 8–1 victory. George entered the record books when he registered a double off of Chicago reliever Jack Pfeister in the top of the eighth inning, the last hit ever at Exposition Park. Cubbies catcher Jimmy Archer struck out to end the game and as soon as the ball snapped George Gibson's leather, the bugler began his farewell calls. The *Pittsburgh Daily Post* captured the final adieu most eloquently: "When the Champions went to bat in the ninth, the notes of a bugle broke the silence. Commodore Charles Zeig, the well known local musician, had quietly taken a position on the circus seats back of middlefield, and as soon as it was certain that Chicago had been hopelessly crushed, he sounded 'taps' through his cornet. At the same time ground keeper [*sic*] Jim O'Malley commenced lowering the big flag, and just as Old Glory touched the ground and the last note of the farewell bugle call ceased, Archer struck out and the historic old baseball lot had passed into history. Commodore Zeig then rendered a few notes of 'Yankee Doodle' and the audience departed."[10] The *Pittsburgh Post-Gazette* spoke of the mixed feelings devoted Pirates fans had after witnessing the park's finale: "Ordinarily, a victory over the Cubs would have sent a Pittsburgh baseball crowd away from Exposition Park thrilled with much talkativeness. There would of been hundreds of faces picturesquely portraying pleasure, fans would have congregated in groups great and small, and there would have been happy exultations over the downfall of the men from the west. None of these were in evidence after yesterday's game. Naturally, the fans were happy because the Pirates had won the game, still there was a painful and touching absence of jubilation. It was goodbye to dear old Expo Park."[11] The sadness turned to elation and utter joy the following day when the brand new, state of the art Buccos home finally opened.

The newly built stadium was given the moniker Forbes Field, after British General John Forbes. While naming the park after a British general might seem an odd choice, Forbes fought in the French and Indian war and gave Pittsburgh its name. So 151 years later, the Bucs returned service and named their home after him. The new ballpark was located in the Oakland neighborhood of Pittsburgh and eventually became known as the Oakland Orchard. The stadium sat 25,000 spectators and was one of the first all concrete and steel ballparks; most of the previous American stadiums were mainly wooden structures. For the project, Pirates owner and president Barney Dreyfuss secured money from aristocratic Pittsburghers such as the Scottish-born Pennsylvanian steel magnate Andrew Carnegie. Luckily for Dreyfuss, the industrialist Carnegie sold his steel company in 1901 and began philanthropic work. He donated most of his wealth to causes he supported; it just so happens that included Dreyfuss's new ballpark. On March 1, 1909, construction of Forbes Field started, and amazingly, only four months later, it was complete and ready for play.[12]

On June 30, the Pirates played their first game at Forbes Field. Gates opened at noon and unsurprisingly, more fans showed up than the building could house. In anticipation, Dreyfuss had temporary wooden bleachers erected in the outfield; however, the added capacity wasn't enough, and the stadium still burst at the seams with excited fans. Even with the crowd swell, the pre-game festivities went off without a hitch. The weather was beautiful and a band played popular and patriotic tunes from 1:30 until 2:30 p.m., at which time the dedication ceremony commenced. Separate bands simultaneously led each team onto the field. Fred Clarke led his team's procession and Chicago followed their skipper, Frank Chance. The clubs faced each other in parallel lines as Barney Dreyfuss, with help from National League president Harry Pulliam, escorted heroic Pittsburghers of the past through the lines, where they were honored by the players and fans. The bands played in a march to center field, where the grounds crew rose the stars and stripes up the flagpole. As Old Glory reached its pinnacle, the crowd cheered, and the players took the field to warm up. Pittsburgh mayor, the Honorable William

A. Magee, declined to relinquish his coveted box seat and in turn, entrusted director of public safety John M. Morin to throw out the first pitch. The public safety man threw a strike to George Gibson and veteran Canadian umpire Bob Emslie yelled "Play Ball!"; with that, Forbes Field was officially open.

The game started on a sour note when Vic Willis hit Chicago leadoff hitter Johnny Evers. The wildness continued and Willis issued a free pass to the next batter, Jimmy Sheckard. The two baserunners each advanced one station on a sacrifice, and then Frank Chance lined a single to center field. Evers scored easily; however, Tommy Leach threw a beautiful ball to Gibson at home who in turn applied the perfect tag to Sheckard to deny the run. In the second inning, Gibson entered the record books again when he hit a "hot duster"[13] past Evers at second; it was the first hit by a Pirate at the aforementioned Forbes Field. The game ended up being a pitcher's duel, but the Cubs captured the first game at Forbes Field, 3–2. Despite the tough start to the month, the Pirates went 19–3 in June and took control of first place thanks to an overall record of 44–15. At the plate, Gibson finished June 25-for-78 with a .321 clip—his highest average any month of 1909.

As soon as the Bucs christened their new home, the schedule sent them on an 18-game Eastern road trip, the club's longest of the season. The Pirates' long trip included a stop in New York to face the Giants, a visit to Brooklyn to take on the Superbas, a journey south to Philadelphia and a final series up in Boston against the lowly Doves. To get to New York City, they likely started on the Penn Special, the Pennsylvania Railroad's quickest train of the time. The Penn Special Line ended at Jersey City, New Jersey, on the western side of the Hudson River, a ride that lasted approximately nine-hours and traversed 440-miles. From New Jersey the club ferried across the Hudson to get to their final destination of Manhattan. Trains did not reach the island until late 1910, when the aptly named Penn Station and the Hudson River tunnel project reached completion.[14]

When the Pirates arrived at the Polo Grounds for a six-game set, the Giants were in third place, eight games back in the standings. Despite the gap, the Giants still had aspirations for the pennant. According to Giants pitcher George "Hooks" Wiltse, his team had a clear objective for the rest of the season: "Beat Chicago and fight for the rag with Pittsburg." Wiltse explained that the Giants pitchers had thrown the ball well all year, and the hitters had started to come around. He knew they'd have a tough time catching the Pirates and told reporter Al Sangree, "Pittsburg is a strong club. I don't know where you can get four better men than Gibson, Clarke, Wagner and Leach. They are among the dozen best ball players right now, and they are the fellows we have to beat by out pitching them."[15]

Wiltse himself took the ball for the Giants in the first game of the series and he put his money where his mouth was. He allowed only eight scattered hits in a 5–1 Giants win. The loss angered the Pirates but so, too, did the condition of the facilities at the Polo Grounds. The visitors' locker room was in horrific condition. Without hot water and proper wash basins, the players could not clean up. Fred Clarke stated: "It is strange how the poorest club houses in the league are the ones in Chicago and New York." Once the players recovered from the poor treatment at the hands of the Giants and found a place to clean up, they spent the night on the town. The Pirates players attended a performance of *The Motor Girl* at New York's Broadway Lyric Theater after being invited by management there.[16]

When the Pirates got back to baseball, they took three straight games from the Giants and won four of the six games in the series. They made it tough on the Giants and thus confirmed Wiltse's earlier statement. The Pirates continued their eastern trip and won the series at Brooklyn, split four games with the Phillies and then swept the underdog Doves in a three-game set. On July 24, Gibson recorded his first, and only, two-error game of the season, but the *Pittsburgh Press* still showed their admiration for him. "It has been due to Gibson's superb catching that Pittsburg's pitchers have been twirling in such smooth fashion this season. His work behind the bat probably has been the best of any backstop in the country up to date, while he hits like a demon."[17] The Pirates won a respectable eleven of sixteen games on the trip, and by the end of July held a six-game lead over the Cubs for the National League flag. The Giants were fading and sat at eleven and a half games off the pace.

As August began, Pittsburgh journalists, fans and management finally realized how important a cog in the Pirates engine Gibson really was. Gibby played an outstanding contest in the first game of the month, a clash at home with the Brooklyn Superbas that Pittsburgh took 9–1. He walked twice and went 2-for-2 at the dish, highlighted by a double in the third inning that scored three runs. George also played great behind the plate and threw out the only Brooklynite who attempted a steal on him. Manager Clarke, impressed with Gibby's performance, decided to give him his first rest since May. Mike Simon took over to finish the ninth inning. The next morning, when asked by reporters if he was all rested up, Gibby joked that he was "greatly refreshed and ready to go through sixty more games without a break." Back-up Mike Simon also discussed what it was like to throw on the chest protector in order to replace Gibson: "Gee but this seems strange. This is the first time I've had this thing on in a real game for an age."[18] The reporter noted that Pirates third-string catcher, Paddy O'Connor, who caught only seventeen innings in 1909, looked envious of Simon's relief appearance.

Gibson's absence from the lineup caused newspapers to be reminded of just how valuable he was. Under the heading, "George Gibson Worth His Weight In Radium,"[19] the *Pittsburgh Press* explained:

Radium, a chemical element discovered a decade earlier by renowned scientists Marie and Pierre Curie, was highly valued for its many potential uses. Gibson's bosses put the same high value on his leadership and work ethic. They recognized Gibby as the reason for the Pirates' success, and so did the press. "Suppose you owned a base ball club that was leading the league along towards the three-fifths mark when the race was hotter than Tombstone, Ariz., in dog days, and suddenly realized that you had but one catcher capable of working. You'd consider said catcher an asset worth pretty near his weight in radium, wouldn't you? Such is the Pittsburg situation today and it isn't violating any confidences to say that Col. Barney Dreyfuss, owner, and Fred Clarke, manager, look upon George Gibson, the reliable backstop, as the one best bet of the Pirate outfit."[20] Gibson masterfully read the opposing batters, and this ability kept the Pirates ahead in the National League pennant race. Fred Clarke called him "Willing George" and knew if Gibby didn't falter, the Pirates would get the flag and turn the value of George from the element radium to the precious metal gold.

Gibson, the man with the majestic arm, began to test his counterparts by trying to swipe bags himself. George showed up his peers by stealing in three straight games. First, on August 18, he took second base on Cardinals backstop Eddie Phelps, and a day later he robbed Phelps again. On the 20th, the newspaper byline proclaimed "Gibson Purloins Two Bases" during the Pirates 4–3 win over the Phillies.[21] In the *Pittsburgh Press*, Ralph Davis wrote about Gibson's three days of pilfering: "George Gibson has added base stealing to his many other accomplishments. 'Hack' is becoming decidedly versatile. Bob Bescher would better look careful, or the Canuck will wrest the base stealing honors of the league from him. 'Gibby' has purloined four sacks in the past three days, and is getting more kittenish on the bags every game he plays. If you find a better all around wind paddist than he, trot him around, please."[22] Not too bad when you consider that Bob Brecher finished atop the National League with fifty-four steals. He remained the best-in-class as he led the league each of the next three seasons as well. Gibby finished the year with a career best at nine steals, third in the National League among catchers behind Red Dooin of Philadelphia, who had 14.

The Pirates ended August with six straight wins, which put them six games clear of the Cubs with just a month left to go in the season. Meanwhile, the Giants trailed the Bucs by 15 games and had essentially played themselves out of contention. The Pirates, aware of the stakes, wanted nothing to do with the humiliation of being caught by the Cubs. George told Ralph Davis: "If we lose that pennant, I'll kick myself all over London, Ont. when I get home in the fall." For his part, Gibby recorded 25 hits in August and pushed his batting average to .258 on the season. He and his teammates made their final run to baseball glory.[23]

As September arrived, George had his ambitions on a significant record for a catcher: most consecutive games started by a backstop. Gibson was chasing 111 straight starts behind the dish, which Charley "Chief" Zimmer achieved in 1890 when he manned home plate for the Cleveland Spiders. When George took his position on September 8 against the Cubs, he tied the 19-year-old record. Just before George broke the record, George L. Moreland of the *Pittsburgh Press* wrote, "Isn't that 'Gibby' who catches for the Pirates the real candy kid? He has been going behind the bat day after day and the fans only recently awoke to the fact that his record for games is coming to a point that will soon place his name among the greatest receivers that ever wore a uniform. The papers all over the country are giving Gibson credit for being a star, but it has taken them a long time to realize the fact. Had Kling or Bresnahan or Meyers or Bergen or Schlei made the record that Gibson has made the fans in the cities they have caught in would have been crazy over their great work, but here in Pittsburg Gibson's work has been taken as a matter of course."[24] The following day, Gibby crouched behind the plate and earned the title of the iron man of the big mitt.

Ralph Davis also wrote his thoughts of Gibson's new record: "Gibson is a glutton for work. He thrives under it. Most windpaddists would get stale if called upon to toil as Gibson has done this season, but not so with 'Hack,' he gets better everyday. Gibson must be given credit for being the greatest backstop in the business today. There is no catcher who can perform so consistently as he. His throwing to bases has been little short of marvellous as is evidenced by the few stolen bases credited to opponents of the league leaders."[25]

Moreland correctly opined that his colleagues in the national press would recognize Gibby's accomplishment. Days after George set the new record, Jack Ryder, renowned baseball writer for the *Cincinnati Enquirer*, gave his take on Gibson's play: "George Gibson is a fine, big fellow, with short, rather fat fingers, which do not get hurt easily and he is a glutton for labor. Griff says that Gibson reminds him very much of Wilbert Robinson, the famous old backstop of the champion Orioles of the nineties, who was also a hard man to put out of the game. Gib is a little taller than Robbie, but is built in the sturdy mold. He is more responsible than any other man, not even excepting the great Wagner, for the fine showing of the Pirates this season. If anything happened to Gib a month ago, the Pirates would not be practically safe for the flag at this date."[26] Gibby was presumably extremely gracious in hearing Ryder's compliment, which stated he was at the very least equal to Honus Wagner in the Bucs' effort to win the 1909 National League pennant. What George thought of the scribe mentioning his "fat fingers" would be interesting to know. Be that as it may, George had more memorable moments in the months ahead, as he was not content to just break Zimmer's record—he wanted to obliterate it.

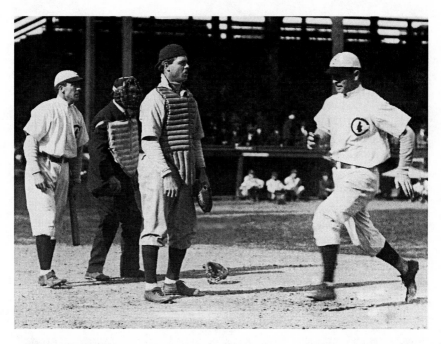

Cubs star Frank Chance crossing home plate as Gibson watches on (SDN-054853 *Chicago Daily News* negatives collection, Chicago History Museum).

On September 28, the Pirates claimed ownership of the National League pennant, after a game they actually lost. The Phillies disposed of the Cubs on that day and in turn helped their fellow Pennsylvanians earn the right to play in the 1909 World Series. As the end of the season approached and with the pennant in hand, Clarke provided Gibson with some rest. On the 28th, against New York, the Bucs trailed 9–1 after three frames, so Paddy O'Connor was sent in to relieve Gibson. The following day, Gibson again only played three innings and reserve Mike Simon got his chance to put on the big mitt. The two replacements combined for three errors in 12 innings of baseball, far below the standard set by Gibson, but by then, the team needed Gibson well rested more than they needed additional wins.

From May 5 through October 2, George started every game behind the plate for the Pirates. On October 3, Clarke finally left him out of the starting lineup and thus Gibby's consecutive games streak ended at 133. Gibson's record did come with some controversy, although it was brief. Jim "Deacon" McGuire, former catcher of the Washington Nationals, claimed he owned the iron man mark when he played in 133 straight games in 1895. That claim did not hold up, as official records showed that McGuire played one of those games as shortstop. Subsequently, with the controversy squashed, Gibson's Pittsburgh friends presented him with a handsome loving cup to mark his great achievement.[27] Gibson's record stood until 1944. That season, Ray Mueller of the Cincinnati Reds and Frankie Hayes of the Philadelphia Athletics each started all 155 of their club's games.

The streak certainly stands as one of the more impressive in baseball lore. Given the immense amount of playing time he logged, it's no surprise that George earned black and blue welts from many foul tips. While he had a chest protector and other gear, equipment in 1909 did not offer the same protections as the safeguards of today. The streak was even more remarkable when you consider Gibson's other injuries. Over the course of the 133 games, he damaged his hand, suffered three spike cuts and seriously bruised his hip. George's official stats for 1909 complete the picture: he played in 150 games and recorded 135 hits, 36 of which were for extra bases. While not impressive by today's standards, his .265 batting average led all qualified National League catchers. Had the Silver Slugger Award existed back then, it's hard to imagine Gibson not winning it, and yet it was his defensive play that made him a star. His .983 fielding percentage topped all National League catchers and he threw out a league best 53 percent of would-be base stealers. He accomplished all of this while playing more games as catcher than any other player in the major leagues. If the Gold Glove Award existed, he would have surely won that too. The Pirates finished the season with a record of 110–42. The Cubs finished in second with a record of 104–49 and, in a distant third, the Giants ended their season with a record of 92–61.

The 1909 World Series broke records for attendance and total gate receipts. The seven-game battle between Pittsburgh and Detroit was witnessed by over 145,000 fans. George performed brilliantly on baseball's biggest stage. He caught every inning of the series for Pittsburgh, recording 28 putouts, 10 assists and no errors. And though the Tigers were expected to run free in the series, they failed as often as they succeeded in challenging Gibson's arm. On the offensive side, George batted .240, recorded a pair of RBIs (one of which was the game-winner in game one) and stole two bases of his own. Gibson's double in the bottom of the fifth inning of game one was the first by a Canadian in the World Series.

Following the series triumph, Barney Dreyfuss somewhat unexpectedly summoned Gibson to the team's downtown office. Gibson recalled walking in only to find manager Fred Clarke standing against a wall and Dreyfuss seated at his desk. The colonel immediately asked him: "What'ya want for next year? What'ya want for 1910?"[28] the implication being that Dreyfuss wanted to secure Gibson's contract for the following year. This surprised Gibson, as he had previously informed his superiors that he would never sign in the fall. Gibson explained: "Now then, if I sign now and our manager makes a deal in the winter to trade me to another ball club, I've gotta go for what's in that contract.

But if I don't sign and you trade me to any other ball club in the league, it gives me an opening that, I can, I've got, go to the new club I go to, and I can dictate terms with them. That's why I don't want to sign."[29]

President Dreyfuss insisted Gibson sign. Barney handed Gibson a blank contract and said: "Make it out yourself. Put your own figure in there."[30] Gibson agreed to sign the contract on one condition. In the event the Pirates felt Gibson became expendable, the Pirates would grant him an unconditional release. George told Dreyfuss, "I do not want you to sell my broken down carcass after you've got all the good out of it."[31] The president agreed to Gibson's request and even offered to write the term into the contract, but George, being a trustful man, took his boss's word and handshake as his bond. George would later regret his error in judgment of not getting the complete terms in writing. In the end, Gibson signed a two-year contract at $6,000 per season (equivalent to $165,500 per season in 2019).[32]

After they concluded contract negotiations and Gibson returned home to the aforementioned adoration of London, he decided to enjoy life with a family trip west. The Gibsons relaxed in Wyoming where George himself got in more than a few hunts. Though he may not have received the national acclaim his play warranted, what happened next clearly demonstrated how badly a select few appreciated his many talents. In the midst of his time in the remote mountains of Wyoming, a vaudeville production in New York tracked him down and requested his services.

In order to supplement their incomes, and have fun, many of baseball's more talented professionals performed on the vaudeville circuit during the off-season. Though Gibson was not just a side piece, Rube Marquard, the Giants future Hall of Famer, garnered the most attention. Marquard regularly appeared in vaudeville shows. The hurler spent so much time there that he met, fell in love with and married his famous co-star, the singer, dancer and actress Blossom Seeley.[33] While New York wanted Gibby, Gibby clearly did not want New York. In a move that suggested Gibson played more than a passive role in his status below the limelight of his baseball equals, he returned to London where he spent the rest of his off-season working in a brickyard. Later, the team invited George to join them in New York to further celebrate their World Series win; Gibson politely declined in a telegram to Dreyfuss:

> I thank you for the kind invitation, and I sure would like to be there. I would be right at home among all those baseball bugs. I think I have been the busiest man in Canada since I left Pittsburgh, but if I can get off, I will be in New York to help make December 15 a big night. I have played over the games of the world's series at least a hundred times since returning home, but I have not yet been able to explain to the fans here how we come to let the Tigers get away with three games. Well, I guess I'd better ring off, or I'll be playing that series over again with you. I am keeping in fine

condition, and expect to be on deck as lively as ever in the spring. The holidays will soon be here and it will not be long until the baseball dope will be flying thick and fast.[34]

George stayed home and celebrated the holidays with his young family, and kept right on working at that brickyard throughout the winter. After only a brief rest, Gibson left for spring training with his eyes on the future and plans to ascend in the clubhouse.

7

Make a Hard Job Easy

Gibson parlayed his success in 1909 into that of a team leader when 1910 kicked off; however, in classic Gibson fashion, it was those around him that spurred on his climb more so than anything Gibson himself demanded. Fred Clarke, now in the 12th of his 17 seasons as Pirates skipper, bestowed a significant amount of responsibility on his veteran catcher. Clarke requested that Gibson lead the advanced team of pitchers and catchers to preliminary workouts in West Baden Springs, Indiana. In addition to the plethora of hurlers Gibson took responsibility for, he also monitored Mike Simon, Paddy O'Connor and rookie Ed Bridges, the three men fighting to serve as catching depth. Given the circumstances, it's easy to say that the move by Clarke served as a demonstrative statement of Gibson's leadership and one that certainly informed Gibson's future as a baseball manager.

The promotion was an obvious vote of confidence from Dreyfuss as well as Clarke. The Pittsburgh press corps also acknowledged the move. "No mistake was made in the selecting of George Gibson to manage the battery squad for the first few days in the Indiana camp. 'Hack' is a clean, capable ballplayer, a hard worker himself, and thoroughly familiar with the methods of his chief. Moreover, he is dependable. The qualities which caused him to develop within a few years from a catcher of only fair ability into one of the greatest backstops in the country are qualities which also fit him admirably for the position of vice manager."[1]

Gibson arrived in Pittsburgh on March 7, one day before the club departed for Indiana. Dreyfuss, ever the dutiful owner, met Gibby at the train station and presented the catcher with a brand-new glove, albeit one the owner carefully made game ready. The equipment change caused quite the sensation and the press described Gibby's new, large leather hand protector: "The mitt was displayed while the piping times of peace were progressing, and everybody who got a look at it, put it on and gave it a regulation punch. In consequence the big glove yesterday showed a cavity in the center of the left palm that made it look like an oldtimer. The cavity will hold at least a pint of saliva. This did not surprise Hack, as Col. Barney had notified him that the glove would be in fine shape for the spring trip, and evidently it is."[2]

George arrived already in fine shape for the spring trip, according to what he told reporters. "I've never felt so well at practice time as I do at present. I spent a very pleasant winter in Canada. My health was perfect all the time and I kept myself from taking on weight by regular exercise and frequent hunting trips. Nevertheless, I am reporting for the season at a lower weight than ever before. I am fairly aching to get down to baseball work again and can hardly wait until we reach West Baden."[3]

On the evening of March 8, George and the Pirates battery left Pittsburgh via a train on the Baltimore and Ohio railroad line. A large contingency of fans gathered at the station to see the Bucs depart and it seems most of the players fed off the energy. George, however, was not most players. While his compadres gallivanted, Gibson displayed a more introspective and focused mood. The reporters in attendance certainly picked up on this energy: "It was noticed that Gibson felt his responsibility, as nobody ever saw him in a more serious mood."[4] Perhaps it was his newfound responsibilities that dictated his mindset, but it's also worth noting that Margaret Gibson, George's better half, decided to attend her first spring training and so she hopped aboard as well. Along with the fans, President Dreyfuss and team superstar Honus Wagner were at the depot to bid their teammates adieu. The two would join the advance team at Hot Springs two weeks later.[5]

The train arrived safely at West Baden Springs and Gibby gave his troops the day off in order to get settled at the resort. While his teammates toiled in the calm of a rest day, Gibson made sure to use the time productively. Consequently, he toured and inspected the baseball grounds

Famous 1911 image of George Gibson used for his Turkey Red tobacco advertisement cabinet (inset) (Canada's Sports Hall of Fame / Pantheon des sports Canadiens—sportshall.ca/pantheonsports.ca; Inset–Healy Collection).

where the team would practice. Had something been amiss, Gibson would have certainly attended to the matter, but as it happened the field was in excellent shape and Gibson used the remaining time to catch up with Heinie Peitz, his former Pirates teammate. Peitz managed the Louisville Colonels of the American Association and also had his club in West Baden Springs for spring workouts. Gibby, once Heinie's understudy, congratulated Peitz as his Louisville club won the 1909 American Association pennant. Peitz reciprocated Gibby's sentiment on account of Pittsburgh's World Series victory.[6] Gibson credited Peitz for helping him adjust to the big-league life. "Peitz was always giving me pointers when I first joined the Pirates. That reflects great credit on Peitz, in my opinion, for he knew he was coaching me to take his job and you bet no person was happier than I when Louisville landed the pennant in the American Association last year."[7] The Gibson-led Pirates shared the West Baden Springs fields with Peitz's Colonels for the duration of their stay in Indiana.

After the reunion, Gibson's focus returned to the task at hand and, unsurprisingly, the spring trip proved to be the first real test of Gibson's leadership skills. The newly minted acting manager ran a tight ship during his first chance as leader of the Pirates club. He presented clear instructions to his men: "You fellows were sent here to drink the water, and drink the water you must. I was instructed by Mr. Dreyfuss to see that you all got up early and unless some of you are ill, you will be expected to be in the spring house at 6 o'clock every morning."[8] Ever the diligent leader, Gibson kept his men on their toes and started every day with cardiovascular exercise. To get their heart rates up, the players walked around the resort's track until the sun appeared over the Indiana hills.[9] Some days, to change the monotony of walking the track, Gibson led the players on hikes. Ever the outdoorsman, Gibson often took his team to the Cross Mammoth Cave. The cavern was a "mere" six miles from the resort and described as a 1,700-foot deep subterranean freak of nature. A trip to the cave not only provided ample exercise, but it also scratched Gibby's itch for nature.[10] Even in his managerial infancy, Gibson displayed a knack for the foresight necessary to manage a team over a long season. During the early parts of spring training, Gibson instructed his pitchers to throw softly; he did not want anyone injuring their arms before the trip down South. Furthermore, Gibby forbade pitchers from throwing any curveballs through a stern warning: "I mean this, and the first pitcher who throws a curve will get a rap across the shins with a bat."[11] The men seemed to take to Gibson's no-nonsense style as there were no reports of disobeyers throughout early camp.

A few days into camp, Gibson was highly pleased with how training was advancing: "The work has been light, and the sole object has been to limber up the muscles of the players. They reported in better form than I have known them to be at the beginning of any practice season since I have been a member of the Pittsburgh club. The weather has been perfect, and we have had two good workouts everyday in addition to the long morning walks, and we have put away a great many barrels of West Baden water. The soreness, which is a general complaint tonight, will nearly be all gone when captain Clarke arrives, and if he is not tickled to death when he looks the pitchers and catchers over next Tuesday, I will have made a very bad guess. They will be in shape to give the fielding squad all the batting practice needed. Each pitcher can work 15 minutes without danger of injury to his arm, and by the end of the week, providing the weather continues favorable, the entire team ought to be in condition. I am certain I will be ready to play ball when we get to Hot Springs."[12] George remained confident in his work and proud of all the work his teammates put in under his tutelage. Gibson knew manager Fred Clarke would arrive soon to meet the players and George boasted that he would not hand the Pirates leader "a bunch of cripples or dead ones."[13]

On the afternoon of March 15, Fred Clarke pulled into West Baden Springs. He insisted that Gibson continue as acting manager for the remainder of the day. In a meeting that night, George jokingly handed his boss a letter of resignation, which all the team found comical.[14] When he finally did resume his managerial obligations, Clarke complimented Gibby for the good job he had done getting the men into playing shape. The Pirates skipper gave his utmost positive approval of Gibson's daily routines and the nature of the drills he requested of his teammates.

On March 20, the Pirates arrived in Hot Springs. To kick off their camp, the team played a series of intrasquad matches, just as they had in springs past. Gibson started hot and rapped a double in his first spring at bat. Defensively, he split time behind the plate with Eddie Bridges. Gibson caught again the following day, but did so with all of the fingers on his left hand in bandages. According to reports, George had a rash on his hand that

Image of George Gibson throwing to second, taken by renowned early 20th-century baseball photographer, Charles M. Conlon (Healy Collection).

was likely acquired when the catcher handled poison ivy while in West Baden Springs.[15] The injury plagued Gibson well into the 1910 regular season, much longer than either the club or Gibby expected. Despite the "itchy hand" Gibson had a great camp. He swatted the ball all over the Hot Springs grounds and handled his new pitching teammates with ease. Ever mindful of the physical impact the 1909 season had on his catcher, Clarke rested Gibson over the last few weeks of spring training. Gibson still provided value as he served as umpire for the stretch games prior to opening day.

On April 14, the Pirates began their National League pennant defense in St. Louis. Howie Camnitz pitched to Gibson in the opener for the second straight year. St. Louis countered with Vic Willis, who the Bucs sold to St. Louis in the off-season. The Pirates won the contest 5–1. George got the better of his catching counterpart, Roger Bresnahan, who vowed to overtake Gibson's ironman record in 1910. Bresnahan failed to even come close to Gibby's record; when it was all said and done, he played in just 88 games in 1910.

Unfortunately, the team's opening day success did not lead to more spoils of war and Gibson's play suffered as well. While George's defense remained on par with his standard, he batted a measly .181 through the end of May. The Bucs' inability to get in a groove at the plate weighed heavily on their overall performance. When the calendar flipped to June 1, the Pirates found themselves in third place thanks to an unimpressive record of 15–18. In spite of Gibson's early struggles at the dish, Pittsburgh reporter Ralph Davis continued to champion his hometown catcher. Davis had watched Gibson since his big-league debut in 1905. His position as Pirates beat writer gave him close access to Gibson before the Bucs backstop drew national acclaim. He believed that George was the world's greatest catcher and felt he was perfectly built and able to work many times harder than other players. He admired how Gibson flourished under a heavy workload, and how Gibby never once complained about it, but rather tried to secure more labor and was delighted when he obtained it. Davis asked Deacon Phillippe for his opinion on George, and Deacon noted, "Gibson makes a hard job easy. He does so because he catches in such a naturally free and easy style that he runs little risk of personal injury. You never hear of his missing a game through being hurt. And yet there are catchers with good reputations who are always getting into the way of the ball. They fight the sphere as it comes to them, and are often laid off with split or bunged fingers. That's not the case with Gibson. He is surely a wonderful backstop."[16] In retrospect, Deacon's kind words may have simply placed an imprecation on George.

Three months removed from his poison ivy incident at West Baden Springs, Gibson's infection remained. George tried to play through it and consequently, his paws did not heal. Team trainers resorted to bandaging his hands, but he really needed to rest. Under orders from Clarke, Gibson sat out from June 4 through June 8, while the Pirates visited New York. Even though the fan base did not properly appreciate their catcher, George's teammates certainly recognized his value. The *Pittsburgh Press* printed a quote from an unnamed Pirate: "Some of our pitchers and even the infielders impose upon the big catcher. They know he has a wonderful arm and the twirlers get careless about guarding first base. They let opposing baserunners get awful leads and count on Gibby's making a snap throw to catch him if he does make a break for second. Too often the runners are allowed to start too far from second, too. But Gibson does not growl and does work well all the time."[17] The Pirates players knew Gibson needed a long overdue break.

Without real insight into the circumstances surrounding Gibson's playing time, when fans in Pittsburgh heard the news, they assumed that Gibson and Clarke were in a quarrel. Both men wrote letters to try to clear the air.

June 4th—Manager Fred Clarke

Gibson and myself have not quarreled. Why should we? I hope I am still sane, notwithstanding our continued run of misfortune, and being so could not have any trouble with Gibson, who besides being the greatest catcher in the game today, is a model player in conduct on and off the field. It is a shame that such stories should be circulated. Although his hands are almost raw, Gibson would not have taken a rest if I had not insisted upon it. He has done too much for the Pittsburg club and too much for me, to be permitted to do himself a permanent injury when a few days' rest will give him time to get his hands in good shape. We are going to be in the race and will need Gibson when the fight warms up, and giving him a brief vacation now is to my mind a wise precaution.

As I must hear the responsibility for our final position in the National League race I must use my own judgement as to the handling of the players. I want to add, however, that in all the time Gibson has been with the Pittsburg club I have never had an occasion to reprimand him for even a trivial matter. From the first he was eager for instruction and for that reason quickly developed into a star. If all players were like Gibson it would be an easy matter to manage a ball club.

June 4th—George Gibson

I have not quarreled with Manager Clarke, and don't intend to. The Pittsburg veterans know their manager better than any outsider could and while they rated him highly in the past they think more of him now than ever before. Our present slump is enough to drive a manager wild, but Clarke knows that the players are as much distressed as he and instead of raving at them he is doing his best to get them going right. He will succeed, too, because his policy is the best one. The players appreciate his consideration for their feelings and they will fight their way to the front yet. Mark my words. My hands are a little sore but I'll go behind the bat Monday if Clarke wants me.[18]

Pittsburgh team secretary W. H. Locke also talked to reporters. He denied that Gibson's performance on the field correlated with his time on the bench. Locke further explained the poison ivy incident in West Baden Springs and also mentioned that Gibson did more damage to his hands when the amateur photographer decided to develop his own pictures. At the time, photography served as George's favorite hobby, and Locke revealed that during a dark room session Gibson spilt acid on his hands and aggravated the injury further. He assured Pirates fans that Clarke and Gibson were swell friends.[19]

When Gibson finally returned to the lineup, he, and by extension his play, immediately quashed any questions about the state of his health. After three days of rest, he put together a thirteen-game hitting streak. During this streak, Gibson slugged a Sam Frock fastball deep over the right field fence, his first home run of the season. In the second game of a doubleheader, the Pirates cruised to a 10–3 win and Gibson put together a 4-for-5 performance with two doubles and four runs scored. Despite improved play by both Gibson and the Pirates, Pittsburgh still lost ground in the standings. At the end of June, the Pirates sat in third place, six games behind first-place Chicago and four games off New York's pace. Halfway through their season, the Pirates needed to show their championship pedigree soon.

Gibson, now nationally recognized, wrote an article in early July 1910 that was syndicated around the country. His essay was titled "How I Win."

By George Gibson;

It is working together and all the time, keeping in condition and having confidence in one's own ball club that wins. With the Pittsburgh club it has been the case. I think Clarke has made us all better ball players by his own example. You see we have a crowd of fellows who like each other personally, and anyone will do anything to help the others. There is a lot in that. Then every man on the team will jump across the river for Clarke, and that helps more. He drilled the teamwork into us, and I think we have it.

No one man won the pennant for us, it was the whole bunch working together and fighting, no matter how badly we seemed beaten. Our style of play and team hitting broke up the other clubs, and we won it by making runs, which are all that count, and forgetting errors just as fast as we made them.

I had a hard season, being in nearly every game, but was lucky. I think the biggest part of the success of our pitchers last year was that they had confidence in my work and in the team behind them. If some of those clubs knew the chances we took they would wonder we ever won. It helps pitchers to know they can put the ball right over straight and feel that someone will go out and get it for them. A fellow does not properly understand the value of teamwork until he has caught a bunch of pitchers who try to do exactly what they are signaled to do and never complain if the catchers' judgement is wrong. It is a pleasure to catch pitchers who will work with you as if you were one. That is the only way for a battery to work. If they get to crossing each other and mixing things up, the pitcher will look bad and the catcher looks worse, and the team will lose.

I cannot tell much about how to catch, because I think a fellow must stay back there and think and study and learn until he gets it for himself. There are some pointers, however, that may be of some use to some fellows who are just breaking in. Stand steady all the time and as nearly in throwing position as possible. Study the batters, what kinds of bats they bring up, how they stand in the box, and try to think out what they are likely to try to do. Always step in as close as possible when expecting to have to make a throw or when the batter is showing signs of bunting. Be ready to go in at all times. Another thing, a catcher can do a pitcher a lot of damage by using bad judgement in what to call for. Do not curve a pitcher to death. Make his work just as easy for him as the situation will permit, if you are giving the signals. It is easier, of course, to catch the curves when they are out. It is a bad idea, too, for a catcher to try to protect himself at the expense of a pitcher. A catcher should not make pitchers pitch out too often and waste balls that may be valuable, just so he can throw from a better position so he can catch runners. A catcher ought to watch the base runners more closely than any other man does. He ought to protect the pitcher by signalling him when to drive runners back, and at the same time to protect himself. He ought to never allow a pitcher to pitch with players out of position, not until he is certain the whole team knows what the signal is, if he is to signal for some throw. He ought to always try to slow up pitchers when they are working too fast, and give them a chance to steady.

No player can tell another one how to play, but each one learns something from experience which may help a youngster, and I hope these ideas of mine will help someone. I think they would have helped me if someone told me at the start.[20]

The Pirates used July to gain ground in the pennant race, and by August 1, they had closed the spread to a half game behind the second-place Giants. The Cubs, meanwhile, still held a comfortable seven-game lead. In August, George caught fire and put together a career-high 14-game hitting streak, bettering his June streak by one game. In the 31 games he played in, Gibson recorded a hit in 26 of them. On August 10, versus the Doves, Gibson reached the apex of his streak when he hit his second home run of the season. The long ball tied the game at 2–2 and then Wagner secured the victory when he hit a solo home run in the seventh inning. Pittsburgh handed Boston a 3–2 loss and the *Pittsburgh Daily Post* captured the event with this limerick:

> Gib and Little Bob
> Were right on the job.
> They got the first man o'er the plate,
> And a four base hit
> By Hackenschmidt
> Tied the Doves—then Hans the Great
> With a mighty swat,
> Sent the ball from the lot
> And the champs had won four straight.[21]

Pittsburgh ended August against New York with a series in which the Giants dispatched the Pirates in three games. Despite the setback, the Pirates used August to move past the Giants in the standings. Now two games ahead of the Giants, Pittsburgh had to contend with Chicago. Unfortunately for the Bucs, Chicago held a commanding 10-game lead. Pittsburgh desperately needed a remarkable final month of the season in order to successfully defend their pennant.

Unfortunately, Gibson suffered a sprained ankle, and without their key cog, the Pirates fell apart. In the critical game, Gibson chased a foul ball into the grandstand and stepped on a bat during the pursuit. Although he finished the game, Clarke ordered two days' rest. George wasn't the only casualty during the final month of play. The Pirates club suffered a rash of injuries down the stretch and by season's end, their poor play landed them in third place, 17½ games out of first. The 1910 pennant went to the Chicago Cubs.

George put forth a solid campaign in 1910, despite so many injuries. At a time when batting averages were notably lower than in today's game, George's .259 average held up remarkably well. Gibson tied his career high for home runs in a season with three, a reasonably impressive total in the midst of baseball's "deadball era." As his offense held up just fine against his counterparts, Gibby's defense set the standard for the rest of the league. For the fourth year in a row, he caught more games than any other catcher in the National League (143), and for the second year in a row he caught more would-be base stealers (137) and had a higher fielding percentage (.984) than any other National League catcher. Gibson's 203 assists led all major-league catchers.

Gibson standing in front of the visitors' dugout at Chicago's West Side Grounds (SDN-056103 *Chicago Daily News* negatives collection, Chicago History Museum).

On October 25, after the season wrapped but before he returned to Canada, George planned to participate in an all-star exhibition tour arranged by D. A. Fletcher, a promoter from Cincinnati. It seems as if some important figures in the baseball community did recognize Gibson's dynamic play. After all, they made sure to include him among a who's who of major-league baseball. The rosters included countless top performers and 14 future Hall of Famers such as Christy Mathewson, Walter Johnson, Honus Wagner, Nap Lajoie and Ty Cobb.

Both baseball's National Commission, a coalition that predated the commissioner's office, as well as many team owners, agreed to sanction the event. When the team owners, who agreed to lend out the use of their stadiums, learned Tex Rickard backed the event, that support evaporated. Rickard earned his living as a boxing promoter, and at the time, this did not sit well with some of baseball's upper class. Fearing the association with Rickard would tarnish the league's reputation, the commission eventually forbade any players from participating. Gibson, always the moral compass for others, returned the $500 in advanced pay that he received. Though many players wanted to defy the league and proceed with the series anyway, neither they nor Fletcher pushed forward. Gibson didn't miss out on barnstorming entirely, though. Fletcher's planned series was canceled early enough that Tommy Leach, leader of previous Pirates post-season barnstorming trips, was still able to pull together a short exhibition tour, which Gibson happily joined before returning to London for the winter.

That off-season, President Dreyfuss insisted on temperance from his team during the winter break. In fact, every player had the order added into their contract prior to 1911. Many reporters worried the Pirates would not respond to the new policy; George disagreed: "That anti-booze contract strikes me as just right, I am heartily in accord with it, and believe all the other boys will be."[22] Gibson continued, saying, "A non-booze team should be a good thing, and the non-drinking rule will never bother yours truly."[23] Of course, as Ralph Davis, noted, the temperance conditions were not intended for players like George, which was a good thing, because he spent his winter working at a London brewery, lugging and loading beer kegs, along with hiking and sport hunting.

After an uneventful winter, George arrived in Pittsburgh before the trip south for spring training in peak condition. He tipped the scales at 185 pounds, the lightest he had been in years prior to the start of a season. Just as in 1910, Gibson took on leadership responsibilities at camp; but, this time, Clarke took the reins and joined him and the advance squad at West Baden Springs. Before the team departed Pittsburgh, George, a bit more comfortable with his burgeoning managerial role, scared the hell out of a few rookies who were on their first excursion south. He told them: "You'll be up at 5am and walking 20-miles."[24] Barney Dreyfuss and veteran pitcher Deacon Phillippe loved that Gibby ribbed the youngsters.

During camp, and especially with the young pitchers, George continued to develop his leadership skills. He enthusiastically promoted their development and helped the pitchers who became frustrated with negative results. He wanted the fledgling gunslingers to keep their wits and taught them to forget about the last batter and go hard after the next guy. He insisted the pitchers keep a steady pace, and not waste energy as they established themselves against highly skilled opponents. Gibson stressed the mental game when he spoke to the Pirates greenhorn hurlers at the 1911 camp. He told them that the "pitcher must use his head and not depend too largely on his arm. Let him study his batter. Look the bad looking chap with the club in his hands square in the eye. Take your time and when you think you have him crossed into hitting at the wrong kind of ball then put it where you want."[25]

George did not want the young pitchers demoralized by anything they read in the papers. He felt that players became demoralized from even acceptable condemnation. Gibson acknowledged that reporters, by their very nature, highlighted many of the player's foibles and knew that might undermine the player's confidence. He used an example from his own start with the Pirates: "When I started with the Pittsburg Club, I had a terrible slump in hitting. I forget how many games I played in without one safe hit. I was absolutely a piece of dead timber with the team. The critics then attacked me. Not personally but my hitting. What they said day after day was all too true and I just kept reading the stuff. Fred Clarke said nothing. Just let me peg along and hope for improvement. Every day it was handed to me and every day it became worse. Finally things began to improve and I shook off a hoodoo that had followed me all because of my sensitiveness for public opinions. Now I do not read these criticisms and employ the newspaper only for such information as I may seek. The public has the right to the criticism but the player should not read it. He should listen to his manager."[26]

Gibson started 1911 just as he had previous seasons: in a slump. His only notable early-season performance took place off the field while in St. Louis. George and teammate Chief Wilson visited a local cigar shop; when the store clerk went to retrieve their cigars, a wall case somehow caught fire. The fire accelerated quickly and reached the ceiling in a matter of seconds. Instead of evacuating, Gibby displayed yet another of his seemingly endless amount of quality traits. George helped the salesperson suppress the flames while Wilson moved the cash register to the front of the store. Firemen eventually arrived and ultimately saved the store. The shop's proprietor presented Gibson and Wilson with a box of cigars as a reward for their fearless efforts. The men gladly shared the prize with their teammates.[27]

Only two weeks into the season, and barely clinging to a .200 batting average, the usually gentile George seemingly became frustrated. He began to act out of character and make kicks toward umpires. In late April, during a close game at Forbes Field, George protested the umpire's strike zone not once but twice. In extreme disgust, Gibson spiked the ball in both instances. Fred Clarke defended the usually well-mannered catcher and pointed out that Gibby had not used profanity. Rigler let him stay in the game.[28] A few weeks later, on May 11, in a game at Philadelphia, George showed up another umpire. Gibson seldom questioned an umpire's decision, but Howie Camnitz was not getting any close calls, so finally George spoke up. On the fourth bad call, Gibson remarked, "There you go again. What's the matter?" Without a flinch, umpire Finneran ordered Gibby directly off the field, the first ejection in George's big-league career. The ejection came with a one-game suspension.

Gibson blew up at the umpire and threw some serious "Canadian Lingo" at Finneran; Finneran returned service and tacked on two additional games on the spot. During the deadball era umpires had the right to suspend and fine players on the spot. The players had the right to appeal the umpires' decisions to the American and National League presidents.[29] Gibby's three-game banishment incensed the Pirates. For his part, Gibson responded with: "Yes, and that is just three days longer than you should be retained as an umpire."[30] Fred Clarke, realizing Gibby's value to the team, hustled onto the field to retrieve his catcher in order to prevent any further reprimand.

Gibson's behavior surprised everyone, including local reporters. George's keen eye and ability to properly assess balls and strikes earned him a great deal of respect over the course of his career. His cool demeanor on the diamond only served to support his reputation. To that end, umpires often trusted his judgment and asked his opinion on close pitches. Finneran's post-game statements created ire in the Pirates clubhouse. Finneran boldly declared that Gibson had no chance in 1911 at breaking his own consecutive games streak. Thomas Lynch, the league's president at the time, upheld Gibson's suspension because George used "Canadian Lingo" that Finneran did not appreciate.[31]

To no one's surprise, the incident infuriated Fred Clarke. Enraged with Gibby's suspension, the frustrated field general fired back at the powers that be. "Gibson has been with Pittsburgh a little over four years, and Finneran, to my mind, removed him without just cause, and President Lynch deprives the Pittsburgh Club of the services of a man, who, although catching every game for a team always in the fight, was never before accused of making trouble for an umpire. Lynch's action is a slap at one of the cleanest and most gentlemanly players the game has ever known."[32] The whole incident sparked a significant change in Clarke's on-field etiquette. For many years, Clarke asked his players to stay away from the umpires. In retaliation for Gibson's suspension, Clarke ordered his troops to take a much more adversarial approach to their play on the diamond. The manager vowed to make things difficult not just for the umpires on the field, but for President Lynch as well. Clarke's order to his team was simple: be just as scrappy as the other clubs and speak up to any umpire's inaccuracy.

Meanwhile, the more subdued Gibby took his suspension in stride. He took the opportunity to see those three games as a spectator in the grandstand. In what might seem odd for the man responsible for keeping his team calm in the midst of even most competitive games, his fierce and competitive temperament again bubbled to the surface in this most unusual of circumstances. Unable to influence the game more directly, Gibson took on the role of rabid fan. He cheered and rooted for the Pirates with everything he had. In his second game sitting with the fans, Gibson spurred on his teammates with vigor. In the end, the Pirates swatted the Rustlers down with a 9–3 victory.

Mike Simon performed admirably in Gibson's absence. During the three games, Simon reached base on a remarkable ten hits in fourteen at bats and also played stellar defense. Ever the upstanding teammate, Gibson applauded Simon: "Mike is a cracker jack catcher. He does not fight the ball nor worry his pitcher, as he has a fine, easy style. When it comes to throwing to bases, he is an artist, and has the nerve to let the ball go at full speed when he thinks he has a chance to catch a runner napping. Some catchers are afraid of making an error, and for that reason only lob the ball. Simon can hit, too."[33] Gibson suffered no jealousy at Simon's success because he just wanted his club to win. Whereas this type of performance from a backup might threaten most men in Gibby's position, George had no such reservations about his playing time.

To no person's surprise, as soon as his suspension ended, Gibson re-turned to the lineup. In his first game back, George did not disappoint. At the plate he settled in with a 2-for-3 performance and added an RBI double. He also walked twice, scored two runs and played a brilliant defensive game. He carried on his improved play towards the end of May, until lady luck pulled the sheet out from under Gibson's feet.

On May 25, Gibson injured the wrist of his throwing arm during a game in Brooklyn. He played through the pain until the end of the month, but as the calendar flipped to June, Gibby knew he needed a rest. Aside from a pinch-hit, walk-off sacrifice fly on June 3, George missed five straight games from June 2 to June 7. The Pittsburgh papers speculated that Mike Simon played more during this time, not because of Gibson's injury but because Gib-son's poor performance with the bat during the first month of play. Gibby returned to the starting lineup on June 8. He caught an errorless game; how-ever, he still had struggles with the bat. It seemed to Clarke that his ironclad catcher still had a chink in the armor. On June 11, a scheduled off-day, Clarke sent George to John Reese, an osteopath based in Youngstown, Ohio, and a superstar in his own right.

John D. "Bonesetter" Reese, a Welsh immigrant, is widely regarded as baseball's first doctor. Reese had the unique ability to manipulate muscles and ligaments, which allowed injured baseball players to return to action much quicker. The bonesetter's impressive client list included Cy Young, Ty Cobb, Walter Johnson and others of that ilk. Reese fell into the practice of joint manipulation while working as a coal miner, where he became known to his coworkers as a healer. He was taught the obscure trade by a fellow ironworker named Tom Jones. Though he tried his hand at medical school at Case Uni-versity, Reese abandoned those ambitions before completing his degree. Ap-parently, he did not take well to the sight of blood.[34] Consequently, he took on the more esoteric role of bonesetter. Bonesetters never really "set bones," and are more comparable to today's physical therapists or chiropractors. That said, Pirates management recognized Reese's talents and tried to hire him full-time back in 1903. Reese declined; he preferred to stay home in Ohio with his family. Despite the rebuff, the Pirates still sent their "cripples" to him all the years later.

When Gibson returned from Youngstown, he was immediately slotted back into the Pittsburgh starting nine. It seems the bonesetter's work had instant results. In the Monday afternoon game upon his return, the Bucs battery of Camnitz and Gibson easily handled the Brooklyn hitters. George helped his pitcher out by snagging a would-be base stealer and tallying seven putouts. Not just a defensive stud, George produced at the plate as well in his comeback. He walloped every ball he saw, with gusto. In three at bats, Gibby lined out hard, doubled and tripled. Not surprisingly, the stellar performance by George helped the Pirates take down Brooklyn, 4–2. The next day, George swiped a cushion and the *Pittsburgh Post-Gazette* sports page headlined "Gibson Steals A Base And Everyone Is Happy."[35] On a team littered with baseball immortals, Gibson had no problem asserting himself with fine play.

Concerns over his recent impairment subsided and Gibson continued to play great ball during the latter half of June. Meanwhile, life off the field seemed on the up and up for the Canadian legend-to-be. Around that time, George bought his first automobile. After looking over many different models of vehicles, Gibson chose a late-model 50-horsepower Inter-State car from the Pittsburgh Inter-State Company. At a time when few cars roamed the streets, this purchase caught the public's attention. Sporting one of the finest automobiles in the city, George spent his evenings tinkering with the car and driving through the city parks. He quickly became an auto enthusiast.

Just as in June, the Pirates started July in fourth place. The New York Giants stood atop the National League; however, five teams remained within striking distance. The Pirates players were in good shape physically, but Gibson wasn't. His injured throwing arm began to flare up, and again, he traveled to visit John Reese. George reported to the Pittsburgh media, "Reese told me that I had gone into the game too soon after he had treated me, and also that I had been 'nursing' my injured shoulder too much."[36] When Gibson returned to Pittsburgh, the doctor instructed him to let loose, and throw as if he hadn't been injured at all. According to Reese, this was the best way to strengthen his lame arm. All in, George missed five games in early July and, like a month earlier, he played great ball after his doctor's visit. Gibby recorded six hits in thirteen at bats in his first three games back. George's performance was highlighted by a 4-for-5 game in New York. He knocked in two runs in a 13–4 victory over McGraw's G-men, but after a week of play, Gibson was again incapacitated. This time his ankle gave out and he sat for twelve games from July 20 until August 1.

When August kicked off, Gibson felt all right and took his regular spot as the starting backstop. Despite his ailments, George started every game save for one in that month. Though he needed a break, the team needed him, as tragedy struck Mike Simon off the field. In the middle of the month, Simon stepped away from his teammates to grieve for his young child, who tragically passed away from pneumonia, and to tend to his extremely ill wife. By this time, Gibson suffered unbearable shoulder pain which in turn prevented him from delivering a proper throw. To complicate matters, he nursed his weak ankle and did not display his usual mobility. The Pirates were forced to purchase the contract of Bill Kelly, the starting backstop of the American Association's St. Paul Saints. As the team waited for Kelly's arrival, Gibby soldiered through and continued to start games while banged up. In fact, Gibson started the day Kelly did show up and he demonstrated the hustle that made him so integral to the Pirates' success. Without hesitation, Gibby chased a foul ball headed for the seats. As he charged forward, spectators scattered and he fearlessly jumped into the grandstand, splayed out across a few seats and snagged the foul ball.[37] A game later, as Brooklyn outfielder Bobby Coulson broke from third base en route to a crash with the Pirates backstop, it seemed the beat-up Gibson might finally crumble. Coulson collided hip-to-jaw with Gibson and the two tumbled in a haze.

Gibson should have left for the hospital, but instead he opted to finish out the ball game. Gibson stated that it was the hardest hit he had taken in his career. Although he did not lose consciousness, he did see stars. George told a reporter the stars "seemed to twinkle wherever I looked. I became deathly sick with nausea and that is why I quickly lay down on the grass. My neck is still sore and the pains have not entirely left the back of my head."[38] The stalwart Gibson returned to the lineup the very next day although he was almost certainly concussed.

In the next two series, Gibson continued to show disregard for his own well-being. Time and time again, he leapt into the grandstand to make plays for his pitchers. In Philadelphia, Otto Knabe sent a towering pop-up into the seats near the fence and Gibby ran over to make a play on it. The Philadelphia faithful tried to distract Gibson by waving their programs and yelling profanities. One fan threw a drinking straw, but Gibson still managed to hold on to the ball … without injury. In New York on August 25, George went after an Art Fletcher foul ball and ended up crashing into the low concrete wall that surrounded the backstop. Gibson collapsed on his way back to the plate. His teammates rushed over, rubbed him down intensely and encouraged him to get back behind the plate. The very next batter, Chief Meyers, popped up another for a Gibson chance and he made a wonderful catch.

During this time, Dreyfuss and Clarke asked the battered and bruised Gibson for his opinion on the team's new prize. Acquired by Dreyfuss from

St. Paul, prospect Marty O'Toole threw a deft spitball and earned his stripes as the strike-out king of the American Association. Not surprisingly, many big-league clubs put in offers for his services. Col. Dreyfuss made the top bid and won O'Toole's arm for $22,500, a tidy sum in 1911.

Gibson relished the task, excited to see what the young man had in his repertoire. As soon as O'Toole arrived in Pittsburgh, Gibson arranged for a throwing session. Gibson liked what he saw and told reporters the same thing he told his superiors: "O'Toole certainly looks good to me. He has worlds of speed, and he shows his experience by varying his deliveries, and mixing them up. His curve balls are wonders. That spitter of his is in a class by itself. I've seen some salivated deliveries in my time, but never anything like his. If the opposing batsmen solve it, I'll lose my guess." Gibson acknowledged the spitballer may be difficult to catch, but was sure he could figure it out.[39]

Gibby's analysis of the hurler proved quite accurate, as O'Toole performed well for the Bucs down the stretch. When it was all said and done, the pitcher compiled three wins and a respectable 2.37 ERA. After O'Toole's first start, a 6–4 win versus the Boston Rustlers, players on both sides marveled at the young hurler's stuff. Veteran Boston catcher Johnny Kling told reporters that O'Toole threw the best spitball he'd ever seen while also noting Marty's free and easy delivery. Bill Kelly, who had teamed up with Marty in St. Paul, claimed O'Toole threw the ball better than he had all season in the American Association.[40] In spite of all the praise and O'Toole's swell start, big-league hitters eventually solved him and his career ended after 1914. O'Toole turned out to be a prolific flop, perhaps one of the biggest in baseball history. Perhaps clouded by the circumstances, George's predictions for O'Toole did not pan out. However, his error in the judgment of O'Toole may have helped Gibson gain insight on how to gauge prospective talent moving forward.

When September started, the Pirates stood a mere three-and-a-half games behind the New York Giants. Still in the thick of the pennant race, injuries decimated the starting nine during the final month of the season. Although Clarke, Wagner and Leach all missed games, no one missed more than Gibby. As the Pirates made their last-ditch push for a title, Gibson sat out twenty-two games. His absence proved devastating. While no one would argue Gibson a superior talent to Wagner, his time off the field suggested the catcher was as important, if not more important, to the overall success of the team. In 1909, Gibson played the full season and the Pirates won the World Series. In 1911, as Gibson missed over 50 games, the Pirates' win total sunk to 85, a full 25 wins less than in their World Series year. There is no doubt that injuries to the three eventual Hall of Famers shattered the Bucs' season, but so, too, did Gibson's failed health.

Still, Gibson served as a base coach during his time out of the lineup. The Giants never wavered and the Pittsburgh club finished seventeen games off the pace. For the second year in a row, the Pirates went home in third place. Further contributing to the team's shortcomings, Gibson had one of the worst offensive seasons of his career. While not as poor as his rookie season, his platework in 1911 was less than stellar. One needn't look past his .209 average to realize that. It's not unreasonable to attribute this poor performance to his failed health. He did, after all, visit "Bonesetter" Reese four times throughout the season. Gibson started just ninety-two games in 1911, his lowest total since 1906. In spite of his personally impaired campaign, George remained Clarke's right-hand man. He traveled on most road trips, coached the bases, instructed the pitchers, guided the rookies and kept his eye on his fellow catchers. It is obvious to even the most casual observer that Gibson's role with the Pirates, up to and, in particular, including the 1910 and 1911 season, propelled him in management's opinion. As 1911 wrapped up, Gibson sat destined for leadership duties within the Pittsburgh club.

8

"Maple Leaf Forever"

In late 1911, Bonesetter Reese consulted Gibson and informed the catcher that he needed to rest his arm and keep it as inactive as possible during the off-season. In early 1912, after a brief respite, Gibson sent a telegram to President Dreyfuss and notified his boss that he had returned to proper form. In that telegram, Gibson told his boss that he had been "so busy doing nothing that I have had time to do nothing else."[1] The news relieved Dreyfuss and Clarke, and all but assured the Pirates that they wouldn't see a merry-go-round of backstops in 1912.

Though Reese requested a sedentary off-season, Gibson kept busy during his time away from baseball. George spent the majority of his time in London at "Fairmount," the Gibson family home's nom de plume. While at home, Gibson, the avid curler, supplemented his daily rest with quite a bit of time on the ice. George previously joined the Thistle Curling Club, and, true to form, took to the sport swimmingly. Considered one of the top players in Western Ontario, Gibby possessed a keen ability to settle the rock near the button and rarely missed the 4-foot-ring. He was the skipper of his team because of his accuracy with the rock. It seems to reason that Gibson's ability to be precise with his pegging arm on a throw to second transferred to his shot-making accuracy on the rink. Gibson loved curling to keep in shape, and once stated, "It keeps a fellow in better shape, than anything I know."[2]

Curling served as more than just a pastime. George competed in tournaments across Southern Ontario and represented his hometown club in Toronto at the Ontario Tankard, the top curling tournament in Canada at the time. When not curling, Gibson took long walks, often accompanied by his brother and his dogs. In addition, he spent time in his home gymnasium, particularly on days when the Canadian winter morphed into a Canadian blizzard. Canadian winters are not to be trifled with but Gibson maintained his upbeat disposition. In a letter to Dreyfuss, Gibson joked that "Santa Claus must have overlooked for Xmas, for he certainly been giving us a cold deal. We call it warm when the mercury hovers at zero. You should see me take a ten-mile walk when it's thirty below and still adiving. Bundled up so strong that Cap. Clarke wouldn't know me."[3]

Gibson arrived for spring training in 1912 excited to teach his team-mates the rules of curling and to show off a gold watch charm he won at the Ontario Tankard. After they had their fun, Gibson schooled the young Pirates recruits, just as he had in years past, on baseball's nuances. Some of the nervous young players wondered where they would play in the upcoming season. Gibby advised the greenhorns not to "let that worry you, get your nerve up and make yourself believe you are going to stick with the show." He continued to draw from his own experience when a young pitching prospect explained to Gibson that he had not performed to his best so far in camp, to which Gibson quickly replied, "No one had." Gibson related to the young man, "Try to be natural. You showed something in the minors or you would not have been tried out here. There are many players that have been tried out in the National League several times before they landed a steady job. Howard Camnitz was with Pittsburgh twice before he finally secured a regular birth. Many of them last for only one season and go back to the minors and pitch the best ball of their careers."[4] Wise words, especially since Gibson never had to go through that kind of an experience as a player. After his purchase from Montreal, his only time in the minor leagues came in a few at bats as manager of the Toronto club in 1919.

When camp moved to Arkansas, games between the Regulars and Yan-nigans began as usual. The *Pittsburgh Daily Post* reported that during one intrasquad game, Clarke had Gibson try out a new pair of shin guards, owing to all of the welts and bruises he always possessed. The paper noted, "He got a big hand from the entire Buccaneer crew when he trotted out as the game started with leather knee caps and shin guards."[5] George was sick of being hit in the shank so often and was tired of playing injured. Gibson did not take to the tibia shields. He later recalled his first (and only) attempt at playing with the bulky leg safeguards. "I took off after a foul ball, just put 'em on the start of the game, and a foul ball went up ... just an inning or two, until I had to run with 'em on ...a high ball went up. A lot of room in those days ... about 150 feet I had to run back behind the plate.... I took off after one of those foul balls.... I got halfway to it and fell down, I got tangled up [in the shin guards], I just sat right down, unbuckled them, took 'em off, and threw 'em away, and never had a shin guard since."[6]

Unfortunately, the Pirates started the 1912 season on a sour note. The club recorded a paltry five wins and seven losses in April. Besides a 23–4 win against Cincinnati on the 27th, the Pirates' bats were silent that month. Gib-son himself had two hits in that rout of Cincy but just seven hits in the other eleven games during April.

May did not bring any reprieve for George or the Pirates. Pittsburgh re-

Gibson and his teammates take batting practice before a game (Healy Collection).

mained under .500 by the halfway point of the month and Gibson continued his downward spiral with the bat. Gibby had no hits in his first sixteen at-bats of May. Manager Clarke responded by resting his catcher. Billy Kelly made the decision easier. Signed the year before from St. Paul of the American Association, he outperformed Gibby to that point in the campaign. During Gibson's 14-game rest, the Pittsburgh club did show a marked improvement. The team won nine games and lost five. Rumors persisted that George was hurt, but those reports were unsubstantiated. On May 30, George finally returned to action. In the first game of a doubleheader, he played well and managed to bag a hit; his only bingle in twenty-one plate appearances that month.

Though his play had started to slip, George still garnered great respect in Piratesland for finding ways to contribute to the team. Clarke's temporary demotion of Gibson only served to enhance his reputation. During this break, Gibby taught Billy Kelly the finer points of catching in the big leagues, just as Heine Peitz did for him years earlier. The *Pittsburgh Post-Gazette* took notice: "George Gibson is giving Billy Kelly the benefit of his long experience and O'Toole's partner is proving an apt pupil. They have their best class sessions on trains and it is a common thing to see the pair in a seat in one of the cars with 'Gibby' doing the talking and Kelly the listening."[7] In June, Clarke felt it was time Gibson returned to action. Unlike years past, when Gibson was ostensibly handed the reins, this time Clarke platooned the veteran. Kelly received spitballers Marty O'Toole and Claude Hendrix while Gibby caught veterans Howie Camnitz and Babe Adams. Clarke also decided that his backstops would never catch both games of a doubleheader. While there is no doubt several other factors contributed to the changes, it's entirely possible the primary reason related to the style of pitcher on the mound. Gibson later remembered that Col. Dreyfuss and Clarke didn't think he could catch a spitball very well, a claim he disputed. According to George, the only difference between a spitball and a traditional curve was that a spitball possessed a little extra break.[8] Once he returned to the lineup, George's play improved. Consequently, the press noticed and in turn attributed Gibson's resurrection to Clarke's decision to rest the Canuck.

Things went smoothly until June 27, when disaster struck. On that day, Billy Kelly broke his finger in a game in St. Louis. This resulted in the catcher staying on the sidelines for most of July. Just as that news started to sink in, Gibson suffered a hand injury of his own. On July 1, Gibson called for a splitter from spitballer Marty O'Toole during a game in Chicago. Jimmy Archer fouled the pitch directly back to Gibby's non-catching hand and the diverted sphere tore off one of his nails. Gibson remembered the instance years later: "I got hit, just with one of those foul tips … lifted the nail, so the nail was standing right up … just that little [cuticle] of the nail was holding it. I just walked over near the bench and I was shaking, and the nail was standing straight up and no one had a knife."[9] George eventually found a knife and used it to remove the nail himself. He promptly taped his finger and then returned to his position. Although he finished out that contest, he missed twelve of the next sixteen games as a result of the injury.

Mike Simon, the Bucs' third-string catcher, suddenly ascended to the top of the depth chart. In the 12 games he filled in for Gibson, the Pirates won eight; Simon played errorless ball, and batted an impressive .333. Even with Simon's strong play, George resumed his role as the Pirates' number one catcher as soon as he was healthy. He caught nine of the club's next ten games, and the Pirates went 6–4.

When the calendar turned over to August, the Pirates stood in third place, fourteen games behind New York, the league leaders. The Pirates won fourteen of their next twenty-one games. Gibby added to his highlight reel during a 4-for-4 performance in a 3–0 win over Boston early in the month. Six days later, he scored the Pirates' only run by smacking a home run off of New York's Rube Marquard in a 2–1 loss. Despite their strong play, the Pirates barely gained any ground on New York. Their record of 71–50 was still 12½ games back of the Giants.

Entering the last month of the season, the Pirates, though not mathematically eliminated, found themselves in too deep of a hole. Despite a fantastic stretch run, the team ended with 93 wins and settled for a second-place finish. George overcame early season obstacles, and finished the year with a respectable .240 batting average. In 94 games, George again led National League catchers with a .990 fielding percentage and caught 54 percent of would-be base stealers.

After that extremely challenging season, Gibson went home and commenced a new undertaking. In early November, Ol' Moon Gibson bought a farm. He purchased a one-hundred-acre farmstead near Mount Brydges, Ontario, for $2,500. Located fifteen miles outside of London, Gibson decided to purchase the land while on a suburban drive.[10] His London friends gladly helped him move to his new place and then granted their town star some privacy. Meanwhile, worried fans feared Gibson intended to quit baseball. However, those feelings subsided when they realized the purchase was only one step towards his life after the game. Gibson later revealed: "I bought it just to get out of the earshot of trains. I'd spent so many years on the trains traveling, I wanted to get some place so I couldn't even hear a train whistle."[11] In fact, he used the heavy farm work to stay in shape and told President Dreyfuss to send other players to work at the farm and keep in good condition. Gibson eventually leased about seventy acres of his land to tobacco farmers and kept a small apple orchard on the remaining land.[12]

That off-season, Gibson befriended his fellow farmers and spent time socializing with them at the local blacksmith's shop. Many of his new friends played for the area's amateur baseball team. Unsurprisingly, they asked Gibson to join the squad for the final series of the season against their rivals. When the opposing club caught wind that Gibson might play, they sent a courier to the blacksmith shop a day before the final game. The message insisted that no "professional pitcher" would be allowed to participate in the game.[13] George let his friends fight their own battle.

The Pirates invited five catchers for Spring training in 1913. The collective included Gibson, Bill Kelly, Mike Simon and rookie Charley Miller. Mike Joyce, a promising young catcher out of Duquesne University in Pittsburgh, also attended camp as a backstop. Pirates management felt that the team had the talent to have an exceptional season. Their success hinged on the team's ability to stay healthy. George, as in previous years, monitored the greenhorn hurlers for the duration of spring. This time, the man of so many talents created a new game the players called "oof." The game, which aimed to improve the players' hand-eye coordination, required a group of six to twelve participants to keep a baseball in the air by passing it using baseball bats. The game drew great inspiration from keepie uppie, a soccer variant that required a collection of players to juggle the ball.

Pirates Spring training games at Hot Springs in 1913 differed from those in years past. Instead of the intrasquad contests, Dreyfuss and Clarke arranged a deal with Boston Red Sox skip Jake Stahl. The two sides agreed to a nine-game duel in Arkansas. The games were anything but practice for the Pirates. The Red Sox won the 1912 World Series and the Bucs wanted to prove the victory a fluke and reestablish National League superiority. As both teams divided their rosters to maximize opportunities for the players, Barney Drey-fuss said, "It will be the busiest training camp in history. While the Regulars of Clarke and Stahl's teams are after each other's scalps, the two sets of Yan-nigans will be clawing at each other."[14] As further evidence of how important Dreyfuss viewed the competition, his rookies played every day during camp. He also sent Forbes Field head groundskeeper James O'Malley south to Hot Springs to ensure that Whittington Park, the Pirates' home field in Arkansas, was in tip-top shape for the Bucs' series with the Red Sox.

Dan Nirella, the bandmaster at Forbes Field, joined O'Malley in Hot Springs and talked to each player about their "walk-up" songs for both the series and the upcoming season. Ever the proud Canadian, Gibson stayed true to his roots and requested that he walk to the plate to the tune of "Maple Leaf Forever."[15] Alexander Muir wrote the song in 1867, in recognition and celebration of Canada's confederation. Muir drew inspiration from his time with the The Queen's Own Rifles of Canada at the 1866 Battle of Ridgeway. Irish Americans, known as the Fenian Brotherhood, invaded Canada at Fort Erie to take colonial Canada captive and force Britain to negotiate Ireland's independence. Muir and his fellow Canadian troops repelled the Fenians. The conflict marked the first time in history that Canadian officers, and not a British commander, led a Canadian battle company. "Maple Leaf Forever" fo-cused on the soldiers' bravery during the battle and remained popular for de-cades. George Gibson chose the song to represent him and honor his country.

The series started well for the Pirates as they earned a 4–3 victory over the World Series champs. Gibson came in as a defensive replacement and managed to count a base hit late in the match. Gibson started the second game, and had a great performance. Unfortunately, none of the other Pirates managed much. In the 7–2 loss, George went 3-for-3 and hit a home run off of Red Sox veteran Charley Hall.

After that match, spring rain arrived and didn't let up for some time. In the end, the teams agreed to cancel four matches and call the series a best of five. Bragging rights came down to the fifth and final game. Surprisingly, Gib-son did not play in the finale; Clarke elected to start Bill Kelly to backstop the Pirates hurlers. He received heaves from Claude Hendrix and Babe Adams, who pitched well and allowed only two runs, but were bettered by Red Sox pitchers Hugh Bedient and Charley Hall, who hung a zero on the Pirates hit-ters. Boston took the series and asserted American League dominance.

The 1913 campaign started off great for Gibson and the Pirates. On open-ing day, they trounced Cincinnati 9–2 en route to a 4–2–1 record in the first week. Gibson, a notoriously slow starter with the bat, finished the week with a

.320 average. The 8–25 opening tear did not last much longer; his 1913 season ended up a disappointment.

On April 20 in St. Louis, in only the eighth game of the year, Gibson was put on the disabled list. Cardinal's outfielder Rebel Oakes popped up a high foul ball back behind the plate at Robison Field. Gibby ran full tilt into the grandstand and severely sprained his ankle when he caught his spikes in some padding along the stands. He made the catch but left the game because the pain was too much. The Pirates won, and the club doctor reported that Gibby did not break any bones. This suggested that Gibson would not be out long.

Gibby returned to Pittsburgh for more tests, where doctor F. M. Storer issued his finding. An X-ray revealed a fracture in Gibson's ankle and meant George would be out of the lineup for at least six-weeks. The disheartened Gibson, now forced to wear a plaster cast, gave up his catching duties to back-ups Kelly and Simon. While Fred Clarke hoped for a speedy recovery, Gibson returned home to London for rest.

About a month later, Gibby sent a letter to Dreyfuss to update the president as to his injured status. Gibson told Dreyfuss that he could move his foot while in the cast, a positive sign to the doctors. They expected to remove the plaster cast within days of the telegram. Ever the consummate teammate, George wanted to get back to Pittsburgh as soon as possible and wrote: "I have had this cast on my leg for four weeks, and they have certainly been the four longest weeks of my life. You may rest assured I will return to the game just as soon as possible. I want to get there and help put the Pirates back where they belong."[16]

On May 28, just five weeks after the injury, George returned to Pittsburgh. Even though he returned without a cast, he required a cane to help him walk. His teammates, excited to see him, wanted to know when he'd be able to play again. Gibson told his cohorts he had no pain in his ankle but admitted to being a little stiff and out of game shape. He assured his compadres he would be catching for them again in no time.

On June 10, the Pirates' record stood at an unexceptional 23–24–2. While the club had not finished lower than third place since 1904, they found themselves in fifth. Then, things got worse. On June 11, the Pirates hosted Brooklyn at Forbes Field without any healthy catchers available. On the 10th, the last man standing, Mike Simon, injured his hand on a foul tip, and he could barely pick up a ball. Bill Kelly split the index finger of his chucking arm in practice, leaving him decommissioned as well. Gibby, in spite of the extended absence, again asserted his "do anything for the team" style of leadership. Without hesitation, he grabbed his mask and prepared to play. Gibson's return seems to have inspired starting pitcher Marty O'Toole. Gibson played outstanding ball and helped O'Toole to his first victory of the season.

In his return, Gibson played errorless defense and recorded two hits in four at bats with two RBIs. After the game, President Dreyfuss moved to shore up his club's defense; he signed twenty-three-year-old Bob Coleman from the Davenport Blue Sox of the Illinois-Indiana-Iowa League.

While Coleman manned the plate for the Pirates, George received additional treatment on his ankle. Doctors recommended that George undergo radium treatment. Radium, at the time, cost three million dollars per pound. Thankfully for Gibson's body and Dreyfuss's budget, the treatment required only small amounts. The doctors mixed the radium with potter's clay and applied the concoction to Gibson's ankle for a few hours at a time. *Pittsburgh Post* reporter Ralph Davis wrote, "Gibson's fractured ankle now ranks as the most expensive injury ever sustained by a ballplayer, without any reference to what his absence from the game has cost his team."[17] A quote from *Syracuse Journal* noted that doctors taught trainer Ed Laforce how to remove and replace Gibson's bandages: "The preparation is one of the most wonderful known to science, and the doctors say the costly application on Gibson's foot will retain its strength for 2,000 years. The Pirate management hopes, however, that Gibson's ankle will get well before the preparation wears out."[18] Even with the expensive treatment, George remained out of the Pirates' lineup for two months and did not return to the starting nine until late August.

In mid–August, Philadelphia Phillies president William H. Locke passed away in Atlantic City. He died from complications due to surgery. Before he left to become president of the Phillies, Locke served as secretary of the Pirates from 1903 until 1912. Prior to that, the *Pittsburgh Press* employed Locke as sports editor. After his death, the paper's Ralph Davis said, "Will Locke is dead! But not in the hearts of his friends, where his memory will forever live—not as a baseball magnate, but as a MAN–A FRIEND."[19] Gibson also made a statement about the man who had been his friend since 1905: "One of the noblest men in the world has been taken. I knew Will Locke from the time I joined the Pittsburgh team as one of my best friends, a man who would go the limit for those whom he knew and liked. The Pittsburgh players know one side of his character better than does anyone else. We know what he would do for others, no matter how tired or worn out he was after his own work was finished, he was ever willing to put himself out to do others a favor. Many a time has he smoothed the way for an unfortunate athlete. I believe no man ever connected with the National League was more highly respected by the players."[20]

The roller-coaster off-field events continued during the team's final road trip that year. On a train from Bridgeport, Connecticut, to Boston, three ruffians boarded the Bucs' private car and began to shout profanities at some of the women present in the rear of the car. Gibson told the men they were on a private train car and politely asked them to leave. In response, one of the hotheads screamed: "Who will stop me?"

In that situation, many a player would certainly throw fists. Gibson, just as he had time and time again, demonstrated his calm under fire. He got to his feet and attempted to de-escalate the situation, but the offender continued to press him. Saving his fierce competitiveness for the diamond, Gibson simply shoved the man, albeit with such force that the perpetrator ended up at the front of the car. Meanwhile, Fred Clarke and Hans Wagner subdued the other men. The fracas was short-lived and ended when Gibson and Clarke dragged the fellows out to the platform. The train then left Bridgeport for Boston and no Bucs were any worse for wear.[21]

The season ended uneventfully as Gibson and Simon split the final games. George appeared in 48 games in 1913, well below the standard that had become expected of him. His absence illustrated how important he was to the Pirates' success. Without Gibson to lead the pitchers and protect the base paths, the Bucs only won 78 games, and finished in fourth place. It was the first time Pittsburgh finished outside of the top three in the National League in Gibson's big-league career. When questioned by reporters in regards to his early season predictions, Gibson relented: "I will never make a prediction of any sort in the future. My hopes ran high last winter. I thought I saw a pennant in sight. As for myself, I was down to fine weight and better than I had been since 1909. To my wife only did I confide my ambition to go in and beat my own record made in 1909 when I caught 138 games. I probably jinxed myself for the season had not gone any length until I broke my leg. Hereafter I will not confide an ambition nor make a prediction of any sort, not even to my wife."[22]

When his off-season commenced Gibson fell into his familiar routine. Over the years Gibson reported back to the Pittsburgh brass a detailed diary card of sorts. In these communiqués, Gibson highlighted his conditioning routine and his holiday activities. The *Pittsburgh Press* often printed these letters and the report that they published in 1914 really caught the attention of the fans. In it, Gibson laid out his facetious off-season routine in a way that certainly shows why vaudeville came calling all of those years earlier:

> 6 a.m.—Lies in bed listening to alarm going off
> 6:30—Still snoring
> 7—Snoring yet
> 7:30—Still at it
> 8—At it yet
> 8:30—Decides to get up
> 9—Decides his former decision was a delusion and a snare
> 9:30—Inquires what time it is

10—Finally arises
10:15—Comes downstairs
10:30—Breakfast
11—Shovels snow
11:30—Reads the papers
Noon—Opens the mail
1—Luncheon is served
1:45—Smokes a cigar
2—Goes for a walk
2:04—Finds the going bad and returns home
2:05—Takes a nap
3:10—Still napping
4—Awakens and stretches
5—Counts his money
5:30—Decides to buy a new automobile next summer
6—Dinner
7—Smokes another black cigar
7:30—Takes a nap by the fireside
8:30—Decides to bat .390 next summer
9—Hits the hay[23]

Coming off his broken ankle, George reduced his workload that off-season. In contrast, the Pittsburgh team management engaged in rebuilding their quickly descending club. In late '13, Barney Dreyfuss traded Bobby Byrne and Howie Camnitz to the Phillies and Dots Miller and Chief Wilson to the Cardinals, and he released catcher, Mike Simon. All five contributed to the Pirates' 1909 championship. In their stead, Dreyfuss acquired three players, all under 25 years old: Max Carey, Jim Viox and Al Mamaux. Finally, and most surprisingly, Dreyfuss sent catcher Billy Kelly, who came from St. Paul with Marty O'Toole, to Toronto of the International League. By the time spring training started, only five members of the 1909 World Series winning team remained: Fred Clarke, Babe Adams, Ham Hyatt, Honus Wagner and Gibson.

The Pirates made another change in the lead up to the 1914 season. They relocated their preliminary training facility from West Baden Springs, Indiana, to Dawson Springs, Kentucky. Dawson Springs sat 165 miles further south than West Baden Springs and the move all but guaranteed better weather during early spring. Dawson Springs spared no expense to lure the Pirates to their corner of the world. Hoping the move would increase tourism, the town's denizens built the team a 100' × 40' indoor practice facility, which the players christened "the Shed."[24] In addition, the Dawson Springs Commercial Club built Tradewater Park field, named after a river that ran nearby Dawson Springs. Still in use today, the field is called Riverside Park. Like West Baden Springs, Dawson Springs had access to mineral spring water believed to have medicinal properties. Gibson was all right with the training grounds change, but admitted he missed the "sprudel" water at West Baden Springs. He was delighted to discover the waters at Dawson Springs were just as good.

The water of Dawson Springs must have been formulated for the Pirates by the gods. George Gibson seemingly wielded Thor's Hammer, in lieu of a bat, at the start of the 1914 season. In April, Gibson batted an earth-shattering .389. The Pirates ripped off a seven-game wining streak and finished the month with a 10–2 record.

April's hot start continued into May, and the Bucs won their first five contests. Then, just as quickly as the young Pirates announced themselves as contenders for the pennant, they ran into their first roadblock. A seven-game losing streak caused Pirates fans to hoot their hometown players, including Gibson. On May 15 at Forbes Field, a rowdy patron began to harshly rouse the Bucs players. The fan called Gibson "slowfoot," as well as a few other choice derogatories. Gibby had heard enough and jumped onto the grandstand, with the intention of going after the ruckus maker. A Pittsburgh police officer stepped in and removed the fan from the ballpark, and charged him with disorderly conduct.[25] Mired in a slump, the team needed to focus on their own disorderly play and not the behavior of their fans. They did just that. With Gibson swinging a hot bat, the club put together a six-game winning streak. On May 25, the team captured first place thanks to a 28–8–1 record. Then, the Pirates' fortune turned again.

On the field, the Pirates floundered. The team went 9–17 and tumbled to fifth place in the National League. Off the field, George's life remained on the up and up. On June 4, George and his wife welcomed their third child, a son named William Edward. William's birth followed the day after a home game against the Cubs and the day before a road game against Philadelphia. His new son's convenient time of arrival allowed George to play in both games. Through June 28, George played in every game that season, intent on besting his iron man record of 1909. Unfortunately, Gibson came down with tonsillitis and that dream ended. After a seven-game absence, Gibson returned to a team one game under .500 and in fifth place.

Gibson returned to action with a short fuse. His frustrations with the Pirates' poor play came to the forefront on July 16 when he was booted from a game in Brooklyn for arguing balls and strikes. The press and fans were not impressed with all the kicking Gibby was doing. Reporter Ralph Davis came down hard on George in one instance, stating, "Gibson acted like an overgrown and much spoiled baby."[26] Davis made this observation during a missed play two days later when Gibson and Ed Konetchy collided on a pop-up that Gibby would have easily caught. George lost his cool and shouted towards the Bucs first baseman. The crowd at Forbes Field was not pleased with Gibson's treatment of his teammate and began to hiss and hoot their long-time backstop. Gibson still fumed upon returning to the Pirates' dugout, and appeared to be looking for a fight with his teammate, but cooler heads prevailed. He settled down and gained control of his temper until the very end of August. Regrettably, on the 29th, Canadian-born umpire Ernest C. Quigley ejected Gibson for arguing balls and strikes. A three-game suspension did little to calm Gibby.

When Gibson returned to the lineup, he was reportedly bitter and not putting up his usual effort. Again, the fans let him know how they felt. During one at bat, the Forbes' crowd booed him mercilessly. George responded by snidely tipping his hat and taking a bow. This further infuriated the crowd and they heckled him even more. After the game, Dreyfuss defended his veteran catcher saying, "If we had ten Gibsons we'd be better off than we are now."[27] In the *Post-Gazette*, James Jerpe, Ralph Davis's crosstown journalistic rival, explained Gibby's 1914 temperament via the eyes of the accused. He noted that George was having the best year of his career in '14 and dreamt of a pennant. He described how Gibby continued to play great ball after all the other players had fallen into a rut. Jerpe excused Gibson for being upset with the fans' hisses and boos and explained to them that what Gibby saw "through the April lens had panned out the bitterest disappointment of his baseball career."[28] In spring, Gibson saw a hopeful club that crumbled in the end. It was his best season with the bat, but griping over things you cannot control will not get you anywhere in life, or with an umpire. The usually docile Gibson was ejected only seven times throughout his playing career. Four of those banishments occurred in 1914.

Meanwhile, with the Pirates well out of contention, Barney Dreyfuss gave up on his spitball experiment. The president sold Marty O'Toole to the New York Giants. Dreyfuss summed up his experiment in one line: "He just couldn't win for us."[29] A report out of Chicago speculated that O'Toole wanted out of Pittsburgh because he was uncomfortable with Gibson as his catcher. The report of Marty's disdain for Gibby was later deemed to be fabricated.[30] O'Toole's poor performance continued in New York. He played ten games with the Giants and ended the season with a 1–1 record and a 4.24 ERA. Following the 1914 season, Marty O'Toole never played in another major-league game.

George played sparingly in September on account of a banged-up hand. In addition, Clarke wanted to get a good look at backup catchers Bob Coleman and Bobby Schang. Consequently, the manager dismissed Gibson prior to the season-ending road trip to Cincinnati. While the season seemed an abject failure by most measures, Gibson led the team in hitting with a .285

batting average. That clip registered 20 percentage points higher than anyone else's and registered over 30 points higher than Hans Wagner's average. The Pirates finished the tumultuous season with a dismal 69–85 record, barely enough for seventh place.

In December, it was published that Gibson was slated to become the next manager of the American Associations' Columbus Senators as a replacement for Bill Hinchman. Fred Clarke called the report hearsay and affirmed that Gibson would "remain in Pittsburg as long as I do. He is the only veteran catcher we have, and I do not consider him an old man. We need men like him, and he will stay."[31] Clarke wasn't lying and Gibson did in fact remain with the Pirates until Clarke departed. The year of 1915, as it just so happened, turned out to be Gibson's 11th year in a Pirates uniform and Clarke's swan song.

When the 1915 squad came together, it included just four contributing players from the '09 World Series winning club. The aging quartet consisted of 33-year-old Babe Adams, 41-year-old veteran superstar Honus Wagner and 34-year-old backstop, Gibson. Player-manager Fred Clarke remained with the ball club as well, but the player's half of his title came to a standstill after 1911.

Native Pittsburgh pitcher Al Mamaux was successful under the tutelage of Gibson from 1914 to 1916 (Healy Collection).

In 1915, Clarke and his three elder statesmen set out to emulate the 1914 Boston Braves' success. The Braves, on the backs of superstar Johnny Evers and manager George Stallings, captured the series only a year after winning just 68 contests. The nearly impossible feat branded the 1914 Boston National League club "The Miracle Braves."

The Pirates' 1915 campaign wasn't miraculous but it was noteworthy. On September 8, Frederick Clifford Clarke announced his retirement, effective at the end of the season. While there were rumors that Clarke intended to jump to the upstart Federal League, he squashed those tales with three little words: "I am through."[32] After the 1911 season, Clarke appeared in just twelve games. He much preferred to be a true player-manager and the stress of managing from the bench wreaked havoc on his nervous system. Clarke took the advice of his doctors, and got as far away from the ballpark as possible. The forty-two-year-old retired to his Winfield, Kansas, farm.

The Pirates finished with a 73–81 record, good for only fifth place in the National League. Al Mamaux was the only real bright spot in an otherwise terrible season. The twenty-one-year-old pitcher and Pittsburgh native won twenty-one games for the Pirates in 1915, and finished with a sparkling 2.04 ERA, good enough for third place in the National League. His eight shutouts helped keep his runs against impressively low. Gibson, on the other hand, had the worst defensive season of his career. He appeared in 120 games, but finished the year with a career-low .965 fielding percentage and a career-high 25 errors. His plate performance suffered as well. Gibson batted an ordinary .251 with one home run, just 15 doubles and only 6 triples. The home run ended up being the last of his career.

After Clarke announced his retirement, newspapermen and fans speculated about his replacement. Ralph Davis suggested Honus Wagner and George Gibson as potential replacements. However, he noted that Wagner's close friends doubted that the superstar would take the position.[33] Meanwhile, local papers promoted Gibson as the man to take over and cited that he successfully directed a brick contracting company and demonstrated superb leadership skills with the team's youthful players.[34] In addition, management liked Gibson quite a bit. For those reasons, Davis felt they would interview George for the position.

The *Pittsburgh Post-Gazette* ran a mock ballot for fans to vote and predict who would be the next man to hold the reins of the Corsairs.[35] Gibson recalled, "This poll in the papers was all running Gibby, Gibby, Gibby!"[36] He was somewhat conflicted in how to handle all the hype, so he went to Fred Clarke for counsel. Gibson asked Clarke, "Cap, you can see the way things is running in the paper. Now what's gonna happen if he asks me to take

Gibson in 1915, nearing the end of his career in Pittsburgh (Canada's Sports Hall of Fame / Pantheon des sports Canadiens—sportshall.ca/pantheonsports. ca).

the ballclub?"[37] Clarke's advice to George was, "Gibby, don't take it in the first year!"[38]

The long-time Pirates manager's guidance was wise, as whomever the newcomer would be, they would never stand up to the great Fred Clarke, especially within the eyes and hearts of the Pittsburgh Pirates faithful. Before the Pirates boss could ask George if he wanted the club's top job, he took Clarke's advice and impassively wrote President Dreyfuss after returning to London. He said: "I have been busy since I reached home, and have not given baseball a thought. I suppose you will be busy this winter signing a manager and lining up your men. I sincerely hope you will get a manager who will give you and the old town a winner."[39] The Colonel looked elsewhere in 1916.

9

You Won't Make a Dime

James Joseph "Nixey" Callahan, the son of Irish immigrants, was born on March 18, 1874, in Fitchburg, Massachusetts. He honed his baseball skills during his teenage years when he played amateur and semipro ball throughout the state. Then in 1894, veteran baseball man Arthur Irwin signed Callahan to his Philadelphia Phillies squad.

Nixey's first attempt at high-level pro ball did not go well. In nine games, Callahan pitched to an abysmal 9.89 earned run average. Irwin relegated his young Bay Stater to the minor leagues to further refine his skills and the move proved beneficial. For the 1895 season, Callahan joined the Springfield Maroons of the Eastern League. He dominated the junior-level batsmen by winning a staggering 30 games and by posting a sparkling 2.48 ERA.

Two years later, after his stint in the minor leagues, Callahan returned to the majors when he joined the Chicago Cubs. As it happened, he remained in Chicago for the remainder of his big-league playing career. After a four-year stretch with the Cubs, Nixey headed to the south side's White Sox for eight seasons. Jimmy proved to be a solid all-round player. He posted a respectable 3.39 ERA and a .273 batting average in 3,610 plate appearances. He also served as a player-manager with the White Sox for four of his eight seasons with the team. Under his guidance, the Sox posted a 70–84–3 record in 1914 and finished in sixth place. The team's poor performance prompted Charles Comiskey, the White Sox's owner, to move Callahan into the front office in favor of Eddie Collins.[1]

On December 17, 1915, much to the surprise of Pirates fans and Pittsburgh media alike, Barney Dreyfuss introduced Callahan as the new manager of the Pittsburgh Pirates. *Pittsburgh Press* writer Ralph Davis who speculated about many potential candidates, went as far as to say that "President Dreyfuss … 'put one over' on the fans."[2]

Dreyfuss gave Nixey every freedom he afforded to Fred Clarke while he was Bucs skipper. Just like he did with Fred Clarke, Barney declared that "Callahan will have absolute power."[3] Dreyfuss believed in his choice and thought he had hired a man with plenty of experience and baseball knowledge. Callahan expressed his feelings about the challenge when he said: "I am delighted with the opportunity of leading the Pirates. I will consider myself fortunate if I can continue the high standard established by my predecessor."[4] Gibson knew that Callahan had big shoes to fill. Happy not to be the one trying to replace Clarke, Gibson publically gave his endorsement of his new boss. "I am sure James J. will deliver the goods, and give the old town what we all want—a winner."[5]

Spring training in Hot Springs moved along swimmingly, as new skipper Jimmy Callahan took notes and learned the intricacies of his new players. With a few seasons of "assistant manager" experience under his belt, Gibson took it upon himself to get to know Callahan and lend him a hand. However, on March 26, after only a few weeks of camp, George received a seriously concerning telegram from home. He learned that his wife Margaret was gravely ill. In the letter, Mrs. Gibson asked her husband to return home to Canada as soon as possible. Callahan insisted Gibson leave for London straight away, so George began the long train ride home from the Arkansas resort. Gibby would have to wait until the regular season to get to know his manager better.

On April 12, the Pirates started their season in St. Louis. With his wife's health greatly improved, Gibby caught up with his teammates in the Gateway City on the morning of opening day. For the first time in ten seasons, George did not start on opening day. Gibby's ten consecutive opening day starts for the Pirates as catcher (1906 to 1915) is still a club record. Jason Kendall nearly bettered the record eighty years later when he caught nine consecutive opening days, from 1996 to 2004. The 17-day absence made it to hard for him to get in playing condition before the season began. He would need to use the first few weeks of the 1916 campaign to get ready.

In lieu of Gibson, Callahan started thirty-year-old Art Wilson, a career backup, in the year's first contest. The Bucs lost Manager Callahan's debut, 2–1. Rookie Walter Schmidt out of Arkansas received the nod from his skipper to start the second game of the season. The Pirates' fortune changed as they topped the Cardinals 4–0 in Schmidt's first career big-league game. Callahan stuck with Schmidt going forward as a result of the victory. The Arkansawyer donned the mask for the Pirates in their next ten games, during which time the Pirates registered four wins and six losses.

On April 29 against the Reds, after watching from the sidelines for the first twelve games, Gibson finally received his first start of the season in the club's thirteenth game of the year. Many people believed George was a pivotal part of Al Mamaux's success during the 1915 season. With Mamaux scheduled to go that day, it seemed as good a time as any to insert Gibson into the lineup. Gibby "caught splendidly"[6] versus the Redlegs and helped Mamaux pitch seven and one-third innings of five hit, one run ball. Though Gibson played well and the team won, Callahan relegated George to the pine until Mamaux's next start on May 8. When the battery secured a second victory while working together, Callahan decided to use Gibson more often. However, the manager remained undecided on his number one catcher. Regardless of the pecking order, Gibson was Al Mamaux's personal catcher for most of the season.

By the end of May, the Pirates were far off the pace in the National League pennant race. With just 17 wins against 22 losses, the team found themselves in seventh place out of eight teams. Gibson played only eleven games through the first two months of the season and Art Wilson also only got the call from Manager Callahan on eleven occasions. Walter Schmidt played the majority of matches through the Spring as he started seventeen games for the struggling Bucs. Nixey Callahan continued the carousel of catchers throughout June and July, but stayed true to his successful battery of Mamaux and Gibson. The results were a mixed bag. When the Pirates started Mamaux, and by extension Gibson, they won 14 games against just five losses. Their next best pitcher, Wilbur Cooper, settled in at 4–4. After that, Babe Adams, Erv Kantlehner, Bob Harmon and Frank Miller all lost more games than they won. Even with their pitching woes, the Pirates climbed into sixth place by the end of July.

On August 2, the Pirates were in New York to take on the Giants. Al Mamaux was scheduled to take the mound, but Callahan surprised the Pirates faithful when he broke tradition and opted to start Schmidt behind the plate. The move ended a streak of 19 consecutive Mamaux starts caught by Gibson. The following day's *Post-Gazette* sports page headline boldly stated: "Al Mamaux Is Hammered By M'Grawmen, 6–2."[7] Mamaux gave up 13 hits in the loss and this left fans wondering why Gibson did not make his usual start with the Pirates' top hurler.

The surprises in New York did not stop with Gibson's mysterious benching. On August 3, Barney Dreyfuss issued Charles "Babe" Adams his walking papers. President Dreyfuss voiced his thoughts on Adam's release: "Adams was a faithful worker. I hated to let him out, but he, as well as I, realized that he was of no value to us. I did not care to send him to the minors after his faithful service here, so I gave him his freedom. He may be able to catch on somewhere, although he tells me he may retire for all time from the diamond."[8] Uncertain of his future, Adams decided to return home to his farm at Mt. Moriah, Missouri, and have a good rest. James Jerpe of the *Pittsburgh Post-Gazette* articulated, "We will miss him, as we will miss Honus and Gibby some day."[9] With Adams jettisoned from the roster, only Honus Wagner and George Gibson remained from the 1909 Pirates World Series championship team.

As it happened, George "Mooney" Gibson didn't last much longer either. Unbeknownst to him, Gibson appeared in his last game as a Pirate on August 11. The great Canadian did so as a pinch hitter in the second game of a doubleheader. Then, on August 15, in a most unceremonious end to his Pirates playing career, Dreyfuss released George. Reports claimed that Dreyfuss attempted to trade the veteran or sell him outright, but no team offered up an asset Dreyfuss wanted. Instead, he put the man that served his club in so many capacities, both on and off the field, for so many years, on waivers. The fans didn't have a chance to say goodbye but Dreyfuss did issue a statement:

> I am sorry that we had to let Gibson out, but we had to make room for the new players who will be tried out shortly. It was not my intention to sell Gibby or trade him. I expected to give him his unconditional freedom, and allow him to map out his own future. But when New York claimed him, I had to turn him over to the Giants. I have had two painful moves to make this season. One of them was the release of Babe Adams, the other was getting rid of Gibson. George was one of the most faithful and hardest working players I have ever had any dealings with. It was a real pain to have to part with him. But baseball is a business, and the fans demand new blood. We have to provide it, and we have to make room for the new recruits by turning loose the men who have passed the zenith of their baseball careers. Gibson has my very best wishes for the future.[10]

Gibson fumed. Barney Dreyfuss broke the promise he made to George after the 1909 World Series. Gibby, who was in Boston when he heard the news of his release, immediately returned to Pittsburgh to confront his longtime boss. The man who earned a reputation for his calmness under pressure on the field took his fiery and competitive attitude directly to Barney Dreyfuss's office. Gibson described the meeting with the club president: "I went down and had a talk with Barney, I said, 'Barney, now you wanna break it?' He said, 'I can't do anything else.' I said, 'You wanna realize $1800 on my worn out carcass after you've got all the good out of me…. You're not gonna do it. Might drive me outta baseball but you're not gonna realize a dime outta my carcass.'"[11]

Dreyfuss either underestimated Gibson's value to the rest of the league or he was being dishonest. The very day he released Gibson, the New York Giants swooped in and claimed him. With his team's regular catcher on the mend, Giants manager John McGraw jumped at the chance to bring the skilled veteran on board.

What happened next drove the wedge between Gibson and Dreyfuss even deeper. In accordance with rules at the time, Gibson, as Pittsburgh's representative in the Baseball Player's Fraternity, should have known he could not be released outright. According to the Fraternity, a precursor to the MLBPA, a player released by his team would not become a free agent if another team put in a waiver claim on that player. Still, Gibson asserted Dreyfuss promised him an unconditional release when the Pirates were through with him.

While Dreyfuss claimed to be upset that another team was able to claim Gibson, his actions contradicted the facts. Dreyfuss implied that he wanted Gibson to have his choice in where to play next. However, Dreyfuss was well aware of the rules. In a time when players were the property of their teams and not merely employees, this was a rather significant detail. In fact, he reiterated to Gibson and the Pittsburgh press that Gibby deserved to be a free agent. However, once the Giants claimed Gibson, they were obligated to pay Dreyfuss $1,500. Thus, Gibson had serious misgivings about Dreyfuss's motivations for the transaction.

Meanwhile, McGraw needed a catcher, and he was ready to put Gibson to work. The Giants offered Mooney a contract for the next season and full pay for the balance of 1916. However, Gibson balked at the offer because he felt betrayed by Dreyfuss. Always a principled man, Gibson refused the contract. By refusing to sign, he voided that aforementioned $1,500 debt owed to the Pirates. He even went so far as to ask that if he did sign, that the money end up with a local charity, so long as the waiver fee did not end up in the pocket of the Pirates' president.

Still, the Giants needed him and McGraw wasn't ready to move on. McGraw offered Gibson an extra $1,500, but Gibson refused this as well. He stated: "I can't afford to let [Dreyfuss] make a dime outta my carcass."[12] Instead of heading to New York, Gibson called McGraw and said, "Mac, I'm going home."[13] Unhappy with the circumstances surrounding the end of his Pirates career, Gibson returned to Canada.

Upon his departure from Pittsburgh, the *Daily Post* printed a statement from the catcher:

GRATEFUL TO ALL FRIENDS,

My regrets at leaving Pittsburgh. Before departing from Pittsburgh I am anxious to have the fans and all my friends know that I have always appreciated the many kindnesses I have received from them; also I am grateful to the newspapers for the fairness with which they have reviewed my work while connected to the Pittsburgh club.

I had hoped that when canning time came, it would have been under the most pleasant circumstances. Coming here in 1905, I had learned to call this my home and during all these years I was under the impression that by giving the club my best efforts, they would be appreciated by the management.

After the world's series of 1909 and during each succeeding year up to 1915, the president of the club told me he would give me my release outright when I was through here, and never even think of trying to realize for my services. Imagine my surprise upon learning without any warning I am released to New York, and he is most anxious to receive $1,500, which is the waiver price.

A word for McGraw, I would surely be delighted to be able to join McGraw, to play under a man I consider the very best in the business and one who knows baseball as it should be played, and I am sure that he takes into consideration my position. I am not holding up Mr. Dreyfuss; having allowed all those chances to slip by. Neither do I care who gets the money, as long as he is made to understand that his word, which to me was always sufficient, cannot be broken to me without some consideration FOR me.

In conclusion, I am sorry for all of this newspaper notoriety, never having cared much for it. I am leaving with my very best wishes for Pittsburgh's ball team.

George Gibson[14]

Meanwhile, the remaining Pirates had to deal with the loss of their leader. Al Mamaux credited Gibby for getting him on the baseball map. When the Pirates cut Mamaux after his first Spring tryout, Gibson assured the young pitcher that he had the stuff to make it with the big clubs. Gibby gave Al the confidence not to give up. The university-educated twenty-two-year-old spoke eloquently of his friend and former teammate:

Mere language fails to frame words to properly express my regret upon having to part from a comrade who has been a [sic] most prominent factor in my success upon the major league diamond. There is something about George Gibson that inspired remarkable confidence and it simply seemed that when he was back of the plate I just could not lose.

Gibson's knowledge of the strong points and weaknesses of opposing batters was marvelous. He had a wonderful memory and always knew whether each rival hitter was having a batting streak or a slump. Is it any wonder I feel sorry to see him go? Not only has he been great as an athlete, but he also furnishes a bright example as a man.[15]

Mamaux went on to explain that Gibson played baseball as a gentleman. The young Pirates hurler felt that the Pirates let Gibson go just as he was rounding into form. Mamaux attributed Gibby's slow start to the fact that he missed out on the benefit of spring practice and the use of the mineral baths. Be that as it may, Mamaux wished Gibson success moving forward and admirably noted that George "has been an honor to the national sport."[16] Had Dreyfuss known what would happen to Mamaux after he sent Gibson packing, it's possible the team owner would have kept the catcher around after all. Mamaux went 4–7 to close out 1916. His fall from grace continued the next season. Without Gibson's veteran hand in 1917, he went 2–11 with a horrid 5.25 ERA. The Pirates traded the once-promising pitcher to Brooklyn after the 1917 season.

As for the situation with Gibson, it seems as if the catcher had some ill will towards his new Pirates manager in addition to his feelings towards the longtime owner. Whether Gibson's feelings directed at Callahan were justified is hard to say; however, based on the circumstances, it is easy to understand Gibson's assessment. In a game against the Cubs, a few days before the Pirates waived Gibson, Callahan heckled Johnny Evers during an at bat. After the Chicago second baseman hit a dud, he made a pit stop at the Pirates' bunker. Evers candidly remarked to Callahan: "You got a lot of guts … try to ride somebody in here. Manager, you're not the manager of this ball club, the guy

[Gibson] that's sittin' right next to ya is manager of the club."[17] While Gibson might only have been a bystander during the confrontation, he seemed to feel that Evers's words triggered some combination of jealousy and insecurity in Callahan. Some years later, when asked about the events, Gibson told it like this: "Well now, Callahan turned around as soon as Evers made that remark, he evidently went to the President of the Pittsburgh ball club and wanted to ask waivers on me."[18]

Publicly, Callahan attributed Gibson's release to the team's desire to provide playing time for their younger players. While this lined up with Dreyfuss's published statements, no one ever questioned Gibson's integrity. As such, it's safe to say that that the situation was anything but simple. It's entirely possible that Gibson was sent packing not only because of the youth movement, but also on account of Callahan's personal feelings.

On August 26, Giants manager John McGraw announced that George Gibson had been suspended by the National Commission on account of failing to report to New York. If George wanted to return to big-league ball, he would have to apply for reinstatement to the National Commission before doing so.

Born on April 7, 1873, John "Little Napoleon" McGraw hailed from Truxton, New York. The son of Irish immigrants, McGraw first ascended to prominence as a star pitcher for his hometown Truxton Greys baseball club. The teenager quickly caught on with a semipro team in the Western New York League, which led him to be picked for an American All-Star team that journeyed to Cuba for a barnstorming tour. En route to the small island nation, the team stopped in Florida for a few games. McGraw played well enough in these matches to garner interest from many semipro and pro ball clubs. After consideration of many offers, John McGraw chose to play for the Cedar Rapids club of the Illinois-Iowa League for the 1891 season. At age eighteen, McGraw played beyond his years with the Cedar Rapids club. It earned him a call up to the American Association's Baltimore Orioles, where he made his major-league debut.

McGraw played thirty-three games with the Orioles in 1891 as a utility player and achieved a respectable .270 batting average in his first attempt at the highest level of baseball. The following season, the American Association disbanded and the Baltimore club joined the National League. McGraw stuck with the Orioles and became one of the game's greatest lead-off hitters. He batted over .320 in nine consecutive seasons from 1893 through 1901. Along with star players Hughie Jennings, Willie Keeler, Joe Kelley and Dan Brouthers, McGraw helped his Orioles club win three straight National League pennants from 1894 through 1896. The Orioles franchise then changed leagues again in 1901, and McGraw partnered with American League president Ban Johnson to run the Baltimore-based club. The two men were incompatible, though, so at the end of the year, McGraw jumped back to the National League to take the position of playing-manager with the New York Giants. Once there, he almost entirely hung up his spikes. Other than the occasional spot appearance as a player, McGraw spent his time with the Giants solely focused on managing the team. He held that position for 30 seasons and captured ten pennants and three championships.[19]

John McGraw had a fiery personality, which made him captivating to baseball fans and non-baseball fans alike. He became a celebrity in Gotham and performed on Vaudeville. McGraw's reputation spread beyond the game of baseball and into the consciousness of the general public. In turn, McGraw leveraged his notoriety, and would do anything in his power to get what he wanted. For the 1917 season, he wanted George Gibson.

Some four months after he had returned to Canada, Gibson's phone rang: "This is McGraw speaking," to which Gibson replied, "Yes Mac." "Are you coming over to the meeting?" Having attended in years past, Gibson immediately knew McGraw was talking about baseball's annual winter meetings in New York. Over the years, Manager Clarke called George in the fall and asked him to journey to the winter meetings. George always ended up

going, stating, "What are you gonna do? He's the manger, [and] wants ya to go over." In his veteran years, Gibson accompanied Fred Clarke to New York and helped with dealings and social events. Gibby did not expect any such call in 1916 as he was no longer part of the Pirates organization. Gibson proceeded with caution: "I had a notion I'd go." Classic McGraw got straight to the point: "I want you to come over, you come over, and come over a couple of days ahead." With nothing more than a simple "All right,"[20] George agreed to travel to the Big Apple.

Once Gibson arrived in Manhattan, he proceeded to the New York Giants' office. The Giants' staff, keen to Gibson's arrival, greeted the ballplayer and sent him down a long corridor towards McGraw's office. George later recollected his first encounter with "Little Napoleon" after

Gibson joined the New York Giants in 1917 after twelve seasons with Pittsburgh (Healy Collection).

his refusal to report. He began: "I walked in, I could see him, McGraw stood out." Then, Gibson elaborated. "McGraw could cuss to note. He cuss to note, and one of the best men that ever walked. He was aggressive, you knew who your boss was when you were playing on his ballclub, and you done what he said."[21]

When McGraw grabbed hold of Gibby and began spitting fire, Gibson simply responded with a laugh. Though Gibson did not mean to coax the fiery McGraw, this response incensed the tightly-wound manager even more. McGraw asserted to Gibson: "If you would of joined us last summer ... we would have won the pennant last year." Gibson, knowing John was seriously interested in his services for the 1917 season, gently replied, "Well, we're gonna have to put it off until next year."[22]

Little Napoleon pleaded with George, "Gibby, I'll give ya anything ya want! I want ya to join this ball club."[23] Gibby explained his situation to Mc-Graw; he did not want Barney Dreyfuss making one cent off him. George told McGraw that he gave one hundred percent to the Pittsburgh ball club and that for every dollar they paid him, the club realized one hundred dollars in return because of his services. When the Pirates brass were through with him, they opted to dump him for a measly $1,500. Gibson exclaimed, "They're not gonna get it." McGraw had heard enough of Gibby's grievances and laid out an offer for him to consider. "I'll tell you what I'll do, Gibby. I'll assume your contract. I'll give you the $1800 [$1,500]. I'll give you your salary from when you went home."[24] Too good of an offer to deny, George, whose most recent job involved picking potatoes and apples, accepted McGraw's offer with careful hesitation. Just as he had mistakenly done with Dreyfuss back in 1909, George consecrated the deal with a hand shake and not a signed contract. For Gibson, his word was his contract. In 1917, George Gibson joined the New York Giants.

Now that he had patched things up with the Giants, Gibson needed to deal with the overseers on the National Commission. Gibson violated his 1916 contractual obligations when he refused to report to New York. Since the Commission suspended him, they needed to reinstate him before he could play or coach with the New York club. With the season fast approaching, time was of the essence.

Though he would not be able to participate in any regular-season or post-season activities, Gibby's suspension did not prevent him from practicing with his new club. While the National Commission debated the merits of his appeal, Mooney headed to the Giants' spring home in Marlin, Texas, where the Giants' spring camp was held. Marlin compared favorably to Dawson Springs and Hot Springs, on account of its access to a mineral water resort. Clearly, any contempt McGraw held for Gibson dissipated after their negotiation session back in New York. Right out of the gate, McGraw tasked

Gibby with chaperoning the team's pitching prospects on their way to Marlin. On March 4, he arrived in the Lonestar state along with his wife and two-year-old son William, a.k.a. Billy. The *New York Sun* reported, "Billy is already the pet of camp."[25]

That spring, seven catchers arrived at the Texas town for spring training with the Giants, all vying for one of three available roster spots. The incumbent backstop was 29-year-old Indiana native, Bill Rariden. Rariden played one-hundred and twenty games for McGraw's G-men in 1916. He batted a mediocre .222 average, but made up for his hitting deficiencies by playing to a solid .972 fielding percentage. Rariden's closest competition for the starting catching duties was 28-year-old Lew McCarty, who hailed from Milton, Pennsylvania. McCarty appeared in twenty-five games for McGraw in 1916 and batted for a spectacular .397 average, to go along with a nearly perfect .993 fielding percentage. Rariden and McCarty were all but assured jobs as catchers with the Giants, so that left only one spot open for the other five catchers in camp. Besides Gibson, only two others were thought to have a chance at making the ball club. First was Brad Kocher, who logged thirty-four games with the Giants in 1916, and second was 26-year-old Chicago native, Ernie Krueger, a minor leaguer in 1916. The young potential stars gave Gibson a tough task in proving his value. Although McGraw guaranteed Gibson a job as a pitching coach, he would have to impress the demanding skipper with his play if he ever intended to don a mask in the big leagues again.

Gibson arrived in Marlin in excellent condition, perhaps due to extended time off. In the team drills he displayed a level of mastery that neither Kocher nor Krueger could match. The papers praised the thirty-six-year-old's performance on the diamond and insisted he make the final roster. "The veteran catcher's show-

George Gibson with his son Billy circa 1918 (courtesy Carol Smith).

ing this spring is a great surprise to McGraw and a disappointment to the young backstops seeking a place in the big league sun."[26] Another paper went even further and predicted a bigger role for George: "Gibson has shown up so surprisingly strong both in catching and fielding that McGraw has thought of using him in regular championship games as well as pitcher coach."[27] Gibson remained confident in his play and felt he could still contribute on the field. He suited up as the Pirates' number one catcher just two years earlier. When the National Commission reinstated Gibson on March 27, Gibby's newfound freedom combined with his great play essentially ended the competition. Now, Little Napoleon would be able to use Gibby in whatever manner he saw fit.[28]

In an attempt to further ready his team for the upcoming season, Mc-Graw scheduled a nine-game exhibition series with the Detroit Tigers, who holed up in nearby Waxahachie, Texas. From March 30 through April 8, the teams barnstormed through Texas, Oklahoma, Kansas and Missouri. Although there was nothing at stake save for bragging rights, tensions between the teams mounted quickly.

On March 31, in a game at Dallas, Tiger star Ty Cobb smacked a single in the third inning and then attempted to steal second. Cobb slid into the bag firmly, spikes high and cut Giants infielder Buck Herzog on the arm and leg. Herzog responded with a punch and a tussle ensued. Other players separated the men in order to end the extracurricular activities and Cobb was summarily dismissed from the game. For what it's worth, Cobb admitted he purposely slid with force. According to reports, "The Georgian admits that he went into Herzog hard in order to teach him not to be so gay."[29] Regardless, he vowed to sit out the remainder of the exhibition series. Cobb's quote in the *Detroit Free Press* serves as just another example of his loathsome personality: "I am not going to be the goat for anybody. McGraw seems to be running this series and the umpires will do just what he says. If I go back in the game there will be more trouble and as soon as I try to uphold my rights, I will be banished. It isn't fair that I will have my hands tied while the New York players get away with anything they please. McGraw is a mucker and always has been and I do not intend to stand for his dirty work."[30]

The drama involving Cobb didn't end on the field. Cobb planned to leave for Detroit, but in doing so, he did not want to appear "yellow" (slang for "cowardly"). To protect his reputation, Cobb decided to save face by reaching out to a leader on the Giants. That evening, Cobb and Gibson convened in front of the hotel the two teams shared. Cobb informed Gibby that Tigers manager Hughie Jennings ordered Ty to return to Detroit. Gibson expressed his approval and went so far as to assure Cobb that he would talk to his Giants teammates so as to dispel any rumors that Cobb fled out of cowardice. Unfortunately, just as George and Ty were wrapping up their conversation, Buck Herzog and Heinie Zimmerman strolled up.

Herzog confronted Cobb straightaway: "I'm gonna get satisfaction tonight. Right now, out of you!"[31] In an era now long gone, street fights went off with a lot more planning involved. The four men went back to Herzog's room and laid out the ground rules. Herzog claimed Zimmerman as his corner man to look out for his interests in the upcoming slugfest. Cobb, without a Tiger in sight, turned to Gibson. Uncomfortable as this made him, for any number of reasons, Gibson agreed to provide the same services to Cobb as Zimmerman would to Herzog.

Gibson recollected: "Here was Heinie sitting on one side, and I was sitting on the other. They just squared off. Ty just hauled off a biggie; hit Herzog right straight on the end of the nose. Herzog covered up his head, covered up his face with both hands and said, 'you win, you win, you win,' and that's all the fight was."[32] The two combatants shook hands but Cobb still went back to Detroit. After that, the series teetered. Ultimately, each team won four contests while rain took care of the remaining game.

After the series wrapped in Kansas City on the April 8, the Giants headed for Boston to kick off their season. Though Gibson easily made the roster, he still took a backseat to Bill Rariden and Lew McCarty when it came to playing time. The season opened on April 12 but Gibson didn't appear until April 24. Even then, he came in as a late-game defensive replacement with Ferdinand Schupp on the mound. Gibson quickly learned that Schupp needed his tutelage. After the game, Gibson explained that he "never saw a pitcher with more stuff and with more deliberation in his use of it."[33] After that, Gibson and Schupp practiced together incessantly, to ensure Schupp maximized his potential.

Meanwhile, the Giants played strong and by the end of the month, they sat atop the standings alongside the Chicago Cubs. Rariden and McCarty continued to platoon for the majority of games with Gibson providing a spot start here and there. On June 7, Lew McCarty injured himself sliding back to first on a pick-off attempt. He fractured his fibula on the play and had to be carried from the field. Bill Rariden claimed starting duties and Gibson slotted in as the backup. When Gibby signed with the Giants, he informed McGraw that he would only be able to catch a few games. However, given his experience with injuries in years past, it's safe to say that George knew he might be called upon. As dutifully as ever, George stepped in to help keep New York atop the National League standings.

While Rariden started all 18 games that took place between June 8 and June 27, Gibson provided support as a semi-frequent defensive replacement. On June 13, the Giants arrived in Pittsburgh for their first visit to the Steel City that season. Up 6–1 going into the eighth inning, McGraw paid a courtesy to his veteran backstop, and put him into the game. When Gibby's name was announced over the loudspeaker at Forbes Field, "he received a rousing welcome from the fans."[34]

New York Giants pitcher Ferdie Schupp had his best career season in 1917 with Gibson as his catcher and mentor (Healy Collection).

Over the 18-game period during which Rariden served as the starter, the Giants collected 11 wins against just 7 defeats. Then on June 28, McGraw elected to rest his first-string catcher; and, with McCarty still sidelined, the manager penciled Gibson onto his lineup card. That day, in Gibson's first start of the season, McGraw pitched Gibby's pupil Ferdie Schupp. Gibson later remembered working with Ferdie at Giants camp: "One of the best left hand pitchers that ever was in baseball, but he could not pitch to McCarty or Rariden, those two catchers … he wasn't successful with them. Well I worked with him in the Spring at Marlin, Texas…. Schuppy said to me, 'I just can't pitch to those fellows. They're moving all over.' I said, 'Listen, when I get that mask on, that's as good a target brother, you're not shootin' at this, or that, or this, or that; wherever I put this [his mitt].'"[35] The duo put on a dynamic showing that day. Ferdie surrendered just two runs on three hits in a complete game performance. Meanwhile, Gibson picked up his first hits of 1917 with two singles in four at bats and the Giants defeated the Braves 3–2. George played so well in the game that McGraw started him the next day in both ends of a doubleheader. While the Giants only managed to split the double dip, Gibson did his part with four hits in four at bats. McGraw rode Gibby the next day, too, before turning the reins back over to Rariden.

Gibson continued to give Rariden rest over a handful of starts throughout July and into August. The team played well, and halfway through August the Giants maintained an eleven-game lead over the second-place Phillies. As a team absent a bona fide superstar, New York relied heavily on cohesive play. The approach paid dividends in the form of 69 wins and just 36 losses. By August 17, the Giants were well ahead in the National League pennant race.

On August 18, at the Polo Grounds, Gibson and Schupp paired up to face the St. Louis Cardinals. In the first inning, Gibson's former Pirates teammate, Dots Miller, fouled back a pitch that dislocated Gibby's thumb. Gibson later remembered the injury: "I was sitting on my heels and that ball was going outside and I went this way to get it … and it just touched the end of his bat and hit the top of my thumb…. I looked around to Bill Klem, I said, 'How do you like the look of that Bill?' He said, 'Is there a doctor in the stands?' McGraw came walking out and he unbuckled the things off me and said, 'Get to the clubhouse.'"[36] The *New York Tribune* predicted a two-week absence,[37] but after doctors examined Gibson's finger, the timetable for his return stretched to at least a month. Gibson's injury left Bill Rariden as the only experienced backstop available for the Giants until McCarty or Gibby returned. Manager McGraw was not worried with such a commanding lead in the standings. In fact, Gibson went so far as to light-heartedly say: "We were so far ahead, we said, let's call it off and start next year!"[38]

As expected, the Giants easily won the National League pennant. The Philadelphia Phillies finished in second, a distant ten games back. Gibson's former club, the Pittsburgh Pirates, finished in last place with only 51 wins. Gibson appeared in 35 games and recorded just 14 hits all season. Still, as was the case throughout his career, the great catcher earned his keep through more than just his playing time. In a sign of Gibson's immeasurable value, McGraw gathered his club and proclaimed: "There's one thing I want every one of you fellows to hear. My pitching staff this year is in the best condition than any pitching staff I've had since Baltimore." The delighted Gibby shook his chief's hands and said: "Thank you brother. That's quite a compliment."[39] McGraw explained to Gibson that the proof was in the pudding. The pitchers had more stamina and pitched deeper into games than they did in 1916. This in turn, at least in McGraw's eyes, led to more wins. George was content. The Giants helped him win just his second career National League pennant and he took a big step towards a promising coaching career.

The Giants faced the Chicago White Sox in the World Series. With Rariden and McCarty healthy, Gibson served as a base coach during the fall classic. The White Sox got a quick jump in the series by winning the first two games in Chicago. The Giants bounced back when the series shifted to New York and tied the series 2–2. In the end, though, White Sox stars Joe Jackson and Eddie Collins proved too good at the plate. Chicago won the 1917 World Series in six games.

The Giants gladly welcomed George back for the 1918 campaign. Just as he did in 1917, Gibson intended to provide coaching support to the team's pitchers and to fill in behind the plate when needed. The year of 1918 marked Gibson's 14th year as a big leaguer and the newspapers took notice. Around that time, the *Reading Times* published an article that pointed out the rarity of Gibson's longevity. Of the 330 men who played in the majors in 1906, only 15 still played when the calendar turned to 1917. Gibson stood, or crouched as the case may suggest, as the lone catcher in that group.[40]

On March 1, the Giants instructed their pitchers and catchers to report to Hot Springs, Arkansas, to begin preseason workouts. McGraw expected Gibson to serve as caretaker during the trip but the catcher made other commitments. Gibson landed at Camp Zachary Taylor, a military installment in Louisville, in order to organize a camp baseball club. It's not clear when Gibson arrived at Taylor but he was certainly there by March 10. A brief note appeared in the *Courier-Journal*:

> George Gibson, the veteran catcher, who was the star backstop with the Pittsburgh Pirates for a number of years, is now stationed at Camp Zachary Taylor as a Captain of a battery. 'Gibby' is organizing a baseball team at Camp Zachary Taylor and in all probability will meet the Colonels in a series of exhibition games. His team will be composed of the best talent at the camp, all of whom are professional players. The team will be under the management of Gibson. Gibson was given his unconditional release by Pittsburgh about two years ago and was later signed by McGraw, of the Giants. He is still on the roster of the Giants.[41]

Just two days later, Gibson left Camp Taylor and trained into St. Louis to rendezvous with the Giants position players. The group then headed to Marlin, Texas, to meet up with the battery folks from Hot Springs. Interestingly, a report out of Louisville on March 14 mentioned an exhibition series between the Camp Taylor baseball team and the Louisville Colonels of the American Association. Newspapers never mentioned George Gibson in association with the Camp Taylor club or with the series.

Coincidentally enough, a report in the *New York Herald* published that very day "confirmed" that Gibson would not play for the Giants in 1918.[42] However, three days later, the *New York Herald* was proven mistaken when the *Houston Post* reported that John McGraw had sent all of his regular pitchers to Rimes Park in Marlin, Texas, "under the careful guidance of Coach George Gibson, the veteran catcher."[43]

The Giants that did land in Hot Springs restricted themselves to light activities. The previous December, the National League issued a ruling that limited clubs to just 30 days of "regular training." After using that time to "straighten out the winter-made kinks of the older players,"[44] the batterymen headed to Marlin to hook up with the rest of the invitees and get spring training started.

With just two weeks to train in Marlin, the Giants jumped into stiff workouts immediately. For the first two days, the Giants, just like Gibby's Pirates, split into two squads. McGraw sent the veteran batterymen to "the old Rimes Park under the command of George Gibson." The remainder of the team "took two sharp workouts at Emerson Field" as McGraw looked on.[45]

When the players reconvened, McGraw instructed McCarty and Gibson to each draft a squad. The two men served as de facto leaders during a best-of-three series of head-to-head matchups. Then, starting on March 25 and lasting through April 4, the Giants played a series of exhibition games throughout Texas. Many of the Giants' opponents for these games were teams made up of enlisted men. Tennis players, boxers, racers and golfers were all holding similar events. Athletic challenges with, and for, military personnel with a common goal: build morale, support the war effort and donate the proceeds to the Red Cross.

After the series of fundraisers, the Giants looked for stiffer competition. Given the bad blood after the previous season's Detroit series, McGraw thought better of challenging the Tigers. He did challenge the White Sox, however, the Sox said a World Series rematch was not feasible. In the end, the Giants kicked off this exhibition against the Cleveland Indians since they were willing to "mix it up with the National League champs."[46] The two teams drew up a 10-game schedule, which started in Texas and then stopped in Louisiana, Mississippi and Tennessee en route to Kentucky. When the series wrapped up on April 13, weather voided three games, one game ended in a tie and the teams split the remaining four games.

On April 16, the Giants opened their season at home with a win over Brooklyn. The Giants then reeled off eight more consecutive victories before they suffered their first loss. On April 28, with their nine-game streak snapped, the Giants headed to Baltimore for an exhibition game against the latest edition of the Orioles, a team unrelated to either of McGraw's previous employers with the same name. George started for the Giants and recorded 13 putouts as backstop. He also carried a hot stick and went 3-for-4 as McGraw's men won 5–2.

On April 30, the Giants traveled to Philadelphia to play the Athletics. "When the game had deteriorated into a romp, McGraw withdrew most of his regulars and the Giants finished with second-string men in the box, behind the bat, at second base, and in the outfield. Still the Phillies were unable to score a solitary run."[47] In his first major-league game of 1918, Gibson did not record an official at bat, putout, assist or error. Many weeks passed before George entered another official game for the Giants, but New York filled their off days with exhibition matches against military teams. George played in a number of these contests.

Even with the supplemental games, the Giants kept winning. Major daily newspapers speculated as to how early they might wrap up the division.

Reporters seemed to agree that they would hit bedrock the first week of July. However, as quickly as that talk started, McGraw's men put an end to it. The team did not exactly implode, but they did lose games in bunches. By the end of May, the Giants' record fell to 26–11, enough for a one-game lead over the 24–12 Cubs. The losing continued and George simply watched from the bench. On June 5, the Cubs moved into first place. Gibson finally returned to action on June 26 in Boston. With the game all but won, George replaced Bill Rariden behind the plate late in the game. Some three months into the season, Gibson finally registered his first official at bat.

The Giants began August by losing 3-of-4 from the Cubs. After the series, United States Secretary of War Newton D. Baker announced there would be "no major league baseball after Sept. 1." The declaration forced every ball player within the draft age to find "essential work."[48] The Chicago Cubs, who used their three wins against the Giants to extend their lead in the standings, did not look back as the finish line neared. McGraw's and Gibson's no-quit attitude permeated the clubhouse and the Giants put up a fight. On August 13, they beat Boston in a doubleheader and thereby registered a 14–0 record against the Braves that season. The pair of wins improved their record to 64–43, and closed the gap on the Cubs to five games.

On August 14, the Giants traveled to Toronto for a matchup with the Toronto Maple Leafs of the International League. Gibson and Schupp teamed up to provide the New York battery. A crowd of 4,000 showed up and witnessed the Giants handily beat Toronto 5–0. Gibson recorded a single in four attempts, seven putouts, two assists and assisted on a double play.

When the Giants returned to league play, they dropped three games to Cincinnati. They found themselves nine wins behind the Cubs with less than two weeks to play. With the fate of their season all but sealed, they headed into Pittsburgh for a three-game set. A doubleheader accounted for the first two games of the series and the teams each won a game. The final game, played on August 20, was never really in question. The Pirates scored early and often on their way to a 10–2 trouncing of the Giants. With the game essentially decided, McGraw again honored the long-time catcher. He sent George Gibson to take up "the mask and protector and relieve Rariden."[49] As expected, the Pittsburgh fans bestowed their adoration on Mooney. In the ninth inning, George managed to wallop a double off of Erskine Mayer in what was his final major-league at bat.

The Giants finished the abbreviated season with a record of 71–53. The Cubs went on to play the Boston Red Sox in the World Series. Babe Ruth and his American League squad won the championship in six games.

For George Gibson, the end of the 1918 season marked the end of his major-league playing career. That season, he appeared in four regular season games, always as a late-inning replacement, and registered a double in two plate appearances. In his major-league career, he played in 1,213 games and finished with a career batting average of .236, recording 1,099 hits, including 15 home runs and 346 RBIs. Gibson finished his career with a fielding percentage of .977 while throwing out 48 percent of would-be base stealers. Although George played his final big-league game in 1918, he was far from through with baseball. Baseball magnates would not squander Gibson's years of knowledge.

10

Gibson to Lead Maple Leafs

Lawrence "Lol" Solman was born on May 14, 1863, in Toronto, Ontario. Solman earned most of his fame and recognition as a theatrical man who cofounded and managed Toronto's famous Royal Alexandra Theatre. Before his involvement with the Royal Alex, Lol spent his twenties chasing different business opportunities across Southern Ontario and Eastern Michigan. In 1893, he returned home to Toronto and settled down to manage the restaurant at the Hanlan's Point Hotel, located on the Toronto Islands. Hanlan's Point is a vacation spot named after early island settler, John Hanlan, who built the first hotel there in the mid–1860s. John's son, Ned, became a world-champion rower when he mastered the craft by rowing to and from the mainland to attend school. Ned Hanlan was a prominent Torontonian, not only as an athlete, but also as a hotelier and city alderman.

Lol Solman married Ned's sister Emily the same year he started at her father's restaurant. After a few years as manager of the restaurant, Lol moved on to serve as the general manager of the Toronto Ferry Company. Solman leveraged his local popularity in order to raise money. Backed by local businessmen and family, Solman morphed Hanlan's Point into a vacation destination that included a sports grounds "inventively" named Hanlan's Point Stadium.

At the end of the 1896 season, the Toronto Canucks, the city's lone professional baseball club, needed help. Due to subpar attendance, the owners looked to offload their franchise. Lol Solman paired with businessman Jim McCaffery and acquired the Canucks. The new owners moved the team to the newly built sporting grounds on Toronto Island.[1]

In Solman and McCaffery's first season as owners, the Canucks won the 1897 Eastern League championship. Many Torontonians used Solman's ferry to visit the Island, and when they did, they watched their hometown team play great baseball. After a few changes of venue, thanks in part to some stadium fires, Solman built his team an expansive steel fortress on the island.

By now christened the Maple Leafs, Solman's team ripped off a string of winning seasons and by the time 1918 arrived, the Leafs owned five championship trophies. That off-season, right about the time the beloved Mooney stepped away from his playing career, Lol traveled to New York in the hopes of finding some fresh blood for his squad.

In New York the Giants brass hosted Gibby at the historic Waldorf-Astoria. The group planned to meet at the hotel to discuss Gibson's future with the club. One day, as Gibby strolled through the lobby, he happened upon fellow Canadian Lol Solman. The two chatted and George later recalled: "Who should I come across but Lol Solman, a theatrical man, head of the ball club, here in Toronto in the old International League. Now Lol Solman come to me and he said, 'Where ya gonna be next year Gibby?' I said, 'Oh, I don't know, as of right now, I'm property of the New York Giants. What's on your mind?' He said, 'I thought maybe I can get you up there to manage that club next year.' Well I said, '...that isn't very far from home, you could throw a stone from there, all the way from there ... my home.'"[2]

The offer piqued Gibson's interest. Not only would the job with the Leafs allow him to stay in Canada and be close to his family, but the offer also provided Gibson with a valuable bargaining chip in his upcoming negotiations with McGraw.

As soon as McGraw and Gibson sat down, George played his ace: "Mac, I had the owner of the Toronto International ball club talk to me, and they want me to go up there and take that ball club next year to manage it. So, what do ya think about it?" McGraw put the question back to Gibson: "What do you think about it Gibby?"[3] George explained to the New York Giants' boss that he knew his playing career had come to an end, but still wanted to be in the game. He also understood that the Giants still held his rights, and he was still with Mac if he wanted him to stay on with the New York club.

McGraw held Gibson in high

Lol Solman, prominent Toronto businessman of the early 20th century. Solman owned the Toronto Maple Leafs Baseball Club when Gibson managed the hogtown team (City of Toronto Archives, *Globe and Mail* fonds, Fonds 1266, Item 15695).

regard and realized the opportunity would benefit George and the Giants. Given Gibson's managerial aspirations, the job with Toronto would provide him with a great launching pad for positions higher up the food chain. For McGraw, having a trusted friend in charge of a high-level minor-league franchise provided him an opportunity to have his younger players develop in a reliable environment. McGraw instructed Gibson to take the job. George agreed and expressed excitement at the chance to work with the Giants' prospects his former boss couldn't utilize in New York.

Before the Maple Leafs could confirm George as their next skipper, he had to go through waivers to gain his freedom. By January 22, 1919, word leaked that the Leafs planned to hire the longtime big-league catcher as their manager. The news elated Toronto fans. The papers celebrated President McCaffery on his choice, perhaps not realizing Lol Solman orchestrated the hire. Those same papers also pointed out that Gibson knew the city of Toronto quite well and that as a Canadian, he came to the position well suited to succeed. Gibson clearly knew the game of baseball; however, the opportunity to work amongst a slew of old friends suggested an easier social transition into his new role.

With the cat out of the bag, team president McCaffery discussed the hiring with the local press. Though Gibson had not yet passed through waivers, McCaffery spoke with certainty: "I am very much pleased at securing Gibson to lead the Maple Leafs. I believe that the appointment of a Canadian to lead the only Canadian team in organized baseball—at least during the past few years—will be a great thing. I had many good men to select from, but I believe the fans are of the same opinion as I am concerning Gibson. He is a veteran of the game, is a quiet, likeable fellow, and I have heard from players who have been with him on the same team that he is a favorite with all. With his years of experience as a catcher he should make a good leader, while his wide connection and ability to know good material when he sees it should prove beneficial to the local club."[4]

These reports made their way to Pittsburgh, where longtime Gibson supporters expressed their approval for the move. The *Pittsburgh Post-Gazette* noted that not since Arthur Irwin in 1898 had a Canadian managed the Toronto club. Then, the paper talked about Gibson's aptitude: "He has the qualifications, including the fighting spirit, and the ability to win respect from his fellow players as well as his rivals. Pittsburgh fans, especially those of Wilkinsburg, where Gibson made his home during the playing season for so many years, were predicting last night that the day is not far distant when this most deserving athlete will be leading a major league club."[5]

The overzealous Pittsburgh fans prematurely had Gibson back in the big leagues as a manager. In reality, that article hit newsstands while George hung in limbo. He had yet to clear waivers and still found his name on the Giants' depth chart. It didn't take much longer. On January 24, George cleared the list and was free to sign with whomever he pleased. While home in London, when Gibson heard the news, he stated: "That sounds good to me, and I expect to get word any day now to go to Toronto and sign with that club."[6]

Before George left for Toronto, some 120 miles away, he decided to make good on his outstanding commitments. As superintendent at the London ice rink, George needed to prepare the arena and its ice for the upcoming bonspiel. That January in Ontario, the weather had been unseasonably warm. Unless the conditions changed, the curling championship would have to be canceled. Gibson believed that with a day of cold weather and a lot of his hard work, he could salvage the event. While it took more than one day of cold, the bonspiel went off without a hitch.[7]

On the evening of January 29, Gibson delivered his John Hancock and officially joined the Toronto Maple Leafs Baseball Club. After he put his pen to paper, Gibson told the press: "I am greatly pleased over the opportunity afforded me in Toronto. Of course I do not know much about the Toronto team and its requirements for the upcoming season, but I know that the policy of the owners is to have a team at the top. It is our intention to take about eighteen players to training camp, which has not yet been selected. The work of selecting and conditioning the team will commence about the middle of April as the season opens on the 10th."[8] After the meeting with McCaffery, Gibson acclimated himself to the local curling scene, now that he had moved on from London. Gibson wandered over to the local arena to watch a much-anticipated curling match between a club from Kitchener and the St. Patricks' rink. George had to take advantage of the downtime as the Leafs planned to get down to business in short order.

Toronto residents took an immediate shine to George and to his family. *The Globe* newspaper reported on his daughter Marguerite's athletic endeavors. As a player on the Princess Pats, a London Collegiate basketball club, Marguerite made her mark during a tournament at the University of Western Ontario. In the tournament, the young Gibson's club defeated the defending champions, New St. James Club. The papers made it a point to highlight young Marguerite's performance: "The great playing of Margaret Gibson ... greatly aided the conquerors of the champions in this well fought game."[9]

As his first order of business, Gibson spent late February planning his team's spring session. McGraw requested that Gibson join the Giants in Gainesville, Florida. Not only would the two squads be able to practice with one another, but Gibson would be able to impart some wisdom on the Giants' young rotation. Before the trip, George took one more chance to enjoy some curling. Gibson joined the London Thistles Curling Club as they attempted to defend the coveted Carew Cup. Skippered by Gibson's good friend F. N. Allen, the Thistles defeated the Galt Granites to retain the trophy. The papers reported that "Mooney Gibson … played brilliantly"[10] as his rink won in an onslaught, 19–9.

On March 21, Gibson made his way south to Gainesville. McGraw, who remained impressed by Gibson's handling of his staff in 1917 and 1918, reiterated his earlier position. McGraw instructed Gibby to "take my pitchers … a week. Instruct them what you want them to do."[11] The new Toronto manager took the opportunity to scout players for his Toronto team; however, other International League managers showed up in North Florida to recruit ballplayers too. Fellow Canadian Arthur Irwin, manager of the Rochester Hustlers, vied with Gibson for big-league cuts and castoffs. Even so, Gibson's relationship with the Giants gave him the upper hand and he snagged three Giants Yannigans. Always one to make the most of any opportunity, Gibson made sure to take a crack at any camp he could find while he trained back to Toronto. Gibby visited the Brooklyn Robins' camp in Jacksonville and the Pirates' camp in Birmingham, Alabama. He secured a few players along the way, and with the first day of spring training on the island scheduled for April 10, Gibby arrived with a full corps of potentials.

One of those possible players happened to be Gibson himself. He did not plan on leading the Leafs from the dugout; instead, he intended to do so from behind the plate. Bad weather delayed the start of camp at Hanlan's Point. That said, the inclement weather gave Gibby an opportunity to see what kind of quality he had in the field. The new playing grounds did not provide the quality Gibby required, so he approached University of Toronto authorities to try and gain access to the school's facilities. Gibby ended up rebuffed as the university field had just been ploughed and seeded. As a last resort, Gibson secured the Toronto Exhibition grounds, the last suitable place in town for proper spring work.

On the 11th, the weather let up and the Leafs practiced on their home field at Hanlan's Point. The stadium's heavy-duty construction shielded the eager players from strong winds, but conditions were far from ideal. As a result, Gibson kept things light. He instructed the team to do some running, throwing and fungo hitting. The fickle Canadian spring weather continued throughout camp; this prompted Gibson to prepare his players indoors at the Old Fort on the Exhibition grounds. Suitable for the pitchers and catchers, the space prevented the position players from performing a full complement of their training activities. Despite the weather problems, the group of players impressed Gibson and he even told reporters that "in all his experience he has never seen a more ambitious squad."[12]

Toronto's first spring test came against the Pittsburg Stars, a black team from Buffalo, New York. In front of twenty-thousand Toronto fans, the Buffalo amateurs blew out the Leafs 7–0. The Toronto papers attributed the loss to a lack of conditioning on the part of the Leafs players, but, in reality, the

Buffalo club just outplayed Gibson's crew. As promised, George competed alongside his players; he caught all nine innings.

As the score suggests, Buffalo's pitcher Dick Redding stole the show. In fact, it's highly likely Gibson expected a performance like that. In advance of the game, *The Globe* wrote that Redding was "said to be another Walter Johnson, and only his color bars him from the major leagues." Clearly, Redding's reputation preceded him, certainly on account of his accomplishments. In a barnstorming match versus the Boston Red Sox, Redding struck out Babe Ruth with the bases loaded. Against Toronto, he lived up to his billing and allowed only five hits in a complete game shutout. Following the game, *The Globe*, confirmed the pitcher's brilliance: "Redding, their big twirler, lived up to advance notices and held the Gibsonites at his mercy."[13] The next day, Gibson's men came away victorious. Redding did not pitch.

During their last week of camp, the Leafs took on local teams. First they tackled St. Michael's College and then they scrimmaged against a team from the Canadian Army's Third Battalion. Once camp concluded, Gibson trimmed the fat from the roster and then headed for Newark, New Jersey, to open the season at Harrison Field.

Every International League team started their season on April 30. Gibson's Leafs matched up against manager Patsy Donovan's Newark Bears of the Garden State. Manager Gibson sent the young Bill Hubbell, one of McGraw's final cuts, to the rubber. *The Globe* described Gibson's opening day pitcher: "Hubbell is regarded by McGraw as one of the best young pitching prospects he has ever had. Hubbell needs experience only, and McGraw believes that with George Gibson in Toronto he will get the coaching and experience necessary to make him a big league star by the end of the season."[14] The Giants prospect pitched a very clean opening day and allowed the Bears only five hits in a 7–1 Maple Leafs victory. In his first minor-league game since his time with Montreal, Gibson worked behind the plate and made one hit in four official plate appearances. Toronto fans, management and George himself were quite pleased with his managerial debut.

Gibson caught his second, and final, game of the season a few days later against Bill Donovan and his Jersey City Skeeters. Bill Hubbell pitched brilliantly again and gave up only five hits in an 11–3 Leafs victory. Gibby went 1-for-4 at the plate again which left him with a .250 batting average for the season (2-for-8). Recognizing that his job was as much about raising talent as winning, George stepped aside to let up-and-coming backstop Gus Sandberg take the big mitt for the rest of 1919.

The Leafs won five of their first seven games, which in turn delighted Gibson: "That's a pretty good beginning, when you consider we had only six days of outdoor practice before we toed the mark. Our team still needs another week of warm weather to get right, but I'm not worried, as other teams are in the same fix."[15] Gibson went on to say that his pitchers were rounding into good form, and also noted that pitchers Hubbell and Johnny "Admiral" Jones had an advantage over his other hurlers thanks to their Giants practices. On May 12, the Leafs returned home for their opener at Hanlan's Point. Seventy-five hundred fans turned out to cheer on their hometown Maple Leafs. Bill Hubbell got the ball for Toronto and pitched a swell match as he surrendered only six Newark hits. Unfortunately for the Leafs, Bears pitcher Eddie Rommel, who went on to become the father of the modern knuckleball, no-hit his opponents en route to a 1–0 victory.

Gibby's crew played tremendous baseball throughout May. This included a sixteen-inning affair at the Buffalo Baseball Park, versus the Bisons, on the 26th. The game got interesting in the tenth inning when umpire M. J. Stockdale delivered a call in favor of the Bisons. Most, if not all, of the Leafs felt the ball was fair despite it being called foul. A contingent of Maple Leafs surrounded the umpire feeling they had been cheated. For what it's worth, the *Buffalo Evening News* proclaimed Stockdale's call a perfect decision. Cooler heads prevailed until the eleventh, when, from the Leafs' dugout, Gibson vigorously insulted Stockdale. The umpire ran out of patience and ordered, "Gibson, to the clubhouse!"[16] Gibby went into a frenzy. He ran onto the field yelling profanities, grabbed the umpire and put his clenched fists in Stockdale's face. Stockdale nonchalantly walked away from Gibson. This only infuriated the Leafs boss further. Again, his players joined him and bombarded Stockdale. The chaos forced the umpire to take action. The *Buffalo Enquirer* reported he "was threatened with bodily harm on one occasion having to call the police to drive away the swarming band of Canucks."[17] City police officers broke up the uneasiness on the diamond and removed Gibson from the field of play. In defiance and protest, George continued to run his team from the grandstand. The Leafs won 4–1. By the end of the month, the Leafs had a half-game lead over Jack Dunn's Baltimore Orioles. Arthur Irwin's Rochester club sat in third place, four games back of Toronto.

Gibby's Leafs continued their solid play through June. Four of the five starting pitchers won at least three games in that time span. Meanwhile, Gibson soured on International League umpires. On June 22, Gibby got into another argument with the ball game's home plate arbitrator. Gibson contested umpire Philben's third strike call. He rushed the adjudicator, shouting expletives, and Philben promptly ordered Gibson from the game. Gibson hesitated to leave the field, but when the umpire pulled out his pocket watch and imposed a threat for a time violation, George thought better of it and left the field unhappily. The Leafs won the game. Despite Gibson's antics, the Leafs maintained a steady pace, albeit they slipped in the standings. When June concluded, Baltimore sat atop the leaderboard, and the Gibsonites found themselves three-and-a-half games back.

Gibby's crew tore the cover off the ball in July. On the 22nd, the Toronto Ball Club entered a series with the Orioles on the heels of a fifteen-game winning streak. While the Orioles held a six-game lead in the standings, the Leafs took two of the three games, which lopped one off of the deficit. Gibson finally had a chance to gloat over Jack Dunn and his Orioles. Gibson expressed confidence in his club and stated that he would not make any changes to the team down the stretch if they kept on winning. A week later, the Leafs found themselves seven games behind the Baltimore Club with just one month to play.

Gibson felt he had to go out and get more hitting because his club was still losing ground. He acquired the services of former Chicago Cub Frank Schulte, a player-manager for the Binghamton Bingoes, also of the International League. Other clubs were upset with Gibson for breaking an unwritten rule against picking up extra players for a pennant run. He told *The Globe*, "If they can get away with it, all right. If I am up there well in the race and I don't get the players, that's my fault. I would never complain if a club wanted to carry forty players."[18] The real question wasn't if Gibson had too many players, it was were his late signings enough to catch Jack Dunn's Orioles?

On August 7, the Leafs remained four games back as they headed into a two-game series in Baltimore. The Dunnmen trounced the Gibsonites in both games by a combined score of 15–4, ultimately ending any hopes the Maple Leafs had of securing the 1919 pennant. Toronto closed out the season at Hanlan's Point, with two wins against Baltimore. They were playing for pride at that point as Jack Dunn's first-class club paced the league with one hundred wins and the first of their seven straight championships.

Near the end of the season, fans started to second guess Gibson's work in 1919. They pointed to, amongst other things, the fact that the team finished seventh in composite batting average in an eight-team league. *The Globe* quickly defended the manager and reminded fans that Gibson had guided the club to a second-place finish. The paper also noted that the club remained in contention primarily because of Gibby's management, in particular, his handling of the pitching staff. They pointed out to readers that Gibson couldn't control when his players would put bat to ball.[19]

Despite their feelings, the fans' behavior suggested anything but unhappiness. Prior to the season, Gibson assured the Leafs brass that fans would show up both regularly and in force. His prediction turned out to be accurate. Gate receipts for 1919 far exceeded ownership's expectations. As Gibby later recalled: "We put people in those stands, in those bleachers, that hadn't been sat in for seven or eight years."[20]

He also recalled an accident during one home game that involved the bleachers themselves. A section of the wooden stands that had decayed due to neglect broke under the weight of the unusually large crowd. Many fans were injured. Gibson headed right into the crowd, tore off his shirt and fashioned a tourniquet for a fan who had cut his arm. The cut punctured an artery which in turn caused blood to hemorrhage whenever his heart pulsed. Without Gibson's quick and compassionate thinking, the fan would have lost a tremendous amount of blood.[21]

In spite of conditions at the ballpark, Torontonians continued to come out regularly to root on Gibson and his club. The successful season led Lol Solman to eagerly inquire about Gibson's availability for 1920. George told his friend that he would not commit to anything until the winter. Gibson didn't disclose that an old boss had also inquired about his availability in 1920.[22] With some off-season commitments already in place, Gibson put next season on the back burner.

Following the season, Gibson scheduled a brief barnstorming tour with three teams from the Class B Michigan-Ontario League. They started the tour against the Brantford Red Sox. Gibson played his top players, including the veteran Frank Schulte, but the Brantford club defeated the International League club, 5–1. The following day, the Leafs faced the London Tecumsehs. Despite hailing from a lower-class league, London topped the AA Maple Leafs by a 3–2 score. In the final game of the trip, the Leafs blew an early 5–0 lead and lost 7–6 to the Hamilton Tigers. In the September 13 edition of the *Hamilton Spectator*, the paper asserted that the teams from the Michigan-Ontario League were on par with Gibson's Class AA squad. The paper spoke of Gibson being sour, with their headline stating, "Manager Mooney Gibson is Through With Barnstorming Forever." The *Spectator* reporter wrote that "Gibson was not only disappointed with the gate receipts, but he also felt a bit peeved at the game finish by his hirelings, three defeats from Class B proving a bitter dose to take. The Gibsonites had visions of glorious financial reception from the 'bush,' but the 'bushers' failed to fall. Possibly next year 'Mooney' may be enticed to visit the fall fairs, Rockton and other places still being open for some of the old-time attractions."[23]

The old boss that had repeatedly called Gibson throughout the final month of the 1919 campaign was Barney Dreyfuss. When Dreyfuss inquired as to Gibson's contract status for 1920, Mooney informed the Colonel that his season closed on September 14, and instructed the Pirates owner to call back after that. Right on cue, Dreyfuss called George on the 15th and offered him the 1920 Pirates' managerial position. The timing was perfect. Gibson, after spending two years under the tutelage of McGraw and one year leading the Maple Leafs, seemed ready to take the helm of a major-league club. Gibby remembered thinking, "Here's the man that I could have hanged, calling me up wanting to know what I was gonna do the next year."[24] George was still upset with Dreyfuss for placing him on waivers and discarding his "old carcass," but was willing to consider the proposal.

Before he accepted the offer, Gibson wanted an in-person review of the Pirates' roster. In 1919, the Pirates, managed by Hugo Bezdek, compiled a 71–68 record resulting in a fourth-place finish. While that may not sound so terrible, they ended up a whopping 24½ games behind the pennant-winning Cincinnati Reds. The bad finish is not why the managerial position needed to be filled. The management job opened up because Bezdek, famed college football boss, received an offer to coach and act as athletic director at Penn State University. It was an offer the football-minded skipper could not refuse. Gibson timed his visit to Pittsburgh to coincide with a Pirates series against McGraw's Giants.[25]

Adding some intrigue to the trip, Gibson didn't tell Dreyfuss about the visit; coincidentally, Dreyfuss departed for New York just as Gibson arrived for the Pirates-Giants series. However, for someone trying to stay off of Dreyfuss's radar, Gibson did anything but keep a low profile.

Prior to one of the contests, he made his way onto the field to chat up McGraw. As soon as he touched the grass, he received a standing ovation from the crowd. The Pittsburgh faithful used the opportunity to try and woo Gibson back to their club. While they were most likely unaware of the reason for the visit in the first place, fans peppered Gibson with suggestions in the form of questions. Gibson recalled hearing "Are ya coming back Gibby? You gonna come to the club?" Gibson continued over to speak with McGraw and as soon as he got within good ear shot, the Giants skipper shouted to George that he wanted him back with the Giants. McGraw frustratingly apprised Gibson on what he thought of his time in Toronto, "What ya do, you made them a million dollars. What did I do? I lost a million dollars by letting you go."[26]

It's hard to think of better statement on just how remarkable people in baseball considered Gibson to be. Here in the midst of a major-league season, one of the most influential owners in the history of the game found himself in a tug of war with perhaps the most famous manager of all time. Quite the circumstance for such an underappreciated individual.

As the conversation between Gibson and McGraw progressed, it became painstakingly obvious to George how much John wanted him back on the Giants. Try as he did, McGraw never had a chance to win him back. Gibson retired to his seat to watch the ball game and get a sense of what type of ball club he would inherit if he took the job in Pittsburgh. Gibson understood the high expectations, so he wanted to be sure he could work with the players on the current Bucs roster.

Meanwhile, in New York, Dreyfuss attended a special National League owners meeting. It's not a complete surprise then that in the midst of baseball folks, he caught wind of Gibson's presence in the Steel City. Strolling onto the field in front of 23,000 fans will have that kind of result. When Barney heard the news, the excited owner hurried home in order to conference with his ex-catcher.

Dreyfuss made it back to Pittsburgh in time to catch George at one of the Pirates-Giants contests. After the game, the two went for an informal meeting and Dreyfuss's desperation really hit a boiling point. Dreyfuss had to wrap up a business meeting and didn't want to lose the opportunity to sit down with the elusive Gibson. In addition, he wanted to keep George sequestered away from outsiders' eyes. He liked to keep his negotiations as private as possible. To solve both problems, the Pittsburgh boss convinced his secretary-treasurer to lock Gibson in the umpires' room. Even more amazing than the request is that they succeeded. After they hid Gibson for an hour, Dreyfuss finally sat down to talk business with the man he knew he needed. The meeting was brief as Dreyfuss quickly laid down the offer. George agreed to take the team on the condition that Barney and he settle their differences. That last hurdle would have to wait, though, since George had a family vacation to take. His old friend asked that George "say hello to Mrs. Gibson and the kids" as the manager left for the South.[27]

Barney's best attempts at secrecy failed. Rumors of the hire persisted throughout the autumn months of 1919. The *Daily Post* told fans there would be no better appointment than Gibby, a man who knew the game inside and out. Despite the papers' adulation of Gibson, President Dreyfuss denied that his ex-backstop would be the new manager. Gibson himself denied the gossip, "My sole idea in coming to Pittsburgh was to see John J. McGraw."[28] Even after being told the managerial position was in doubt, the *Pittsburgh Daily Post* assured their readership that George was the frontrunner for the gig.

President Dreyfuss had a long list of candidates which included Johnny Evers, Jack Hendricks, Patsy Flaherty, Lee Fohl and Joe Doyle, among others. But just like in 1916, the rumor mill counted Gibson as the top man. Gibson studied opposing players with great diligence and learned each athlete's style, weaknesses and strengths. Though he certainly acquired this information by watching opposing players, Gibson also studied the newspapers to get tips on opposing lineups and mentally recorded which players were hot with the stick. He would have his pitcher approach the hot hitter in a stingy manner which greatly benefited his staff. Former manager Fred Clarke often asked Gibby his thoughts on game situations and rival players. Gibson enthusiastically accrued that information and went so far as to say: "What I'm interested in, is the players on the other teams. The ones we must oppose. It's always easier to beat an enemy if you can get a line on his tactics."[29] As if that were not enough, the *Post* continued to heap on the praise. They acknowledge the job he did with Toronto and how he tutored those many young Giants.

National League umpires were also in favor of hiring Gibson to manage. In the experience of most umpires, Gibson handled his discrepancies in a gentlemanly way. Gibby would say his piece and go sit down. He was always honest with the umpiring crew, so they trusted him. One National League adjudicator told a Pittsburgh paper, "There isn't a man in the game for whom I have a higher regard. Several times after close plays I have asked Gibson for his opinion, and he has informed me without hesitation that the decision was correct or that it was wrong, as the case might be, and no matter whether it went in favor of his team or against it, I've never known him to speak anything but the truth."[30] This umpire thought of George as a shining example of how a baseball player should behave on the field.

Near the end of November, the minor-league meetings were held in Springfield, Massachusetts. Barney Dreyfuss called Gibson to tell him about the meetings and told him that he was traveling by way of Buffalo. He asked Gibson to meet him there. Gibby agreed to get on a train and traverse the 143 miles from London to the Lafayette Hotel in Buffalo. After pleasantries were exchanged between the men and lunch came around, Barney Dreyfuss took Gibson into the dining room and said, "Well, we've got something to settle. You said you'd take the ball club, if. What is it?" Gibson pointed out to his one-time boss that he didn't receive any salary from July 1916 until the end of the season that year. George informed Dreyfuss, "You realized $1,800 [$1,500]. The very thing you said you wouldn't do, you got $1,800 [$1,500] off of my broken down old carcass. Now then. Let's settle that one!" Dreyfuss immediately agreed to give Gibson his past salary, simply saying, "All right … you'll get it." Gibson said that the contract that he signed in 1909 was for $12,000 and agreed to manage for the same salary plus bonuses: $500 if they finished fourth, $3,000 if they finished third and $5,500 if they finished second. That's as far as Gibson went. Dreyfuss responded, "Well as long as you win the pennant I'll give you the damn ballpark."[31] No papers were signed, but a gentlemen's agreement had been made.

Secretary Leslie Constans announced the hire to the press. Constans told reporters that Gibson had been weighing the contract terms offered by Dreyfuss, and on the morning of December 8, Pittsburgh brass received a

Pittsburgh Press **cartoon of George Gibson (courtesy the** *Pittsburgh Post-Gazette*).

telegram from Gibson. The telegram related this message: "Your terms accepted. More than pleased to be with the Pirates again. Will meet you in New York Wednesday."[32]

On December 11, Gibson met with President Dreyfuss at the baseball winter meetings in New York. The two discussed important club matters such as the team's spring training sites. After Gibson departed in 1916, the Bucs rotated their preseason homes. In 1917, under manager Jimmy Callahan, the team trained in Columbus, Georgia. Under Hugo Bezdek, the Pirates held camp in Jacksonville, Florida, in 1918 and then in Birmingham, Alabama, in 1919. Always a man of routine, Gibson selected Hot Springs, Arkansas, for spring training and suggested either West Baden Springs, Indiana, or Dawson Springs, Kentucky, for pre-camp conditioning. These were the Pirates' training facilities when Gibson caught for the Pirates in his glory days.

Gibson also formally spoke at the winter meetings about his return to Pittsburgh:

> I am delighted to be at Pittsburgh and expect to make a flying trip there within a few weeks. I hope to reside in Wilkinsburg next summer, as usual. I will give the fans and the ball club the very best that is in me, and that's just about all one person can give. Having a pretty good opportunity to keep in touch with Pittsburgh, I am able to have a very fair knowledge of the timber on hand. Not a few of the present Pirates are former teammates of mine. Such as Babe Adams, Wilbur Cooper, Walter Schmidt, Max Carey and several others. I know just what they can do. As for deals, I've tried to start something, but in each effort it's been the old story of everybody wishing to capture two or three of your brightest stars in exchange for some player they don't need and whom nobody else would want. If any of our players are turned loose, believe me, it will be in trade for something that is sure to add strength to the team.[33]

After the meetings, the Bucs made reservations at the Hotel Eastman in Hot Springs; the early booking assured them lodging, meals and first crack at the hot baths. George explained: "I consider Hot Springs the best place in the world for ball players to prepare themselves. I have been at many training camps in much warmer latitudes, but they are not equipped with such bathing facilities as are to be found at the Arkansas town."[34]

Gibson's old friend, renowned Pittsburgh writer Ralph Davis, explained to his readers how well-qualified Gibson was for the job: "No one can deny that Gibson knows baseball. He learned it under Fred Clarke, and afterwards played under John McGraw, the most sagacious leader the game has known. President Dreyfuss does not deny that the fact that Gibby had a course of instruction under New York was a point considered in his favor when it came to thinking about a manager here for next season. Gibson not only knows baseball, but he knows the ballplayers, as well, and what is more to the point, he knows human nature, and has the knack of getting along amicably with his fellow man. Probably no more popular player than Gibson ever wore a

Pittsburgh uniform. He was well liked not only by the players on his own team, but by all the rival athletes, and by managers of other teams, too."[35] The *Pittsburgh Daily Post* wrote a lighter note in regards to Gibson's return to the Steel City:

> When Gibson first enlisted with the local club, somebody sent his name in as George H. Gibson. As it was impossible to ascertain what the middle letter stood for, one of the baseball writers referred to him as George Hackenschmidt Gibson. Because of his great strength he was named in honor of the old wrestler. This nickname clung to him and he is still referred to by many local admirers as "Hack" Gibson. As a matter of fact, Gibby never possessed a middle name or even an initial.
>
> In the International League, where he started his professional career, the big catcher is known as "Mooney" Gibson. How he came to get this moniker has been explained in various ways from time to time, but Gibby says he never could give a reason for acquiring such a handle. When he was a small boy in his native town of London, Ont., one of his playmates bestowed the name of "Mooney" upon him and it continues to be the popular way of referring to him among his many Canadian admirers.[36]

No matter what people called him, the hiring pleased the Pittsburgh faithful and they could not wait for the 1920 season to get underway.

11

Back in the Big Leagues

At thirty-nine years old, George Gibson found himself back in the "Grandes Ligas" after a one-year absence. He took the helm of his former team, the Pittsburgh Pirates. George reported to Pittsburgh in early January for a meeting with President Dreyfuss.

When Gibson arrived in Pittsburgh, the Pirates greeted their newly appointed manager with a surprise dinner at the Concordia Club. Barney Dreyfuss, members of the Pirates' staff, players, local reporters and dignitaries all attended. For his first order of business, Gibson relocated the team back to West Baden Springs and Hot Springs for their preseason training.

Gibson must have been excited to return to the comforts of Whittington Park, the field in Hot Springs that the Pirates usually occupied. Unfortunately, other professional clubs had grown wise to the playing grounds. In 1920, the Boston Red Sox swooped in to secure the field, thus leaving the Pirates to find alternate digs. The Bucs arranged to use Fordyce Field, a solid consolation prize. Still, Gibson must have been disappointed. While other big-league clubs had used Fordyce Field in the past, Gibson didn't know its comforts as he had never played there.

Meanwhile, Gibson had to contend with changes to the environment while his players got used to the new world order. Previous skipper Hugo Bezdek did not hold early camp for his pitchers. That changed when Gibson took charge. Gibson clearly felt pitchers needed more seasoning than position players. He elaborated his feelings to local papers:

Nothing pleases me better than the idea of taking the pitchers to West Baden for an extra week of work. I would not want the entire team to start training at that time. After seeing several clubs go through their spring training practice I have made up my mind that the old system which was carried out by Fred Clarke for so many successful seasons is just a little better than all the rest.

By taking the entire team to training camp at the same time, it is my belief that the progress of players is greatly retarded. The pitchers cannot start in all at once using all their speed. They must go about it gradually in order not to overtax the delicate machinery of their salary arms.

…

The pitcher requires a more complicated course of treatment. He carries some wonderful muscular mechanism in the arm in which he delivers the ball to the batsmen. He would not dare take a chance at wrenching any of those dainty nerves and tendons by beginning with a rush. After the long winter's rest, he must start off gradually, and then it requires little more than a week to ten days to bring him to that stage of the game where he can cut loose without danger of injuring the wing that earns him his bread and butter.

That is why I am not taking anybody except the pitchers and catchers to West Baden. It will not hurt the catchers to take a little extra time to develop their arms, for the valuable backstop must be able to peg with great accuracy. However, the prime reason for having them on hand so early is to aid the pitchers in warming up. Oh, Yes! I have planned all along to have the men get into their uniforms every day they are at the Indiana camp.[1]

Before he had to battle the rigors of the marathon that was a major-league season, George returned to London for a little rest and relaxation. Even so, there was no way for him to do that given his new title and the accompanying duties. Serving as a manager at the highest level of the game brought a lot of at-

George Gibson circa 1920 (Healy Collection).

tention and admiration; however, it also brought a great deal of obligation. On February 28, Gibby returned to Pittsburgh and attended a big birthday bash for his good friend Honus Wagner. The Flying Dutchman's party took place in Butler, Pennsylvania, a small town approximately thirty-three miles north of Pittsburgh.

The Butler County stove leaguers, a group of baseball fans who discussed the sport around a "hot stove" in the winter months, organized the event. Four hundred guests packed the local Masonic Temple to listen to a bevy of speeches from various Pirates supporters. Both Dreyfuss and Gibson provided brief statements that honored Wagner's baseball career. Then the icon himself took the stage. Even in the midst of his own celebration, Honus Wagner doled out praise onto the Pirates' beloved George Gibson. The fact that one of the greatest ballplayers in the history of the game took time to praise Gibson is noteworthy enough. That Wagner did so in the middle of his own party is another thing altogether. The Flying Dutchmen went on to say:

> Mr. Gibson is the type of fellow who is fair as long as the other fellow is fair. Gibby is broad, but if anyone tramps on his toes he'll be on top of 'em before they know what has happened. I played long enough with Gibby to know him. He may not grab off the pennant right at the start, but you can feel safe that there will be action every day, every hour and every minute that the Pirates are playing with Gibson at their head.
>
> George Gibson got his schooling under Fred Clarke, who, in my opinion, was the smartest manager of baseball. Gibby was brought up under Clarke's idea of baseball, and that idea was good enough to win four pennants and a world series. George knows that Fred had the proper system and he will use much of it in running the Pirates. All he needs is the proper opportunity.[2]

The succeeding day, Gibson led a squad of hurlers and backstops to West Baden Springs. Then, on March 2, the club engaged in their first workouts in preparation for the 1920 campaign. The morning activities included a vivacious exercise program composed by Gibson. The routine included running and throwing drills as well as bunting instructions. The activities helped players limber up after a long off-season of relaxation and idleness. Then, just as he did in his playing days, Gibson led a two-hour afternoon hike through the Orange County hills. In between workout sessions, the Pirates chief made sure all of his soldiers drank the revitalizing water of the famous Arkansas springs.

Over the next few days, Gibson led his team through a few light exercises and drills. Even with the lighter workload, Gibson insisted his players drink the natural spring water. At one drinking session, Gibby's five-year-old son, Billy, who was designated the team's mascot, took down a second large glass of the pungent liquid and expressed to his father and the players that he did it to wash down the first glass. The Pirates players must have seemed like a boisterous bunch of big brother types to the young Gibson. Billy's antics stemmed from his eagerness to be accepted by his father's men.

Terrible weather plagued the final days in Indiana. Heavy downpours of rain and even a brief spell of snow hampered the Bucs' remaining outdoor training plans, but Gibson pressed his team onward. Gibson told the papers: "We can't manufacture our own weather, but we can do one thing, and that is to make the best of it."[3] The avant-garde manager had the men do their baseball work in the hotel's gymnasium and their cardiovascular activities at the resort's covered bicycle track. Some of his men, including veterans Babe Adams and Wilbur Cooper felt it all right to take the ball outside in the unfavorable conditions, which prompted Gibson to tell them: "You fellows take to this work like ducks to water."[4] Impressed by their dedication but concerned about potential injuries, the skipper ordered his players back to the sheltered gym.

At 9:15 a.m. on March 7, George and the Pirates batterymen departed Indiana via train en route to St. Louis. When they arrived in the largest populated city of the Show Me State, the men transferred to the Iron Mountain train. The long-haul, overnight locomotive brought the ball players from St. Louis to Hot Springs on the Southern Railway. There, the squad convened with the rest of the team.

When the team got to work on March 8, they did so two men down. Outfielder Billy Southworth did not show up to camp on time, but reported within the week. The other man, top catcher Walter Schmidt, whose holdout caused Gibson a good bit of anxiety, stayed away for much longer. Gibson stated: "The fellow who likes to play ball and desires to remain in the game has no excuse for wrangling all spring over the terms of his contract. He is hurting himself more than anybody, for if he loses the benefits of the training the chances are that he will not be worth much to the club all the year."[5]

Despite the absence of those two well-regarded men, Gibby wasted no time and held the first practice the very day they set foot in Hot Springs. The *Pittsburgh Post-Gazette* reported: "Gibson led his men to the field and soon had his boys 'snapping into it' like a real top sergeant."[6] Clearly, Gibson felt that strict discipline gave his players the direction and foundation they needed to succeed in the upcoming season.

Save for the missing men, camp went off without a hitch. Early in camp, Gibby watched as his team played back-to-back days against the Boston Red Sox. Though his team lost both games, Gibson seemed satisfied with the performance. Gibby's Pirates lost by only one run in each game and out-hit the Bostonian's in both matches. The Bucs' offence wasn't a problem; it was the club's fielding. The team made six errors in the two games, something Gibson was sure he would remedy by the start of the regular season.

As the team headed towards opening day, roster moves were not the only changes to contend with. In an attempt to help diminish the overwhelming advantages the rules provided to pitchers, baseball outlawed "freak" pitches prior to the 1920 campaign. To help make sure teams caught on, the league dispatched officials to the various team camps around the country. Umpire extraordinaire Bill Klem visited Hot Springs.

Klem advised the Pirates that pitchers were no longer allowed to doctor the ball with bodily substances, thus reducing the use of the spitball. Nor were they allowed to scuff the ball excessively, thus eliminating the pitch made famous by Russ Ford. However, pitchers who already threw the spitball were grandfathered in. The rules only prevented new arrivals from tossing it. Umpire Klem concluded the Pirates had no freak pitchers: "'Am I correct?'

inquired Klem, turning to Manager Gibson. 'That's right,' replied Gibby, 'We have no spitters on our club.'"[7]

Back on the field, the Pirates marched on towards opening day. The club's tour of the Texas and the Southern leagues went as well as could have been envisioned. From April 2 through April 12, the Pirates racked up 10 victories against 0 defeats. After the dominating road trip that included stops in Fort Worth, Dallas, Shreveport, Little Rock and Memphis, Gibby's club stood ready to open the season in St. Louis. Although the team looked ready, George knew he had a major problem on his hands: Walter Schmidt remained AWOL.

On the eve of the new season, Gibson sided with his catcher. However, Gibson encouraged the catcher to meet with club management: "The ball player cannot be blamed for trying to induce his employer to pay him more money, but he should use judgement in his method of going after it. I would advise any young man in the business to reason the matter over fully with the club owner and if at first they cannot come to an understanding through their correspondence, let them get together personally and talk contract. They can do better this way than in any other."[8] Gibby eventually put his foot down and warned President Dreyfuss that if the Bucs did not bring back Schmidt, he would voluntarily leave his managerial post. Before George signed the contract to manage the Bucs, he stipulated he wanted no interference from the club president on baseball matters. The *Pittsburgh Daily Post* published an excerpt from an argument between Gibson and Dreyfuss:

> GIBSON: "We must have Shmidt."
> DREYFUSS: "Not unless he accepts terms."
> GIBSON: "We must have Schmidt, at his own terms if necessary. The club is bad enough, even with him. Without him, it's hopeless. And furthermore, the pitchers insist on having him."
> DREYFUSS: "We will not have Schmidt unless he will play for the terms I offer him—and I am running this ball club."
> GIBSON: "If you don't get Schmidt, you and your ball club can go to _____."[9]

Gibson's scare tactic paid off. The Bucs skipper received a telegram from Walter Schmidt just three days before the start of the season. Schmidt informed Gibson that he had signed; however, he would miss the season opening series on account of the missed practice time. Neither Dreyfuss nor Gibson spoke to the press about the signing, but Schmidt himself reported he would receive $8,000 for the season.[10] Gibson, even without his top catcher, or a full understanding of his team's talents, seemed optimistic when he spoke to reporters on the eve of his managerial debut:

> I think we have a dandy ball club and I'm not looking for any alibis. To my way of thinking, it is foolish for a manager to say where he is going to finish. I am confident we have a good team, but don't know just how strong the other clubs in the league

are going to be. Nearly every fan knows we have been doing some experimenting in several positions, but I can say without reservation that I feel satisfied that the holes will be plugged successfully.[11]

In Gibby's first game as bench boss, the Pirates defeated the Branch Rickey–led St. Louis Cardinals 5–4. The hotly contested match stretched 10 innings and included contributions from a number of Canadians. In addition to the Canadian on the bench, J. J. Clarke represented Canada on the field and served as the Pirates' catcher. Meanwhile, longtime umpire and fellow Canadian Bob Emslie adjudicated.

The Pirates started the season 5–1, an encouraging sign for the club faithful. The hot streak seemed to discourage the Pirates' opponents as much as it excited the fanbase. After the Bucs swept the Reds, winners of the 1919 World Series, Cincinnati manager Pat Moran said that any team managed "by a man as brainy as George Gibson is bound to be dangerous at all times, if it has any native ability at all."[12] While Gibson's lineup had native ability in spades, the comment spoke to Gibson's managerial prowess. Sure, two of the Pittsburgh starting nine went on to the Hall of Fame, but Moran knew that a team with Gibson in charge and even a hint of talent would be dangerous at any time. The Canadian possessed the talent for both instructing players and managing personalities. President Dreyfuss expressed optimism, "There is no doubt that we have an improved team this year, and I believe Gibson will get the very best out of the men."[13]

On April 23, Pirates fans had their first chance to see the Gibsonian Buccaneers. The Pirates hosted the St. Louis Cardinals in the home opener. *Pittsburgh Press* reporter Ralph Davis wrote that "18,000 enthusiasts braved pneumonia and kindred ills to see the opening game of the season in Pittsburg."[14] Honus Wagner memorably marked the occasion and threw out the ceremonial first pitch to Gibson. Unfortunately, the ritual turned out to be the only positive moment for the Pirates that day as the Cardinals toppled the Bucs 9–7.

As April turned to May and eventually early June, the Pirates' hot start became but a distant memory. During the two weeks between May 22 and June 11, the club imploded and finished the abysmal stretch with four wins against twelve defeats. The sixteen-game set obliterated any hopes for the pennant. When it started, the Pirates sat on top of the National League standings. By the time they returned to playing decent baseball, the Bucs stood in sixth place. Even as they dropped in the standings, though, Gibson never doubted his club: "A team that has not been hitting a lick for the past two weeks and can stick up within four and one-half games of the top certainly looks to me to have the stuff, and, with 115 games left to be played, we are going to show the fans of the National League circuit the brand of stuff of which we are made."[15] By the end of June, the Pirates sunk to a game under the .500 mark. Surprisingly, they found themselves just five games behind the first-place Reds.

On the heels of their poor performance, the *Post-Gazette*'s Charles J. Doyle noted the Pirates to be just the eighth-best hitting team in the National League. Pretty terrible considering the league included just eight teams. Still, the Pirates used August to climb into third place in the National League. Doyle concluded that Gibson's managing allowed the team to stay competitive. The reporter postulated that Gibson's experience as a pitcher's sage, and by extension his management of the pitching staff, kept the Pirates in the hunt.

Further to the point, he was impressed by Gibson's ability to build the team's morale: "Gibson has exerted a spirit of harmony which has kept the club off the rocks in the absence of hitting power and the plentitude of infield wobbles. There are clubs higher in the race than the Bucs whereon the practice of co-operation is far below the standard of the 1920 Pirates. Anyone who has been with the club and who has observed the morale of other teams must of fairness commend Gibson for this important phase of leadership."[16] *Pittsburgh Press* scribe Ralph Davis echoed Doyle's sentiments. He noted that

during Hugo Bezdek's tenure, the Pittsburgh players arrived at the ballpark seemingly already beat. Conversely, with Gibson at the helm, the Pirates played "as hard as they know how at all times."[17]

Even with his mediocre lineup and lackluster record, journalists from all over the country took notice of Gibby's excellent job. Joe Vila, the sports editor of the prestigious *New York Evening Sun* and perhaps the most lauded sports writer of the era, sung Gibson's praises. Vila wrote that Gibby had "won the respect and admiration of his players, and they are working with him in perfect harmony."[18]

Even late in the season, Barney Dreyfuss, perhaps oblivious to his poor job in assembling a roster, felt good about the team's chances. Having a great field gen-

Manager Gibson looks over his club from the Forbes Field dugout (Healy Collection).

eral seems to have clouded his judgment. On a road trip late in the season, Dreyfuss told George: "Gibby, I think you're gonna win this pennant."[19] The colonel's audacious statement caught Gibson off guard. Gibson knew better and informed Dreyfuss that they wouldn't get into, let alone win, the World Series with the bunch of inexperienced kids on the ball club.[20]

Regardless of the team's record on the field, Dreyfuss sensed that he needed to keep Gibson in the fold. With a month remaining in the season, Dreyfuss re-signed Gibson for the 1921 campaign. Unlike their previous negotiations, which stretched out over months at a time, Dreyfuss and Gibson settled these terms in a single sit-down.

Barney handed George the contract and told him to look it over. Dreyfuss provided Gibson with identical terms in 1921 as he did in 1920. Gibson quickly accepted the terms and promptly signed the document. Gibby later recalled his interaction with the club president: "Now I go up into the office and of course Barney, he paid me … he said, 'How about your contract?' I said, 'Let it ride.'"[21] Later, in talking about the negotiations, Dreyfuss went on to say that "George Gibson's first season as a manager has been entirely satisfactory to me. Conditions have been most discouraging this year. Illness and injury have weakened the team just when it needed all its strength. Despite such drawbacks, Gibson has kept his players keyed up to a high pitch and they have done all that could be expected under the circumstances. He certainly has done his best and is deserving of an opportunity to lead the team in 1921."[22]

By mid–September, the Brooklyn Robins had run away with the National League pennant. Despite their National League dominance, the Robins lost the best-of-nine World Series to the Cleveland Indians five games to two. Meanwhile, the Bucs wrapped the 1920 season with a record of 79–75, good enough for fourth place but 14 games behind Brooklyn. Clearly, the Pirates had a lot of work to do in order to field a competitive team in 1921.

Leading in to the winter meetings, George knew, above all else, he needed better middle infielders. All told, the Pirates' keystone combination combined for 94 errors in 1920, with the shortstops responsible for 65 miscues. While Gibson had a diamond in the rough in Pie Traynor, the 21-year-old had a horrid first crack at the majors. Gibson was smart enough to keep the eventual Hall of Famer on the roster, but also smart enough to keep him on the sidelines until 1923. To serve as a stop-gap, Gibby eyed Rabbit Maranville, the Boston Braves' 29-year-old star shortstop. It just so happened that George Grant, the Braves' owner, offered Maranville up at the winter meetings. Easily the best player available for trade that off-season, Maranville's appearance on the trading block tantalized many of the owners, but Grant established an extremely high asking price. When approached about the acquisition, Grant told reporters that "Maranville is on the market and the Pittsburgh club knows what I want for him, so it's up to them."[23] Meanwhile, Gibson, who finally received free rein from Dreyfuss to have full control of negotiations, played things close to the chest and offered up a cloudy response: "Well, I've told [Grant] just what we will give for Maranville, and now it's up to the Boston club to say yes or no."[24]

Then, the Giants' John McGraw got involved in the hopes of pulling off a three-team trade. The Giants man joined Gibby and Braves manager Fred Mitchell at the negotiating table. Unfortunately, friends of McGraw started showing up uninvited, which in turn incensed Gibson. George walked out so peeved that he told reporters: "I am going to ask for a showdown inside of an hour. I intend to either get some real information from McGraw and Mitchell, or I will call off the Pittsburgh club's negotiations."[25]

The trio reconvened but to no avail. Gibson left abruptly for unknown reasons; however, it is entirely possible this was a negotiating ploy. The Braves realized they missed out on a good deal and reopened negotiations with Gibson after all parties returned home. Pittsburgh exchanged Billy Southworth, Fred Nicholson, Walter Barbare and $15,000 for Rabbit. The hefty package raised the eyebrows of more than a few Pirates fans; however, George thought the reward outweighed the risk. Gibson and Dreyfuss went to New York to sign Maranville. Immediately after the New York trip, George returned to London and took a much-needed vacation.

On the eve of the new season, Gibson exuded confidence. "We have had a successful training season and we're going out there tomorrow to give them all we have."[26] While the Pirates' strong off-season certainly helped, Gibson's family decided to join him in Cincinnati as the Pirates kicked things off with the Queen City's finest. Both Gibson's wife and daughter made the trip and their presence served as extra contentment for George. His daughter Marguerite had recently recovered from a serious bout with blood poisoning and her recovery gave the manager a sense of optimism.

Back on the field, Gibby's old pal Babe Adams started and cruised through seven innings. In the eighth inning, Babe fatigued and he surrendered four runs in the frame. The Reds took a 5–1 lead and finished the contest with 5 runs to Pittsburgh's three. Despite the unfavorable start, the Pirates finished April with an 11–3 record. This, in turn, sparked the Pirates faithful, who felt confident in their team's chances that season.

Gibson's men carried their good play into May. Before they embarked on a 13-game road trip, the Bucs rattled off 5 straight victories. Prior to traveling east, Gibby brought the Pirates north to his hometown to participate in an exhibition match against the London Tecumsehs, the defending Michigan-Ontario League champions.

Four thousand London rooters witnessed some great baseball. Gibson and his 1909 batterymate Babe Adams recaptured their former glory and shut down London in the first frame. George delighted the crowd by taking an at bat in the exhibition and made a single. Gibson was awarded with a loving cup from the London Kiwanis Club as a token of thanks. After the ceremonial first inning, the clubs participated in a well-played game. The Pirates narrowly defeated the London Tecumsehs by a final score of 8–7.

Back on the Senior Circuit, the Bucs took both Boston and Philadelphia to the woodshed. Gibson's crew then traveled to New York for a four-game set against Brooklyn followed by a two-game series versus the Giants. The Pirates swept the series versus the Robins, and then managed a split with the Giants. The results seemed encouraging even though the Robins had fallen off considerably in 1921. The Giants fielded a strong team and the split series left the Pirates with a solid three-and-a-half-game lead over McGraw's men. After the series wrapped, McGraw talked to the press about Gibson and the Pirates: "Gibson has a great ball club, and he deserves a lot of credit for the way he has his players hustling on the ball. Even the fans at the Polo Grounds were amazed at the way the Pittsburgh players carried on when they scored six runs in the ninth inning on Sunday. That's the kind of fighting spirit that helps a team to win ball games. Gibson has a lot of young players who move fast both in the field and on the bases. They know how to run bases, too, and a good base running team is going to win a lot of ball games if it gets fair pitching and a little bit of hitting."[27] Gibby's spark plugs continued their winning ways throughout May and finished with a record of 29–10, good enough for first place.

One need not look further than the Maranville acquisition to explain the strong play. The high-minded and advanced baseball lieutenant finally had a topflight talent on the field. Maranville's hitting and fielding exceeded expectations, and his great play seemed to rub off on his teammates. Meanwhile, the newest Pirates player had a straightforward rationale for his strong start to the season: "Gibson is a great manager and a fine fellow. He's a wonder at handling men and he is endowed with as much baseball knowledge as any other manager in either of the two big leagues. The boys like him and they will win the pennant for him."[28] If Rabbit and the Bucs continued their strong play, Gibson's team would coast to a National League pennant. In fact, Gibson's leadership really resonated with his team. The players responded to his discipline. Outfielder George "Possum" Whitted opined: "A fellow who wouldn't hustle for George Gibson ought to lose the uniform for the rest of his life."[29]

In June, the Bucs got their first real taste of defeat. The Giants swooped into Forbes Field and snatched three of four games from the upstart Pirates. Following the club's downturn, rumors of unrest in the Pirates' clubhouse surfaced. One rumor spoke of a bunch of Buccaneers appearing at a saloon after curfew, on the fringes of the city, only to return home extremely inebriated. Another story involved pitcher Moses "Chief" Yellow Horse and fellow hurler Wilbur Cooper. Cooper accused Yellow Horse of being a quitter and Moses responded by punching him.[30] Reports also told that Gibson gave his men free reign to let loose and relax after the disappointing series with the Giants. It just so happened that the tales were hearsay. Gibson did not allow such unruliness among his club, but even when a small slump developed, the rumor mill began to spin. Ultimately, the Pirates' harmonious clubhouse contributed to strong play on the field, and the rumors subsided. Pittsburgh finished June at 46–22, a comfortable five games up on the Giants.

In mid–July, the Pirates made another East Coast trip. The club started with a four-game set in Manhattan against the Giants followed by another four-game trip across the East River in Brooklyn. Sitting in the visitor's dugout at Ebbets Field, George spoke to Gotham City reporters about his club's chances in the National League pennant race: "Fightin'est ball club I ever had anything to do with. Never know when they're beat. That's the kind of club I got." While a lot of games remained to be played, Gibson expressed confidence in his club but stopped short of predicting a World Series appearance: "I've never won any pennants, and I never make predictions. Think it's a Jinx."[31] The New York media men proclaimed McGraw's Giants as the biggest threat to the Pirates' pennant chances. Gibby concurred in the most direct way possible: "Right now it looks that way."[32] He reiterated that the season was only midway finished, and other clubs were also playing good ball. Unfortunately, the Pirates broke even in the Big Apple which did little to help their standing in the league. The following week, back at Forbes Field, McGraw's men took three of four contests from the Pirates, which surely dampened Gibby's title hopes. Now with sixty victories on the season, the Giants pulled even with the Bucs in the win column. With August upon them, Gibson had two months to win just one more game than the Giants.

The Pirates caught fire in August. They swept a home series versus the Phillies, and then won five in a row against the Bill Killefer–led Chicago Cubs. From there, they won four of six at the Baker Bowl in Philadelphia. Over that 21-day stretch from August 1 through August 22, the Pirates won 16 of 21 games. On August 24, the Pirates arrived in New York for a crucial five-game series against the Giants.

When the series started, the Pirates held an impressive seven-and-a-half-game lead over the second-place Giants. The five-game set began with a doubleheader and the Giants easily dispatched Gibson's team in both games. The next day, the Giants won again. Things did not get any better in the fourth game of the series. Gibson's men notched more hits than the Giants batters but the Giants still came out on top. In the series finale, the beating concluded when the Giants put the Pirates out of their misery by a score of 3–1.

More than any other aspect of their play, the Pirates' hitting languished at the Polo Grounds. Over the five games, the Pirates plated just six runs. It is hard to imagine that type of production being sufficient in the deadball era of Gibson's playing days, let alone in the live-ball era. Regardless of why they lost, the fact remained that the Pirates failed to capitalize on the opportunity and instead of stretching their lead to 12 games, they found themselves just two up in the standings.

Gibson told reporters: "We've certainly found the going rough during the last few days, but we have no alibis to offer. Five straight defeats by New York was a hard blow. The Giants simply played better ball than we did, however, and our hats are off to them. We're going back home to fight it out to the finish. Two-thirds of our remaining games will be played at Forbes Field. That's something of an advantage. All our players are in good shape, I haven't a kick of that score. Our pitchers, especially the young fellows, are going fine and I am not worrying over the possibility of the staff cracking. Of course a good many things can happen in a month's time, but as we've gone this far on high, I don't see why we can't stick it out."[33] Entering September, both New York and Pittsburgh had 78 wins (Pirates 78–47, Giants 78–50).

On September 9, after leading the National League all season, the Giants caught and passed the Pirates for first place. On September 16, the Pirates trailed the Giants by 2½ games as McGraw's men marched into Pittsburgh for a critical three-game series at Forbes Field. It seems everyone recognized how important the series happened to be as reporters pegged it as the last chance for the Bucs to stay in the championship race.

Unfortunately for Gibson and his club, the Giants took two of the three games, and extended their division lead to three and a half games. After the series defeat, Gibson reiterated the statement he made after his club's defeat in New York: "The Pirates have not quit. We are not out of the pennant race by any means and do not intend giving up until the last game is played. There is one thing that happens to every ball team and that is what is known as the slump. Seldom in a season does any club escape it. The Pirates were no exception this year, but unfortunately our slump came at a period in the race where it hurt the most."[34] Gibson also addressed rumors that the players were upset. He explained that all players get excited in the heat of the moment, and sometimes the players' anger or frustration shows at inopportune times on the ball field. He noted that frustration is part of baseball when playing bad, just as happiness is when playing well: "We have been fighting all the year and intend to give the very best we've got as long as the slightest thread of hope remains."[35] Meanwhile, the team held out hope until September 29, when the Giants clinched the National League crown. The Pirates finished 1921 in second place with 90 wins and 63 losses, just 4 behind the champion Giants. Although of little consolation to Gibson, New York won the 1921 World Series over Babe Ruth and the Yankees, five games to three.

Despite the late-season collapse, many people inside and outside of the Pirates organization credited George for keeping the team in contention throughout the year. Most Pittsburghers wanted Gibby to have another chance in 1922. *Pittsburgh Daily Post* writer Edward Balinger noted that "when a pilot which can pick up a ball club which is not much better than a third or fourth-rater and hold its head in front of the procession for the greater portion of a campaign it would appear that he should be given a further opportunity to show what he could do if provided with more reliable timber."[36] On December 7, President Dreyfuss agreed, and signed Gibson to a one-year contract while the duo attended the minor-league meetings in Buffalo, New York. Although Dreyfuss offered Gibson a longer contract, Gibson felt the flexibility of a one-year agreement benefited both the manager and the team.

Even though the team played better in 1921 than they did in 1920, Gibson still wanted more from his team. In an attempt to keep his players fresh during the 1922 season, Gibson put limits on the players' extra-curricular activities, golf in particular. The skipper felt that the excessive amount of walking that took place during a round of golf in advance of game days drained the players' energy. He even went so far as to tell the players that he "was not opposed to golf, but that I was opposed to playing the game before baseball practice or before a ball game. Some might argue that a few holes of golf does not interfere with their work on the diamond, but it does, and the man who says it does not is a stranger to the truth."[37] In addition, papers reported that players spent more time talking about their golf game in 1921 than they did discussing their profession. Those writers deduced that the play on the field suffered in part because of that distraction. Gibson wanted his new rules to have some teeth, and so he insisted on stiffer penalties for any violation of his rules, be it golf or otherwise.

Despite Gibson's new approach, the team played uninspired ball to start the 1922 season. They started the year by taking on Branch Rickey's Cardinals at Sportsman's Park. The Cards promptly swept the Pirates right out of the stadium. Their lackluster and inconsistent play continued and the team wrapped the month with a pedestrian 7–8 record.

In an attempt to right the ship, Gibson opted to work his men during an early May rainout. Gibby explained to Dreyfuss that their club needed practice more than they needed the day off. Dreyfuss concurred and, along with Gibson, outwitted the weather man. They ordered their club to skirmish at the 107th Field Artillery Regiment's armory. The officers of the military installation happily allowed the Pirates players to make themselves feel at home. Manager Gibson put his men through their paces and had the club exercise until an ample sweat manifested on each man's brow. Then, to help build their stamina even more, the skipper finished the workout with sprints. The Buccaneers had not had a strenuous workout like that since spring training in West Baden Springs. The extra training paid off, and the Pirates exhibited new pep during an 11–2 stretch from May 7 to May 25. By the end of the month, Gibby's club sat in a respectable second place, just 1½ games behind New York.

Just as the team started to settle in, Gibson himself derailed things. After a late–May incident during a game in Cincinnati, the umpire ejected Gibson. The occasion marked the first time Gibson received the boot as a big-league manager. The experience seems to have made Gibson snap and subsequently, his usually calm disposition gave way to that of irritation. Gibby became angered when he noticed that many of the baseballs put into play were unusually scuffed to the point of unfair advantage. He asserted the Reds were manipulating the balls. Umpire Hank O'Day gave Gibson his ear for a time, but eventually the skipper's bench jockeying got him tossed from the game. The Bucs picked him up and won the second game, giving them a split on the day regardless of the possibility of doctored balls.

In June, the Pirates club played the rolls of Dr. Jekyll and Mr. Hyde. Despite their inconsistent play, Gibson's team remained in second spot, this time four games behind the Giants. Again, like so many other times in Gibby's reign as Pirates skipper, a four-game series at the Polo Grounds proved to be pivotal. And, like almost all of those other times, the Pirates did not have the talent on the field to compete with the Giants. Gibson's men lost all four contests, found themselves eight games off the pace and languished in third position in the standings. Needless to say, Gibson worried about the rest of the season.

Gibson's fears manifested and Pittsburgh slumped. A week after being scrubbed by the Giants, the Reds visited the Pirates for a three-game series and promptly dispatched the Bucs in all three matches. When Gibson returned to the ballpark after the series concluded, he skipped the clubhouse and went to visit Dreyfuss. Gibson did not feel well, perhaps because he hadn't had coffee yet. Unfortunately, he was about to feel worse.

As soon as Gibson walked in, Dreyfuss started to second-guess and question him about the Reds series. Dreyfuss concluded that since his team finished in second place in 1921, and because they had brought in some more firepower, that they should be higher than fourth in the standings. Not an unreasonable opinion, but be that as it may, the Pirates stood at 32–32 on June 29. Gibson did not take kindly to Dreyfuss's feedback and the meeting devolved from there.

When Dreyfuss broached the topic of the Cincy series and what caused the Pirates to lose, Gibson replied, "That is baseball…. Those are the breaks of the game." The interrogation upset George and he took the opportunity to remind his team's owner about their recent contract negotiations. Gibson, not Dreyfuss, insisted on the shorter term. With a one-year contract in place, he told Dreyfuss: "You don't lose any money, you just look for another manager."[38]

Although a team-first individual, Gibson did not want the Pirates to fire him. However, he also had had his breaking point. In fact, Gibson insisted on just one thing during the contract negotiations. He said: "I can't stand anybody second guessing me ... Barney, I want you to leave me alone!"[39]

The one-on-one continued the following day. Though both men had a night to sleep on things, the meeting culminated with George putting his hands on Dreyfuss's desk and telling the owner: "Barney, do you remember what I told you in the Lafayette Hotel in Buffalo about second guessing me? What I'd do, if you second guess me and didn't leave me alone? ... This is my last day with you."[40]

Gibson left Dreyfuss's office and proceeded to the clubhouse in order to confirm that the entire team had showed up for that day's game. But instead of causing a scene and jeopardizing his team's chemistry, Gibson kept the news to himself and quietly slipped out the door. He drove home, penned his resignation letter and then returned to Forbes Field. When he arrived at the ballpark, George found the office doors locked. He slid the letter under Dreyfuss's door, then proceeded to the clubhouse just as he would have on any other day.

After reviewing the Cardinals' lineup for the day, he advised his pitchers on which strategy to use against St. Louis. Then, he pulled the team together for a meeting. "Fellas, this is one ball game. Now, you've won a lot of ball games for me. You've lost a lot. This is one ball game I wanna win. This one, today, I wanna win it." It was not to be. Branch Rickey's club trimmed the Bucs 6–0. In the locker room after the game, Gibson explained to his men why he spoke prior to the game in the manner that he did: "Well, now fellas, we wasn't fortunate enough to win today. I'll tell you why I wanted to win today.... Today is my last day with ya. Tomorrow you're gonna have a new manager. This is my last day with ya, that's why I was so anxious to win."[41] In front of the captive audience, he explained his decision: "The club is not going as it should, and I feel there may be men on the roster who can get better than those attained recently. So I think I am doing what is right by stepping aside for somebody else. But I want to thank every fellow on the club for the way you have helped me. Everybody on the team hustled and I want you to know I appreciate it."[42]

The news flabbergasted the Pirates players, the Pittsburgh fans and even the Steel City's press corp. Out-of-town reporters provided more insight and more titillation. A Boston newspaper headline read: "Barney Dreyfuss Should Resign."[43] The attached story explained the Pittsburgh club president's failure in the way he handled the Pirates. The *Brooklyn Eagle* also told of Pittsburgh's baseball woes. The sarcastic headline declared, "Barney Dreyfuss Not to Blame for Downfall of the Pirates? Gibson Seems to Be the Goat."[44] George Daily, of the *New York World*, wrote: "George Gibson has ever been such a credit to baseball both as a player and manager that it is regretful to have him resign as leader of the Pittsburgh Pirates. Whatever the reason back of it all, he retired as the sportsman he is, without a single word of complaint and wishing the players the best of luck."[45] *Pittsburgh Press* reporter Ralph Davis, however, backed the owner and said that he felt Dreyfuss had been unjustly condemned by the national media.[46] At the time, only the president and manager knew why George had to retire. Gibson promptly traveled home to devote his time to his 100-acre farm near Mount Brydges, Ontario.

12

Yearning for the
Glory Days

Rumors of George's plans for 1923 began to spread almost immediately following the news of his resignation from Pittsburgh. In August, the *Reading Times* reported that Gibson would return to Toronto to manage in the International League for the 1923 season.[1] Then, in early November, the *Pittsburgh Daily Post* reported that the Reading Aces were in pursuit of Gibson.[2] Eventually, the *Toronto Daily Star* caught up with George at his home in London, where he admitted that he had been negotiating with a number of clubs. He informed the reporter that he had not interviewed for the Reading position. George planned to attend the winter meetings in New York to explore options to reignite his baseball career.[3] He didn't remain out of baseball for long.

When Gibson arrived at the meetings on December 12, he was warmly greeted by those who mingled in "Peacock Alley," the stomping grounds of the rich and famous at the Waldorf-Astoria Hotel. While in New York, Gibson also searched for a manager to lead London's Michigan-Ontario League team at the request of the club's owners.[4] The rumor mill cranked up almost as soon as he stepped foot in the Waldorf. Even though Reading had signed Spencer Abbott weeks earlier,[5] rumors persisted that they were still in pursuit of Gibson.[6] The *Courier-News* also reported that he "may manage the Peterson team in the new Atlantic League."[7] Despite the rumors, George had his sights set on remaining in the big leagues.

Gibby's big-league ambition found him quickly. Frank Chance intercepted Gibson as he headed to another meeting. Over the course of that brief discussion, Chance, the newly appointed manager of the Red Sox, informally offered Gibson a coaching position on his staff. He asked that Gibson not sign with any other club until the duo had the chance to sit down. George had every intention of waiting for that meeting; however, as the hours ticked by, other opportunities presented themselves. Donie Bush, who had just taken over as the Washington Senators' manager, ran into George, and told him: "I want you to come with me. Now, I never managed before. You have. You've got an idea what it's like. I want you to come with me."[8]

While Gibson had inclinations for the Red Sox position, he waited until 1 a.m. before he decided that the Red Sox skip may never come back.[9] Eventually, Gibson received an offer from Boston; however, he had already put pen to paper with Washington president Clark Griffith. Gibby's deal for 1923 paid a salary of $12,000. The *New York Evening Leader* felt that Clark Griffith was "certain to have made a ten strike when he added the veteran catcher, George Gibson, to the Nationals."[10] Griffith agreed and said: "Really, I think my best stroke in New York was to sign up Gibson. A great catcher himself, he knows how to get all there is out of his pitchers."[11] Unsurprisingly, Bush planned for his new assistant coach to develop the Nationals' young pitching staff.

On February 28, a contingent of Senators arrived in Tampa to begin spring practice. The entourage included George and his wife as well as Mr. and Mrs. Griffith, manager Donie Bush and a small group of players. The rest of the team, save for one major exception, would not arrive until March 8. That notable exception, legend Walter Johnson, did not arrive for another few weeks. His 18-month-old son Bobby developed a serious infection and needed life-saving surgery. Instead of traveling to the Sunshine State, Walter took his son to Children's Hospital San Francisco (now known as the UCSF Benioff Children's Hospital), where doctors performed multiple surgeries.[12] Thankfully, Bobby survived. However, the missed training time and stress of the ordeal had a noticeable impact on the aging superstar. While Johnson posted an impressive 17–12 record with a 3.48 ERA in 1923, it served as one of the worst statistical outputs of his entire career.

Given the absence of their staff stalwart, even more responsibility fell to Gibson. The pitching staff needed a leader and George set a firm tone for his pupils. The papers pointed out that "Gibson is not letting any of them loaf. He is behind each and every one either with a word of advice or driving them a little harder."[13] On March 10, George reported that he had as many as four pitchers ready to throw three to five innings in practice contests. While he possessed plenty of enthusiasm for the new recruits, he tempered expectations. A strong performance in spring helped, but ultimately, preseason scrimmages were a very different test from regular season contests.

After Johnson made his way to Tampa, the pitcher and his new coach quickly established a good rapport. By then a 35-year-old grizzled veteran, Walter Johnson quickly grew to appreciate Gibson's brilliance and his approach to the game. One day, George peppered his pitching staff and clued them into the nuances of fielding bunts. Even Walter, who by then had cemented himself as one of the greatest pitchers in baseball history, past or present, took to the drill.

Clark Griffith, a heck of a pitcher in his own day, watched Gibson run

George Gibson with Washington Senator star Walter "Big Train" Johnson (Healy Collection).

Johnson through bunting exercises. Gibson focused on having Johnson approach the ball in such a way that when he picked it up, he was already in position to throw. This approach saved invaluable seconds against speedy runners. Johnson eagerly adapted to the advice. While perhaps not a surprise considering Gibson called Walter a "perfect gentleman,"[14] Johnson had every reason not to listen to the new coach. Here was a man who dictated the terms of his career, who developed such a keen mastery of the game that he landed on the All-Century Team and who was anything but a novice. He knew the game and played it better than most anyone before or since.

Griffith later made a comment to Johnson, in earshot of Gibson. Griffith didn't like Walter fielding bunts and didn't think it'd help him. Johnson responded: "Listen Griff, I've been with you for 13-years and today I just learned how to field a bunt." Gibson "never saw Griff on the training ground after that."[15] The training session spoke volumes about Gibson's ability to help any pitcher improve, rookies and veterans alike.

On April 18, Washington opened their season in Philadelphia and Walter Johnson served as the starter. The Senators lost 3–1 and went on to lose their first four games. From Philadelphia, they traveled to New York to face Babe Ruth and the Yankees. On April 22 and 23, Washington held Ruth hitless; this allowed them to steal a pair of one-run victories, and improve to 3–3. The Senators' winning percentage would not equal or top .500 at any time the rest of the season. By the end of April, they were 4–7 and in fifth place. On May 20, things got even worse, when, in St. Louis, Walter Johnson injured his left knee while throwing a pitch. George worked with Johnson daily and instructed him to chase fungoes in an effort to strengthen his legs. Johnson's leg problems persisted despite his enthusiastic work.[16] Near the end of May, the Senators traveled through George's hometown to play an exhibition game against the London Tecumsehs. The game proved to be a challenge for the big leaguers. London held a 5–0 lead as the seventh inning arrived. However, Washington capitalized on some defensive miscue and won the contest 13–9. Gibson performed managerial duties, and piloted the Senators "before a highly pleased crowd"[17] at Tecumseh Park. From London, the Washington club journeyed to Boston, where they fell back off the wagon. With two losses in that three-game series, they ended May in sixth place, with a record of 14–21.

At the beginning of June, George received a phone call from his wife, who was at home in Canada. Her father passed away. George left the club immediately and traveled to London from Washington to attend the funeral, and be with his family.[18] Shortly after Gibson's return to the team, Clark Griffith pulled him aside and told him that he was being released from the ball club. George recalled years later that he had been discharged from the ball club because the team was having financial difficulty and could not afford his services. However, according to Henry W. Thomas, author of *Walter Johnson: Baseball's Big Train*, the real reason for Gibson's release was that despite his efforts to strengthen Johnson's legs, he actually made them worse.[19] Whatever the reason, George accepted Griffith's decision and felt he had been treated fairly. His only question to Griffith regarded the timing: "Why didn't you tell me that when I was going home?"[20] In George's mind, if he had been told this news prior to leaving the first time, he would have saved himself a trip. George gathered his belongings and left quietly, without even saying goodbye to his friend, Donie Bush.

After he returned to London, Gibson received word that Donie Bush was through as manager. On August 1, the *Washington Post* reported a rumor that although he would be kept until the end of the season, in 1924 Bush would not manage in Washington.[21] When the season ended, it was made official. Clark Griffith relieved Donie Bush of his managerial duties. Though Walter Johnson did get back into form, it took until mid–September, and the best Washington could do was sneak into fourth place, with a 75–78 record.

With his baseball career on hiatus, George jumped back into the contracting business. In addition, he spent time tending to his farm in Mount Brydges. Never one to stay still, Gibson added to his workload when he rejoined the London Thistle Curling Club that winter. Even with the busy schedule, Gibson still wanted to be part of the game of baseball.

That December, he traveled to Chicago for the winter meetings in search of employment. While at the meetings, George used the opportunity to re-unite with old friends Barney Dreyfuss, Bill McKechnie, Sam Dreyfuss, Chick Fraser, Bill Hinchman and Lefty Leifield. Curiously, rumors persisted that the Washington Senators wanted Gibson back to manage the team in 1924; just as with previous rumors, this never materialized. In the end, Gibson departed Chicago without a job offer, returned to London and spent the year out of baseball.

One year later, Gibson got back in the swing of things. He traveled to Springfield, Illinois, for the minor-league winter meetings in order to "renew acquaintances."[22] While there, Chicago Cubs manager Bill Killefer approached Gibby. Killefer, like Gibson, played catcher in the big leagues and graduated to bench boss when he hung up the big mitt. He played with the St. Louis Browns and Philadelphia Phillies before he joined the Chicago Cubs in 1918. In 1921, when the Cubs deposed of manager Johnny Evers mid-season, Killefer succeeded him. At the meetings in Springfield, Killefer searched for a new bench coach, having just released Oscar Dugey, who previously filled the roll. On January 12, 1925, after about a month of very secretive negotiations, Chicago Cubs president Bill Veeck announced George Gibson was "a coach, buffer, assistant pilot, and general all-around handyman" for manager Bill Killefer.[23]

Three days later, Gibson returned to London for his daughter Margue-rite's wedding to Firman "Bill" Warwick. Warwick, a fine catcher himself, first appeared on George's radar in 1921. After a standout career at the University of Pennsylvania, the Pirates acquired his services during one of the team's eastern road trips. On July 18, Warwick made his major-league debut when Gibson inserted him into the lineup as a late-inning replacement. Bill logged two innings as catcher, and went hitless in his only at bat. He never played another major-league game for the Pirates. Warwick banged around the mi-nors for a few years after that, landing back in the big leagues with St. Louis in 1925; but his one-game Pittsburgh career reaped benefits off the field that surely topped anything that happened on the field. During his time with the Bucs, Warwick met Gibson's daughter Marguerite.[24] The relationship culmi-nated with the wedding, just before Warwick returned to the topflight base-ball league. Two years and 22 games later, Warwick concluded his big-league career with an impressive .304 career batting average. Bill and Marguerite kicked around the minors for a few more seasons until 1929, when the couple settled in Texas, where Bill became a city engineer in San Antonio.

After the wedding, Gibson headed to Catalina Island in California for the start of the Cubs' spring training. Mel Kerr, a Canadian outfielder, joined the Cubs on his way to becoming just the 95th Canadian to appear in a major-league game. At the end of March, the two countrymen and the rest of the Cubs ramped up for the regular season with a series of exhibition matches against nearby teams. They started in Los Angeles against the Pacific Coast League's Angels. On March 29, the Cubs departed Los Angeles for Sacramento and eventually Kansas City. By April 14, the Cubs had traversed the country and arrived back in Chicago ready to open the season against Gibson's beloved Pirates.

Thirty-eight thousand fans watched as the Cubs drummed the Pirates 8–2. Pittsburgh answered back the following day, but Chicago still started the campaign 3–1, which put them in first place. St. Louis cooled off the Cubs when they came to Cubs Park and swept a three-game series, but Chicago still found themselves in second place on May 2 with a 10–6 record. The season went all downhill from there. By the end of May, the Cubs were 17–25 and in 7th place. President Veeck, knowing his team needed a spark, sent Gibson out on scouting trips in search of help. On June 29, the Cubs bought Art Jahn, on George's recommendation. The astute baseball man saw Jahn as he racked up a .344 batting average for the Flint Vehicles in the Michigan-Ontario League. The 29-year-old Jahn played in 58 games for the Cubs in 1925 and batted a respectable .301 with 37 RBI.

After his road trip, George returned to Chicago intent on settling back into the routine of an assistant coach. That plan soon changed. One night in

Gibson (left) in 1925 with Chicago Cub manager Bill Killefer at Weeghman Field (SDN-065330 Chicago Daily News negatives collection, Chicago History Museum).

early July, George made plans to dine with his wife and daughter. As he departed Cubs Park and left his day's work behind, Gibson "bumped into" Bill Veeck. The owner informed his coach that Bill Killefer would no longer be the Cub's manager. The position was George's for the taking.

George, forever loyal, declined the offer. He told Veeck: "Listen, it's not that I have to be in baseball. I don't have to be in baseball. I come here as a favor to Bill Killefer to try and help him. I've failed to help him.... You wanna release Killefer and let me take his job.... I will not take it."[25] When word of the impending move reached reporters, they published articles pegging Gibson for managerial duties. Gibson insisted he would remain with the Cubs but that he had no interest in taking over the top position. When Veeck finally issued Killefer his walking papers, he replaced him with Cubs infielder Rabbit Maranville. Maranville, who learned from Gibby back in Pittsburgh, continued to play shortstop while he managed the team.

The Cubs' fortune did not turn around as a result of the change in management. With Maranville at the helm, Chicago continued to play to mediocre results through July and August. As August rolled into September, rumors began to circulate that Maranville, too, was through as manager of the team. Once again, newspapers predicted George as the likely successor.[26] However, when the Cubs arrived in Toronto for an exhibition game against the Maple Leafs on September 3, neither Maranville nor Gibson held the title of pilot. Instead, Charlie Grimm had been assigned acting manager duties. The Cubs won the rain-shortened battle 2–0, but were unimpressive. Coverage in the following day's paper noted, "This major league team is only a shadow of the old Chicago machine, and the line-up they used here yesterday would have a hard time finishing in the first division in the International."[27] On September 4, Rabbit Maranville resigned his position as manager, and George Gibson was appointed as his replacement for the remainder of the season. Rabbit hopped back to his regular shortstop position to finish out the season.

With the Cubs well out of playoff contention, Veeck asked Mooney to focus on the development of younger players. Gibby did just that. Interestingly, perhaps as much out of duty to his countrymen as to anything else, Gibson made sure to give Mel Kerr his whack, albeit a brief one. On September 16, Gibby inserted Kerr as a pinch runner against Boston. In his only appearance in a major-league game, Kerr scored, but Chicago still lost 8–6. On October 4, the Cubs wrapped up their season against the Cardinals. The baby bears needed a win to finish in sixth place, but they lost 7–5, dropped to 68–86 and finished in the National League's cellar.

Given the losing hand Veeck dealt him, Gibby's 26-game stretch as manager proved again just how sharp a baseball mind he had. The Cubs finished their first 128 games with a .438 winning percentage. Gibby's men showed a marked improvement. Though they still finished eighth, they improved their winning percentage to .462. Not a remarkable number by any means, but when you consider that Gibby fielded mostly second stringers, many of whom never had the talent for major-league stardom, the record begins to shimmer just a bit.

With neither the Cubs nor the White Sox capturing a pennant, the two teams renewed their crosstown rivalry with their annual post-season series. They kicked off the best-of-seven showdown on October 7. Ted Blankenship, a 24-year-old righty, started for the White Sox. Gibson countered with future Hall of Famer Grover Cleveland Alexander, the 38-year-old elder statesmen of his staff. Both men pitched a complete game, which ended after nineteen innings in a 2–2 tie. The series resumed the following day, and the Cubs eventually won in six contests. Thanks to his team's "decisive trimming of the White Sox in the city series,"[28] Gibson earned a full share of the gate receipts, worth $561.93. Before the series wrapped, Gibson and Veeck had already laid the groundwork for the Cubs' future. On October 14, 1925, the *Alton Evening Telegraph* informed readers that the franchise hired Joe McCarthy away from Louisville.[29] Meanwhile, Bill Veeck retained George as a scout, but it is unclear how much work Gibson did for Chicago in 1926. From his home in London, it would have been easy for him to catch games in and around Ontario, Michigan and Ohio. However, there is no record of Gibson finding any talent worthy of signing that season.

By the end of 1926, George had happily receded into the background. He skipped the winter meetings and seemed to be content living the family life that he missed out on during his long baseball career. Over the next five years, Gibson built or helped build multiple houses in London. Some of those still stand and remain in his descendants' possession.

Also during that time, Gibson, along with his wife and their son William, frequently traveled to Wilkinsburg, Pennsylvania, to visit his eldest son, by then established as Dr. George Gibson. Those trips also extended to San Antonio, their daughter Marguerite's city of residence. They were fond times for George and may have been what inspired William, who followed in his brother's footsteps and went on to study medicine at the University of Western Ontario, just as George Jr. had.

Even with his focus on family and on seclusion from public life, nearly two decades removed from the peak of his career, Gibson had by no means abandoned the game. When those trips to Wilkinsburg lined up with Pirates' home games, Gibson would stop in Pittsburgh to watch. He attended the games as often as possible, accompanied by his old friend Barney Dreyfuss. Of course, the fans at Forbes Field made sure to acknowledge their beloved World Series backstop, a fact that did not escape Barney.

In spite of Gibby's resignation in 1922 and the tumultuous contract negotiations in years prior, Dreyfuss remained fond of George. Dreyfuss valued

Gibson's baseball insight; and, as the two old campaigners sat and watched the Pirates languish on the field, they discussed the current state of baseball. Jewel Ens, the current Pirates skipper, never managed to deliver much. Despite a team laden with Hall of Fame talent, seasoned veterans and exciting prospects, Ens's teams hovered around the .500 mark during his more than two years at the helm to that point. Dreyfuss yearned for the glory days with Mooney. As Gibson and Dreyfuss spent more time together during the 1931 season, newspapermen, doing what newspapermen do, began to read between the lines.

Why else would a brilliant baseball mind and experienced manager sit with his long-time boss unless the two were planning something? Reporters suggested that Gibson was scouting

George meets with former teammate, Bill McKechnie, in 1928, when Bill was manager of the St. Louis Cardinals (courtesy the *Pittsburgh Post-Gazette*).

the team for the following season. As late as September 22, those claims appeared far-fetched. Gibson claimed that "they have me taking the place of everyone here but Jack Fogarty and his ground-keeping gang."[30] For the second season in a row, Pittsburgh wrapped up the campaign in fifth place.

By 1930 the game had changed. The deadball era gave way to Babe Ruth and an offensive onslaught known as the "long ball." Dreyfuss disliked this approach in favor of "small ball." In his idealized game, teams succeeded by relying on great pitching, outstanding defense and mastery of the basepaths. To spearhead his team's renaissance, the Bucs president could only think of one man: it was George Gibson. Dreyfuss convinced George to meet. Despite George having been out of the game for half a decade, Dreyfuss offered him the manager's position for 1932 on the spot. Gibson did not hesitate. He also did not change his immediate plans. As in years past, the Mooney clan headed to Texas to extract every last drop of vacation they could. After a few days in the south, he journeyed back to Pittsburgh to watch the final few games of the season.[31]

Seeing no reason to rock the boat, perhaps out of respect for the current manager and/or the Pirates' place in the standings, Dreyfuss and Gibson agreed to keep the deal to themselves. After the season, Gibson returned to London confident he could do a good job with the club. He returned to Pittsburgh in early December and was officially announced as the new manager, having "beaten out" a long list of candidates for the position. While it's hard to say how much of an opportunity the other men had, Gibson bested Frankie Frisch, the great second baseman of the St. Louis Cardinals, Art Griggs, who managed the Pirates' Western League affiliate in Wichita and other pros such as Joe Devine, Otis Crandall and Dave Bancroft.

The *Pittsburgh Press* explained the move as such: "In selecting the Canadian, Dreyfuss is thought to be attempting to capitalize on his theory that the deadening of the baseball by the National League will return the game to a basis of strategy such as was in vogue in Gibsons heyday. The Pittsburgh owner frequently has been quoted as saying that he believes the day of free hitting is over and that it will be supplanted by former methods of scoring—with base stealing, sacrifices and similar means of advancing the runner becoming paramount."[32] Pittsburgh baseball writer, Edward F. Balinger, chimed in: "Gibson is back among old friends and if given proper encouragement I believe he will be the man to lead his men out of the wilderness of the second division. He learned his baseball at a time when ballplayers combined skill with scrappiness, but from the moment he broke into fast company as a rookie, some 27 years ago, the sturdy Canuck never was known to seek a back if trouble was threatened."[33]

Profile portrait of Gibson during his second tour as Pirates skipper (Canada's Sports Hall of Fame / Pantheon des sports Canadiens—sportshall.ca/pantheonsports.ca).

The optimism for the upcoming season received some serious challenges in the months that followed. Dreyfuss had hoped to keep the Pirates in the family. However, his son Sam passed away prior to the start of the 1931 season. Barney, who had his own health problems, continued as the Bucs' top boss. Between his duties as vice president of the National League and his obligations to the Pirates, not to mention the death of his son, Dreyfuss did not seem to hold up very well. Sadly, on February 5, 1932, Barney Dreyfuss passed away after his own battle with pneumonia, complicated by two glandular surgical operations. Barney's passing rocked George. Although they had their differences, the men always resolved any unpleasant circumstances that occurred while they worked together. Gibson counted Dreyfuss as one of his very best friends. He made a statement upon his friend's death:

> Throughout my acquaintance with President Dreyfuss, which began in 1905, I have found him to be an ideal employer and, after serving practically my entire diamond career with his club, I long ago learned to look upon him as a father. We had differences of opinion, but the most friendly feeling has always existed between us and his passing is indeed a severe blow to me. I know I am going to miss him, but his absence will cause me to work harder than ever to provide what was his foremost wish in life—a winning ball club. It is my resolve to carry on along the lines he mapped out, just the same as if he still was with us.[34]

With both Sam and Barney gone, family matriarch Florence Dreyfuss earmarked her son-in-law William Edward Benswanger to be Barney's successor.[35] In addition to being Barney and Florence's in-law, Benswanger was already deeply familiar with the organization as he had been the team's treasurer for some time.

While Gibson dealt with the personal turmoil, he remained steadfast in his obligations to the club. He vowed to bring the old style of baseball back to the big leagues just as he had promised his old friend. When Gibby outlined his training plans, he dropped the relatively new workout practice of calisthenics from the team's regimen in favor of pedestrianism, a 19th-century from of competitive walking. Gibby believed walking, running and jogging were the best forms of exercise for a ballplayer.

During the club's four-day journey to Paso Robles, California, for spring training, George planned to get his men some extra cardio work: "Whenever the train stops long enough to permit the players to get off at any station along the route to California, every player will be given a chance to limber up his leg muscles. All must get out of the sleeper on such occasions and indulge in a jog up and down the platform." Gibson disdained for callisthenic exercise, which had become popular in baseball training camps. He thought maybe for other sports or general exercise calisthenics was OK, "but for baseball NO! ... Baseball was different."[36] The baseball season was long, and Gibson believed cardiovascular exercise was superior to sustain each player's endurance throughout the year. Gibson had seen too many clubs lose their gusto by the end of the season. "The legs and the wind will be given special attention throughout the training period. When an athlete can run consistently and can breathe steadily and naturally he will find no difficulty in getting his throwing arm into proper shape. If a pitcher is lacking in condition and especially if his breathing is not normal, he cannot expect to work more than six of seven innings at the furthest."[37]

Despite their lackluster performance during Ens's tenure, Gibson inherited a talented roster. That season, Arky Vaughan debuted as short, veteran Pie Traynor guarded third base and the Waner brothers, Paul and Lloyd, played right and center field. All four men were eventually inducted into baseball's Hall of Fame. Meanwhile, Gus Dugas filled one of the reserve spots. When he premiered in 1931 he became the 96th Canadian to sport major-league threads. Clearly the Pirates had the offensive talent to contend for the pennant.

However, the pitching staff, without any notable hurlers, needed attention. Devoid of any topflight talent on the rubber, Gibson's years as a horse-whisperer to many a pitcher made him perfectly suited for the challenge. As soon as the chance arrived, Gibson began the arduous task of coaching up his boys while at the same time, instilling a new clubhouse culture. Gibson didn't feel he was a new manager for the Pittsburgh club. He felt he knew the team fairly well and spoke to reporters on his familiarity with his Bucs club:

> I studied this club last summer pretty carefully. I saw what I thought were weak points, and saw some good points as well as faults in individual form. We have practically the same club as last year. The boys have been working hard in training camp and have enjoyed it. Why, just this spring, the improvement in teamwork has been wonderful. The pitching staff is in shape, and the infield looks mighty good. We have some extra outfielders that will keep the regulars hustling to hold on to their jobs.[38]

The Pirates began the 1932 campaign with a disappointing road trip. They finally set foot in Pittsburgh on April 20, where Gibson stepped into the manager's box for the first time in ten years. After a scoreless three innings, one of the Cardinals illegally blocked a Pirates runner on the basepaths. Gibson decided to set a fighting example for his uninspired club and stormed out of the dugout to protest. The umpire promptly ejected Gibby, which is exactly what the manager had hoped for. Gibby's riot act energized the Pirates as *Pittsburgh Post-Gazette* Edward Balinger explained:

> George Gibson, new pilot of the Pirate brig, was exiled from the activities by Chief Umpire Charley Rigler for storming over a play at the plate in the fourth inning just after the struggle had been decided. The absence of the leader, however, had little effect on the galiant performance of his athletes, for the big Canadian already had infused into their systems all the fighting spirit that was to be needed.[39]

The Bucs won their home opener, 7–0. The win sparked a streak and Gibson's no-nonsense managing propelled the Bucs to play a more inspired type of baseball. By the end of July, Gibson's club stood 19 games over .500 with a 59 and 40 record. Their play landed the Pirates in first place, 5½ games ahead of the Cubs. However, just as Pittsburgh fans became excited at the possibility of a first National League pennant since 1909, Gibson's crew slid unexpectedly. From July 30 through August 25, the Pirates went a dismal 5–22, which resulted in a 13-game swing in the standings. Although the Pirates fought valiantly to chase down Chicago, they finished four games back with a record of 85–68. Of little consolation to the Pirates, the Yankees walloped the Cubs in a four-game World Series sweep.

When the 1932 season ended, so, too, did Gibson's contract. While he pondered what to do as a lame duck manager, he headed to Texas to see, for the first time, his new granddaughter. As Gibson and Benswanger did not meet before the trip, reporters and fans speculated about Gibby's status as Pirates skipper. Signs pointed to him coming back. On the surface, Gibson and Benswanger had a good working relationship. Furthermore, the team performed exceptionally well in 1932 thanks to Gibson's leadership. Reporters certainly gave their vote of confidence. They suggested that Gibson deserved a salary increase, quite the declaration considering that the country was in the throws of the Great Depression.[40]

Honus Wagner (left) and George Gibson enter the players' entrance at Forbes Field in 1933. Gibson hired Wagner to be a coach for his club (Healy Collection).

Still, nothing was going to happen until the two sides sat down. Gibson facilitated that meeting with senior management when he returned from Texas in mid–October. The two sides quickly hammered out a deal; however, they did not disclose the details to the public or press. Gibson offered up a few earnest sentiments: "Nothing pleases me more than to be chosen again to serve as manager of the ball team with which I was associated for so many years. It was in Pittsburgh that I began my major league career and I have learned to feel that this is my home. I expect to reside here this winter, but will leave here in a few days for a short sojourn in London, Ont. Then I will come back and take up the work of planning for next season and will attend the minor league meetings at Columbus and also the December sessions of the majors in New York City."[41] Gibson later recalled a brief part of a conversation he had with Benswanger after resigning. The Pirates' president told Gibson, "Gibby, I hope we stay together until our whiskers touch the floor." Gibson could only reply with, "Don't worry Bill. We won't."[42]

Going into 1933, Gibson, a lifelong National League member, was mildly disturbed with all the talk amidst the baseball world about which American League slugger, Lou Gehrig of the New York Yankees or Jimmie Foxx of the Philadelphia Athletics, had the most power behind their bats. Gibson thought that many National League players could give those American League fellas a run for their money. "If the American League pitchers think they are in trouble when Foxx and Gehrig are at the plate, they should try facing Riggs Stephenson of the Cubs, Paul Waner of the Pirates or Chick Hafey of the Reds through an entire season." Gibby explained his reasons for his assumption, "I believe Stephenson hits a harder ball than anyone else in our league. That old boy is liable to handcuff an infielder any time. He doesn't drive out a particularly long ball, but it goes into the outfield like a bullet. The beauty of Riggs' batting is that he hits with equal strength to all fields. Next I would place Paul Waner. Paul, like Stephenson, isn't noted for getting distance, but I have never seen a man who can smash the ball so hard past first base, nor a left hand hitter who can wallop them into left field so fast. Chick Hafey is third, according to my way of looking at it, although he is almost a dead left field hitter and when he drops them into another field, his hits do not have the same steam."[43]

George had high hopes for 1933. In addition to his own team, he felt the Cubs and Giants possessed the talent necessary to take the pennant. He even went so far as to raid the Giants' roster of Fred Lindstrom and Waite Hoyt, which brought the Pirates two more future Hall of Famers. The acquisition led Gibson to say that he needed to be mindful of the cold weather "or fear my face doesn't freeze in a perpetual smile."[44]

With Lindstrom inserted into the outfield, over 60 percent of the starting lineup would end up in the Hall. On days when Hoyt pitched, two-thirds of the lineup registered as baseball immortals. Gibson, not surprisingly, felt that he had the best outfield in the big leagues; with Forbes Field's cavernous dimensions, the team needed that kind of talent out there. Gibson knew, for better or worse, that his team would sink or swim on the arms of their pitchers. While not the best rotation, Gibson hoped his arsenal of batters and their strong defense would carry them to a top-line finish. In addition to their new gem on the field, Gibson added some coaching firepower in the one and only Honus Wagner. Gibson pegged Wagner to coach the infield and the Flying Dutchman, when asked about his new role, said: "I want to be of every possible assistance to George Gibson."[45] For the first time since he retired in 1917,

Wagner donned the Pirates rags. Needless to say, Gibby was ecstatic to have his old friend along for the pennant hunt.

Before leaving for spring training in Paso Robles, Gibson received a letter of encouragement from the subcontinent of India. A former Pittsburgh native, the Reverend Marsh, had moved to India to do missionary work. He couldn't get over his love of the Bucs and penned a letter to the Pittsburgh pilot. "You doubtless receive many fan letters, but I venture to think you will not have received a letter of a fan as far away as I happen to be. For years I have followed the ups and downs of the Pirates. I have rejoiced in their victories and bemoaned their defeats...." He gave George his best. "I rejoice to know that a man of your character is identified with my favorite team. So here is wishing you good luck and a fair share of the breaks in 1933. Your success will bring real pleasure to me."[46] George, living in Canada and working in the United States, likely got used to being an international star, but to have fans as far away as India really shows how loved he was among the Pittsburgh faithful.

Unlike the previous year, the Pirates started off 1933 by scorching their opponents. By the end of May, the club owned a 24–15 record, good enough for first position. They slipped to third at the end of June, but bounced back in July and ranked in second place, 3½ games behind the Giants. However, the fanfare

Left to Right: W. W. Bensanger, president of the Pittsburgh Pirates; Honus Wagner, former star and Pirates coach; and George Gibson, 1933 Pirates manager (Healy Collection).

that accompanied the announcement of Gibson's extended contract came with high expectations. In spite of his club's second-place standing, around Pittsburgh, George was said to be on the hot seat. Bucs president William Benswanger quickly defended his man and went so far as to say that "Gibby is doing as well as you or I or the other fellow could. We are trying to win with the material we have. The fact that our outfield hasn't hit as we expected and some of our pitchers haven't delivered as we anticipated is not Gibson's fault. No one is more disappointed than myself or Gibson that the club hasn't won more games. But don't forget we aren't out of the race yet."[47]

Pittsburgh Press **cartoon of George Gibson (courtesy the** *Pittsburgh Post-Gazette*).

Pittsburgh Press **cartoon of George Gibson (courtesy the** *Pittsburgh Post-Gazette*).

A heated early August series with the St. Louis Cardinals had the teams in fisticuffs. The teams threw spikes and fists during the three-game series which boiled over in the second game. Pittsburgh shortstop Arky Vaughan hit a ground ball and headed for first. Meanwhile, Cardinals pitcher Bill Walker sprinted over to serve as the de facto first basemen; the men collided at the bag with a thunderous smash. Walker didn't take too kindly to Vaughan's hustle and started throwing haymakers. The benches spilled onto the field, each looking for a dancing partner, but the umpires stepped in and ended the fracas quickly. The next evening, the press asked Gibson what he thought of the Vaughan/Walker situation and about any potential melees in the series closer:

Anytime any player takes a swing at my boys I will order them to swing back. What else could the kid [Vaughan] do when Walker hit him. We won't play rowdy baseball, but we also won't stand for that kind of stuff they pulled on us yesterday and today without swinging back. However, there is no bad blood between our two clubs. It's merely a case of two such incidents happening on successive days.[48]

Gibby's Pirates lost the final game of the series to Cardinals pitching stud Dizzy Dean. There was no rough stuff but the loss kept the Pirates 3½ games behind the Giants. The stage was set for a pennant race that looked to be going right down to the finish.

The Bucs did make up ground on the Giants down the stretch but finished the season four games back. Gibby led his club to an 87–67 record, second place for the second straight season. With six future Hall of Famers on his club (Waite Hoyt, Lindstrom, Traynor, Vaughn and the Waner brothers, "Big and Little Poison"), the Pirates faithful expected and seemingly demanded the flag. In the end, Gibson did not get a strong performance from his arms, and that doomed the team. Gibson ended 1933 just as he had 1932, and with no pennant in two seasons Gibson headed to Texas. However, this time, his future was anything but certain.

That off-season, local press steered clear of the previous year's optimism. Fans remained in limbo and George appeared to be on thin ice. On October 19, President Benswanger informed fans that he would choose a manager soon. He wanted to have his skipper in place as soon as possible so he could start shaping plans for next season. Benswanger gave himself an early November deadline to make the hire so his manager could attend the annual minor-league meetings with him in Galveston, Texas.

The following day, William E. Benswanger announced Gibson had accepted his offer to manage the club for the 1934 season. They communicated by telegraph because Gibby was still vacationing in Texas. George signed the papers early in the new year but even before he put pen to paper, Benswanger stated: "We have weighed all of the evidence carefully, considered the wishes of the fans and scanned the field of managerial timber from top to bottom. We considered the problem of a manager first after the World Series closed and have been working on the matter ever since. Gibson is our choice."[49] When Gibby returned from Texas to meet with Benswanger, he told reporters about his time in the Lone Star State. George told them he did get some golfing in and noted he did not get any birdies, "but almost landed a couple of deer."[50]

Even if fans and newspapermen seemed to be on the fence about Mooney's return, Pirates players, wintering all over the country, wrote letters to President Benswanger regarding their delight with the reappointment. Paul Waner was one of the first to send a letter. From his off-season home in Florida, he stated how glad he was that George was retained. Larry French, Pittsburgh's lefty ace, wrote from Los Angeles that Gibby could get greatness out of his ballplayers better than any skip he had ever played for. Pitcher

Waite Hoyt penned from Brooklyn and expressed his satisfaction with Gibson managing again in '34. Steve Swetonic, Lloyd Waner and Hal Smith all sent the president notes telling how pleased they were with the decision. Of course, coach, ex-teammate and good friend Hans Wagner was more than ecstatic that George would still be around.[51]

Despite Pittsburgh's yearning for years gone by, the game continued to evolve during Gibson's second stint as manager. At the 1933 winter meetings in Chicago, the owners and managers debated the actual baseballs used. Recently, the American League had started using a ball with thinner covering and fewer stitches. This resulted in more potent offenses which seemed to excite more fans, increase the attendance and generate more money for the powers that be. In the end, the National League adopted the more lively "jackrabbit" ball,[52] which provided Gibson with yet another obstacle to overcome: a new style of baseball. While Gibson knew deadball era baseball and preferred the strategy and small ball style of play, he was willing to change and adapt. In the end, he took the challenge head on and never once used it as an excuse for any misgivings on the field.

When the Pittsburgh club arrived at Paso Robles for the start of spring training, there were concerns among the ranks with how Gibby would condition his pitchers. In 1933 the Pirates pitching staff ran out of gas down the stretch, which caused them to miss out on the pennant. Gibson believed in vigorous running to build up his pitchers' stamina for the work of a season, but some of the pitchers didn't agree; they did not like all the running. In 1934, some members of the pitching staff expressed their displeasure with that new routine. Gibby had none of it and his pitchers ran. However, the ever-thoughtful Gibson tried to appease his disgruntled hurlers by changing up the drills.

Many pitchers took much pride in their batting, so instead of suicide sprints and things of that nature, Gibson let his moundsmen partake in batting practice, with a notable condition. After a few hits, Gibson made the fellas run the bases. Adding an element of baserunning accomplished two things: it established the pitchers' confidence on the base paths and it had them do the cardiovascular exercise that Gibby wanted. Gibby resigned to have his men stay on their feet and insisted they walk to and from the ball grounds each day. They were not allowed to use their own vehicles or accept an automobile ride from their friends. A week into camp, pitchers ran nearly 4 hours daily. Gibson believed that "if a pitcher's wind is perfect his arm will get into condition, too."[53]

Gibson's men kicked off their season playing ordinary baseball and finished the first month of the year at 5–5. After their slow start, Pittsburgh won 15 and lost 11 in May. Just four games behind the league-leading Cardinals, the Pirates expected to continue their climb in June. Unfortunately, the sea-

The 1934 Pirates, Gibson's final club (Armstrong Collection).

son soured, and the club lost 8 of 9 games from June 8 through June 19. A shake-up was imminent.

In the midst of the prolonged slump, President Benswanger called a meeting with Gibby to discuss the team. He was concerned that George was losing the reins on his club. Despite the scores during the streak, Gibby felt his hitters performed admirably and felt the pitchers held their own. He admitted that he did not know how to solve the problem. William issued an ultimatum: "If there isn't a change in this ball club in the next two or three weeks, I'm gonna change managers." A disheartened Gibson responded to his boss, "Bill, listen. Two or three weeks? It'll be two or three years before there is any material change for the better in this ball club. Now, if you feel like you do, now is the time to do it."[54] The men agreed that Gibson would leave the club. Just like that, Gibson's storied career in the major leagues, the highest level of baseball in the world, came to an unceremonious conclusion.

Third baseman Pie Traynor took over as Pirates manager. Upon his leaving, Gibby wished Traynor well. "I'm sorry I couldn't come through with the Pirates, I had my heart set on a winning team and a pennant. The executives of the Pittsburgh Baseball Club thought a change was necessary in the management of the team and I'm glad to step out in accord with their wishes. I wish Pie Traynor all the luck in the world." Then, George relayed his disappointment to Pittsburgh's fans: "I am still an ardent supporter of the Pirates, and my heart always will be with them. There's nothing I wouldn't do to help them and I sincerely trust they will get out of this slump. It is with regret that the time has come when I must part with them, but under the present conditions it was the only thing left for the club to make a change. I intend to remain in Pittsburgh where most of my family now is located. We probably will drive to San Antonio shortly for a visit with our daughter who resides there, but I propose to continue living in Wilkinsburg and rooting for the team with which I was so long and pleasantly associated."[55] At the time of his release, Pittsburgh found themselves on the right side of the .500 mark with a 27–24 record. In his absence, the club fell even further. They finished in fifth with a record of 74–76.

Eventually, Gibson pardoned Benswanger for his mismanagement of the team. Gibson recollected that Benswanger was an insurance salesman who could not have possibly understood how to run a baseball club. He further explained that the president pilfered through fan mail addressed to George. In many writings, fans offered up uninformed advice on how to improve the club. Consequently, Benswanger questioned Gibson for not considering their counsel. George knew better than to take direction from know-it-all fans. Benswanger, however, felt pressure to appease the Pirates faithful. Because Benswanger catered to the public, Gibby's last official day on a big-league roster was that late spring day. For "Moon," it was not a sad day, because he knew, on the subject of baseball, "The fella didn't know anything."[56]

13

Forever a Baseball Man

After the Pirates released George in 1934, his career as a member of Major League Baseball officially ended. Following Gibson's retirement, he returned to Ontario and tended to his Mount Brydges farm. George and Margaret also maintained a residence in London, which kept them close to family. Their residence near Victoria Park was in a neighborhood inhabited by many influential Londoners. Two prominent men, John Jr. and Hugh Labatt, sons of the famous brewer, John Labatt, became close friends with George. According to George's nephew, George Lambourn, when the Labatt family decided to purchase Tecumseh Park, they did so based on a suggestion by Gibson himself.[1] The park previously belonged to London residents Arthur and George Little. Throughout the Great Depression the park had fallen into disrepair and had become a mere shadow of its former glory. On December 15, 1936, John Sackville Labatt acted on Gibson's advice and purchased the grounds with a pledge of $10,000 for restoration. They donated the ball field to the city of London on the condition the ballpark be renamed in remembrance of John's father.

In the spring of 1937, the Thames River overran its banks and caused mass devastation to both the ballpark and the city. The river reached twenty-one and a half feet above its usual summer flow. It caused five deaths and destroyed an estimated eleven hundred homes. Property damage was estimated at $3,000,000 (equivalent to $51,600,000 in 2019).[2] Many of the Gibsons' relatives occupied affected homes, and in some cases, George himself rescued them by boat. He brought his family back to his Central Avenue home, where they remained for a week until the flood waters receded and their homes were safe to return to. The flood totally washed out Tecumseh Park, which rested on the shore of the Thames. The grandstand toppled, and the water ravaged the ball field so much so that at initial glance, the grounds were left forever unplayable. The Labatt family, however, stepped up in a big way and donated an additional $10,000 to help recover from the flood.

Later that year, George's youngest son William graduated from the University of Western Ontario with his Doctor of Medicine degree. William then began an internship at Pittsburgh hospital. The move allowed him to be closer to his brother, George Jr., already an established physician in the Pittsburgh area, dating back to his father's time in the city. This gave George and Margaret another excuse to travel to Pittsburgh on a regular basis. Following William's appointment, George and Margaret sold their London home and moved out to their Mount Brydges farm full-time. The large farm offered plenty of space for George to host his children. Now that George was not playing baseball in the summer, his children had the opportunity to visit him during the warm months when his grandchildren were out of school. George's granddaughter Bucky Smith, now in her 90s, still fondly recalls loading into the family car and making the three-day trek from Texas to London to visit her grandparents.

Despite moving out of the city, George was still very present in the Lon-

Undated photograph of George (left), with his sons Billy (middle) and George Jr. (right), enjoying a day of fishing after George's baseball career had ended (courtesy Carol Smith).

don baseball scene. In the late 1930s, George spotted a player by the name of Frank Colman playing in the London City League; George convinced the Pirates to offer Frank a contract. Colman's father refused to allow his son to accept the deal because he wanted him to finish school first. Colman eventually joined the professional ranks, and made his major-league debut with the Pirates in September 1942. Colman played parts of five years with the Bucs before they sold him to the Yankees. Frank Colman credited Mooney for providing his path to the big leagues.[3]

In 1939, the Pittsburgh Pirates lost $8,000 on account of the location of their minor-league affiliate's ballpark in Jamestown.[4] When Jamestown officials failed to assure the Pirates that a new stadium would be built, the

George Gibson greets fellow London big-league player, Frank Colman (The *London Free Press* Collection of Photographic Negatives, July 9, 1955, Archives and Special Collections, Western University, London, Canada).

team decided to move the club.[5] On February 8, 1940, the Pittsburgh Pirates announced that they were relocating their Pennsylvania-Ontario-New York (PONY) League farm club from Jamestown, New York, to London, Ontario. George's influence on the Pirates played heavily in that decision.

London wasn't the only city to show interest in hosting the Pirates' farm team. However, Joe Schultz, head of the Pirates' farm clubs, visited London and knew it was easily the best option. In his official report, Schultz noted that he found baseball fans in London to be particularly enthusiastic about having the Pirates come to town. A feeling, he noted, existed towards the Pirates "ever since the days when one of their fellow citizens, George Gibson, put them upon the baseball map by blossoming into one of the catching stars of the major loops."[6]

On July 13, 1940, the fully renovated and newly named John Labatt Memorial Park, with its new locker rooms, new seating and an art deco entrance, officially opened. Many prominent Londoners attended the London Pirates game against the Batavia Clippers. George participated in the opening ceremonies and served as the club's ambassador. In addition to his duties as ambassador, he also acted as a scout. Gibson put a lot of faith in Francis G. Brewer, a 19-year-old backstop from London. Gibson felt Brewer possessed a particularly strong and accurate arm and thought he could turn out to be a real find. Brewer failed to live up to Gibson's expectations, but two London Pirates did ascend to the major leagues. Vic Barnhart, an infielder from Hagerstown, Maryland, played for London for two years and then went on to play three seasons with Pittsburgh. Andy Seminick, a catcher and left fielder from Pierce, West Virginia, played with London in 1940, and eventually went on to play 15 major-league seasons. After two seasons, the Pirates decided they preferred to have all of their farm clubs within the United States, and relocated the London Pirates to Hornell, New York.[7]

The lack of a major-league affiliated team in London didn't stop George from finding ways to stay connected to Major League Baseball. During the Second World War, Canada's colonial mother, England, was devastated by continuous bombing by the German Air Force. The initial bombing of England's capital of London began in October 1940 and continued until May 1941. The Blitz, as the German bombing campaign was known, killed more than 40,000 civilians and destroyed more than one million houses. After England retaliated with an air assault on German targets, the Luftwaffe attacked the British mainland again. Beginning in March 1942, England was shelled during an offensive called the Baedeker Blitz, which led to even more casualties.[8] The city of London, Ontario, planned a benefit baseball game to raise money for the victims of the air raids in their namesake city. They called upon George to recruit baseball men with star power to attract fans and ensure a maximum turnout for the benefit game. He didn't let down the cause. Longtime Philadelphia Athletics manager, Connie Mack, accepted an invitation from Gibby to attend the match, as did his former Pirates teammate, Honus Wagner. The Flying Dutchman's letter of response said, "Hello Hack, In reply to your letter, I will make the trip to London August 14, so look for me unless something happens in the meantime. I will have to ship you a uniform for the game as I could not carry two sets. The border men would pinch me. I have told Benswanger to ship you a uniform."[9] The Queen's Fund Benefit Game was the first time Gibson dawned a Pirates uniform in almost a decade. George, at 63 years old, caught the first inning for the London Old-Timers team as they routed the local police club, 15–5. Many fans turned out to watch the famous baseballers of years past and a tidy sum of $1,500 (equivalent of $23,000 in 2019) was raised for air raid victims.

The scout/coach teacher bug in Gibson's veins never went away. In 1947, the local Thamesville Board of Trade, and his former club from Pittsburgh,

World War II charity game at Labatt Park, London, Ontario. Left to right: Honus Wagner, Connie Mack and George Gibson (The *London Free Press* Collection of Photographic Negatives, August 13, 1943, Archives and Special Collections, Western University, London, Canada).

called and offered him a chance to teach youngsters at a development camp. George jumped at the opportunity. The Pirates' Canadian development camp attracted 300 players from as far away as Detroit and Ottawa. During the week of lessons, the Pirates hoped to find at least a few players to sign to contracts. George was impressed with a young battery he discovered at the camp: a pitcher who was 16 years old and catcher, 13. The boys were too young for big-league contracts though. He also helped the London Majors' star shortstop Don Cooper with infield drills. George got "just as much bang out of the showing of the young Canucks as the kids."[10] George got the call again in 1951, when the Cleveland Indians ran a development camp of their own in London. Despite being seriously ill, George made his way to Labatt Park to look over the players and chat with old friends Hank Gowdy and Tris Speaker, who were in town representing the Indians.

George returned to health, but in the spring of 1953, tragedy struck. Margaret Gibson, George's wife of more than 50 years passed away due to a heart condition. Some years later, Bill reflected on the impact his mother had on him in an interview with Forbes Health System:

> "I was guided more by her than anyone," he said. "She was a very disciplined woman. Both her and my father stressed getting an education. Back in those days (the 1920's

Gibson instructs Don Cooper, star shortstop of the Intercounty Baseball League, London Majors (The *London Free Press* Collection of Photographic Negatives, August 22, 1947, Archives and Special Collections, Western University, London, Canada).

and 30's) it was a great accomplishment just to graduate from high school. And I know if I would not have done that, they really would have tanned my hide," he said with a smile. What about his father, was he strict? "God, yes!," he bellowed, throwing his head up and leaning back in the chair. "He was a very strict disciplinarian—but also a sincere man." Perhaps some of the disciplinary traits came because of his profession. His father was a professional baseball player and manager for the Pirates in the early 1930's as well as coaching on an number of other teams in baseball. Because of this, he was not home too often during the summer so Bill's mother had to run the show.[11]

The family interred Margaret at Campbell Cemetery in Komoka, Ontario. George dealt with the loss by keeping himself busy. He made regular trips to Pittsburgh and continued to trek to Texas. Shortly after Margaret's death, Gibson made a pilgrimage to Pittsburgh. A *Pittsburgh Press* reporter found out George was in town, tracked him down, and offered to drive him out to see his old friend, and longtime teammate, Honus Wagner. Wagner was delighted to see Gibson. The two caught up, and of course talked baseball. The reporter got a kick out of their banter. "What would our 1909 team have done today, Honus?" Gibson asked the Flying Dutchman. Wagner chuckled and replied: "Win the pennant with eight men!"[12] On April 30, 1955, Honus

Gibson meets with Cleveland Indian representatives Tris Speaker and Hank Gowdy at London's Labatt Park in 1955. Cleveland held open tryouts for London players in 1955. Left to right: Gowdy, Gibson and Speaker (The *London Free Press* Collection of Photographic Negatives, July 5, 1955, Archives and Special Collections, Western University, London, Canada).

Wagner was honored with a statue in Schenley Park in Pittsburgh and George made sure to attend the celebration. George wanted to be there to support his friend and affirm to those in attendance that Wagner happened to be the best player ever to work on a baseball diamond.

In early 1955, Forest City baseball supporter Gordon Berryhill pitched the idea of creating a serious baseball league for the youth of London. Former big-leaguer and London Majors owner Frank Colman agreed with Berryhill and advocated for the league. They named the league the Eager Beaver Baseball Association. Berryhill acted as commissioner and Colman as president. They established the league with a motto: "The objective of the association is to implant firmly in the boys of the community, the ideals of good sportsmanship, honesty, loyalty, courage and reverence, so that they may be finer, stronger, and happier boys and will grow to be good, clean, healthy men." To encourage the growth of the league, the association appointed George Gibson as honorary lifetime president; no one else could better inspire young players as a role model.[13]

The new league opened on June 4, 1955. The players paraded down Dundas Street to Labatt Park, where city dignitaries took the field for an opening ceremony. City mayor George Beedle threw out the ceremonial first pitch and George Gibson acted as his 74-year-old backstop. Meanwhile, Frank Colman served as batsman and gave the ball a good whack. The umpire yelled "Play ball!" and the inaugural game of the Eager Beaver Baseball Association began. Gibson's lifelong love for the game never waned and he saw this new league as an opportunity. Gibby hoped, in part due to his involvement, that many of the Eager Beavers would be big-league stars in the future.[14] In their first season, the league involved 300 players on 12 teams. It has since grown substantially, and as of 2019 is still in operation.

A month later, some thirty-five years removed from his days on the diamond, George made headlines again. While visiting Pittsburgh, Gibson made an off-the-cuff comment to a journalist about the durability of mid-century catchers. Gibby still despised the use of shin guards, saying "they made a sissy of the catcher."[15] Hundreds of papers across the United States, from Wilkes-Barre, Pennsylvania, to Salem, Oregon, syndicated the comment. George still knew how to draw a crowd.

George and his wife, Margaret, circa 1950 (courtesy Carol Smith).

George always preferred the game to be played like it was during his playing days. However, in his later years, just as he had done during the deadball-era debate in 1933, George knew the game needed to evolve to keep fans' attention. By the 1960s, he felt play in Major League Baseball had deteriorated and that the minor-league system had followed suit. Gibson blamed the situation on money: "Babe Ruth, when Babe come up, Babe started that home run business and they built the present Yankee Stadium to suit Babe. They brought that right field bleachers in for Babe.... Babe could hit 'em down there just as good as anybody. Well, that's what the people wanted, the Yankees were drawing the crowds … if you're in a business, no mat-

ter what business you're in …
you gotta swing the business
to satisfy the public."[16]

Though he understood
the necessity of that change,
his fondest memories from
baseball often recalled incidents from his time on active
duty, when things just seemed
different to him. Gibson loved
to recount those stories to
anyone who would listen and
did so in fine fashion. One
day, Frank Bowerman, who
Gibson called "the gamest guy
who ever put on a uniform,"
fell in front of a beer cart. The
cart went right over Frank's
chest. The big fellow arose,
took a moment to regain his
wind, smiled and proceeded
to the Polo Grounds. When
John McGraw asked Frank
about the accident, Bowerman
informed his manager that "it
didn't amount to anything …
it hardly left a mark." As Gibson told it, McGraw wasn't
satisfied, and asked Frank to

Gibson instructs a few young lads on the inaugural opening day of the Eager Beaver Baseball
Association (The *London Free Press* Collection of Photographic Negatives, June 4, 1955,
Archives and Special Collections, Western University, London, Canada).

take off his shirt. The big catcher complied, promptly disrobed and proudly displayed the imprint of the wide steel tire on his chest. Gibson greatly admired
that kind of toughness and certainly practiced what he preached as well.[17]

In his book *Touching Second*, Hall of Famer Johnny Evers relayed a story
about George. Evers mentioned a time in 1909 that Gibson "had black and
blue spots imprinted by nineteen foul tips upon his body, a damaged hand, a
bruised hip six inches square where a thrown bat had struck, and three spike
cuts."[18] One might wonder why a man who took such a tremendous beating
never donned shin guards. After all, catchers back then played with all sorts
of bumps, bruises and cuts. It's clear that Gibson was far more hardened than
his fellow catchers of the time. He considered the wear and tear of a 154-game
season inevitable and if he was going to get beat up, he might as well be comfortable while doing it.

Gibby shows his mangled hands thirty years after his playing career ended (The *London Free Press* Collection of Photographic Negatives, August 22, 1947, Archives and Special Collections, Western University, London, Canada).

Gibson didn't need any help to make it through the grind. From 1907 to 1910, George appeared in more games as catcher than any other player in the National League. Not only did he appear, he also performed. From 1907 to 1912, he finished in the top three in the National League for putouts by a catcher. While his volume of appearances helped pad that stat, he also registered fielding percentage superiority in three of those seasons. From 1908 to 1910, Gibson ranked in the league's top five for defensive WAR. Over those four seasons, no other catcher appeared in the top ten in every campaign. Had the Gold Glove Award existed between 1907 and 1912, Gibson would surely have secured a few of those trophies.

Further consideration shows that George excelled at the plate as well as in the field. In 1909, the year of his ironman streak, George set career highs in hits, doubles, triples, RBIs and stolen bases. Had the Silver Slugger Award existed, it's hard to believe Gibson wouldn't have won it. He ranked in the top ten for offensive WAR, making him and Hall of Famer Roger Bresnahan the only National League catchers during the deadball era to appear in the top ten of both offensive and defensive WAR in the same season.

As a manager for parts of seven seasons, he led his clubs to an overall record of 413–344 and finished in second place three times. In recognition of his long tenure as a professional baseball player and Manager George received a lifetime pass from National League president, Ford C. Frick.[19] The Commissioner's Office presents long-tenured players, umpires, scouts, executives and employees with passes that allow them, plus a guest, admission into any major-league park for the rest of their lives.

Time and time again, Gibson played and performed alongside the best of them. He dominated baseball in ways many people overlook. Aside from recognition by the Canadian Baseball Hall of Fame and the lifetime pass, he never saw his just deserts in his lifetime. By the late 1960s, Gibson's age caught up with him. By then in his 80s, cancer crept in. Due to his advanced age, doctors considered operating too risky.[20]

From there, George's health slowly declined and nurses regularly visited. In the winter of 1967, Marguerite traveled from her home in Texas to stay in Mount Brydges to look after her father. In January, Victoria Hospital admitted George, where he passed away on January 25, 1967. Announcements of his death spread across Canada and the United States. Hundreds of reporters disseminated the sad news but used the opportunity to affirm his status as a deadball-era iron man. Though many of his teammates had already passed on, Commissioner of Baseball William Eckert, along with a large entourage, traveled to London to attend Mooney's funeral. George's great niece, Julie Anne Baskette, who was ten years old at the time, remembers being impressed not only by the men's fancy suits and fancy cars, but by the fact that they made the trip to small-town London in the middle of winter to pay their respects.[21] As expected, the family interred George in Komolka in a shared plot with Margaret.

The National Baseball Hall of Fame has been notoriously stingy with catchers from Gibson's era. Of the 18 catchers inducted all-time, only Roger Bresnahan played alongside Gibson. George played in an era where catchers made their contributions on defense. Men like Jimmy Archer, Johnny Kling, Larry McLean, "Chief" Meyers and Red Dooin were all essential to their team's success. Bill James, father of SABR-metrics, refers to the era of catching between 1903 and 1909 as "The Kling-Bresnahan-Gibson Era," as he considers them "the three best catchers in baseball in that era."[22]

Even if the Hall overlooked Gibby, others have recognized his achievements on the diamond. In 1950, George was named Canada's Baseball Player of the Half Century, and in 1958, he was the first baseball player elected to Canada's Sports Hall of Fame. On August 5, 1982, fifteen years after his death, George was honored by the Pittsburgh Pirates at Three Rivers Stadium between games of a doubleheader. His son, Dr. William Gibson, was present to accept the award on his behalf.[23] In 1987, the Canadian Baseball Hall of Fame drafted Gibson into their ranks. Seven years later, on August 19, 1989, a plaque was installed on the side of the grandstand of John Labatt Park,[24] and in 2002, George was part of the inaugural class inducted into the London Sports Hall of Fame. As of 2019, George is the last Canadian to manage full-time in Major League Baseball.

When George Gibson's baseball career ended, he spoke to the *Pittsburgh Post-Gazette* about his greatest baseball thrill. The catcher's favorite baseball memory was not winning the 1909 World Series, was not achieving the record for most consecutive games caught and was not the myriad of accolades he received throughout his career. Gibby's greatest thrill was when he was trusted as a leader. He recalled a moment in his career which brought him great joy. Before a game, late in the 1909 pennant race, Fred Clarke, unsure of what pitcher to use in the important game, turned to George. He told Gibson: "George, I'm not going to pick the pitcher today. I'm going to put that up to you."[25] George was greatly honored by his skipper's trust in him. He relished being the go-to guy. During his young career, Gibby wanted to be on the field regardless of any physical ailments. As a veteran, he treasured teaching young players and leading club outings. As a manager, Gibson found satisfaction in developing players and providing them with the skills and discipline to become the best ballplayers they could be. George Gibson's career has gone underappreciated in baseball history. But whatever you call him, be it Gib or Gibby, Hack or Hackenschmidt, Moon or Mooney, one thing is certain: his skill, durability, determination and leadership make George not just a baseball icon, but also a great man to be inspired by.

Epilogue

George Gibson ended his playing career in 1918, and throughout the century since his retirement, over 150 Canadians have appeared in the major leagues. But unlike Gibson's era, when the Great White North produced many catchers, since the deadball era Canada has produced very few backstops. Two Canuck catchers made lightning quick appearances in the big leagues during baseball's golden age. Eric Mackenzie of Glendon, Alberta, caught one inning for the Kansas City Athletics in 1955, and Jim Lawrence of Hamilton, Ontario, was behind the plate for three innings in 1963 as a member of the Cleveland Indians. Thirty years later in 1993, when Joe Siddall of Windsor, Ontario, caught on with the Montreal Expos, the occasion marked the first time a Canuck backstop started for an MLB club on his native soil. Siddall's appearance began a small surge of Canadian catchers to the show, albeit, most often, only for a cup of coffee. Greg O'Halloran, Pete Laforest, Andy Stewart, Maxim St. Pierre, Cody McKay, George Kottaras and Mike Nickeas all took their place behind a major-league plate. It wasn't until 2006 that a Canadian-born catcher began building the same credentials as Gibson had throughout his career.

Russell Martin, who grew up in Montreal, hit the ground running when he was called to the show. He was selected to the All-Star Game in his sophomore season. Through his 2018 season, Martin has played in four All-Star games, made eight playoff appearances, and won a Silver Slugger and Gold Glove award. Martin is noted for possessing the same type of grit behind the plate that George displayed during his career a century earlier. Martin played two seasons with Gibson's "alma mater," the Pittsburgh Pirates, and led the Bucs to two straight playoff appearances in 2013 and 2014. Russell compelled long-time Pirates announcer Greg Brown to scream "Clear the Deck, Cannonball Coming!" on account of the many mammoth home runs Russell swatted for the Pittsburgh club. Martin stood behind the plate with the storied Los Angeles Dodger and New York Yankee franchises, and also wore the big mitt for his native Toronto Blue Jays.

It took even longer for a catcher from Gibson's hometown of London to stand behind the dish in a major-league game. In September of the 2013 MLB season, Chris Robinson, a 29-year-old minor-league veteran received a call to the show by the National League's San Diego Padres. Although he played in only eight games, his first hit, a home run, drew one of the greatest calls a Canuck long ball has ever received. Legendary sportscaster, the late Dick Enberg, gave Robinson one of his famous "Oh, My's." On September 25, Padres manager Bud Black called on Robinson to pinch-hit in the bottom of the eighth inning in a game against the Arizona Diamondbacks. Chris rewarded Black when he launched a ball into the left field bleachers of Petco Park. Enberg could not contain his excitement and exclaimed, "Oh, my. That's wonderful. Chris Robinson, a lifetime minor leaguer, a hockey player from Canada, loves baseball. He has his first hit, and it's a home run. Oh, my. A three run shot for Robinson."[1]

Other Londoners have had fruitful baseball careers. Paul Quantrill played fourteen seasons in the majors. He was a member of his native country's Toronto Blue Jays for six seasons and received one All-Star nod during his career. Adam Stern played in the big leagues with the Red Sox, Orioles and Brewers. In the baseball world, Stern is best known for the inside-the-park home run he hit for Canada against the United States during the 2006 World Baseball Classic. Jamie Romak had a cup of coffee with the Dodgers and Diamondbacks before taking his talents to the Korean Baseball Organization. In 2018, the Canadian slugger helped his club, the Incheon Wyverns, to victory in the 37th Korean Series. The newest London baseball sensation is Adam Hall, a middle infielder selected by the Baltimore Orioles in the second round of the 2017 MLB draft. He is a sure bet to cover the orange birds' infield in the not too distant future.

George would be proud so many of his fellow countrymen dedicated themselves to the beautiful game of baseball, the game he loved. His hometown of London has produced the most big-league players per capita in Canada's history, with a total of 15. Only the large centers of Toronto and Montreal have sent more players to the majors. Although Gibby was not the first professional ballplayer from his hometown, he certainly left the greatest baseball legacy in London, and hopefully all the yannigans playing now remember him.

Appendix 1:
Major League Statistics

George "Moon" Gibson
Height: 5'11" Weight: 190lb Batted: Right Threw: Right
Born: July 22, 1880, in London, Ontario
Died: January 25, 1967, in London, Ontario

Batting Statistics

Year	Team	G	AB	R	H	2B	3B	HR	RBI	BB	SO	AVG
1905	PIT	46	135	14	24	2	2	2	14	15	--	.178
1906	PIT	81	259	8	46	6	1	0	20	16	--	.178
1907	PIT	113	382	28	84	8	7	3	35	18	--	.220
1908	PIT	143	486	37	111	19	4	2	45	19	--	.228
1909	PIT	150	510	42	135	25	9	2	52	44	--	.265
1910	PIT	143	482	53	125	22	6	3	44	47	31	.259
1911	PIT	100	311	32	65	12	2	0	19	29	16	.209
1912	PIT	95	300	23	72	14	3	2	35	20	16	.240
1913	PIT	48	118	6	33	4	2	0	12	10	8	.280
1914	PIT	102	274	19	78	9	5	0	30	27	27	.285
1915	PIT	120	351	28	88	15	6	1	30	31	25	.251
1916	PIT	33	84	4	17	2	2	0	4	3	7	.202
1917	NYG	35	82	1	14	3	0	0	5	7	2	.171
1918	NYG	4	2	0	1	1	0	0	0	0	0	.500
TOTAL		1,213	3,776	295	893	142	49	15	345	286	132	.236

Fielding Statistics

Year	Team	POS	G	TC	PO	A	E	Fielding %
1905	PIT	C	44	263	200	54	9	.966
1906	PIT	C	81	446	336	97	13	.971
1907	PIT	C	109	642	499	125	18	.972
1907	PIT	1B	1	2	2	0	0	1.000
1908	PIT	C	140	764	607	136	21	.973
1909	PIT	C	150	862	655	192	15	.983
1910	PIT	C	143	850	633	203	14	.984
1911	PIT	C	98	581	452	117	12	.979
1912	PIT	C	94	591	484	101	6	.990
1913	PIT	C	48	219	182	34	3	.986
1914	PIT	C	101	497	358	126	13	.974
1915	PIT	C	118	710	551	134	25	.965
1916	PIT	C	29	181	140	39	2	.989
1917	NYG	C	35	145	116	27	2	.986
1918	NYG	C	4	2	1	1	0	.977
TOTAL		C	1,194	6,753	5,214	1,386	153	.977
		1B	1	2	2	0	0	1.000

Appendix 2:
Photo Gallery

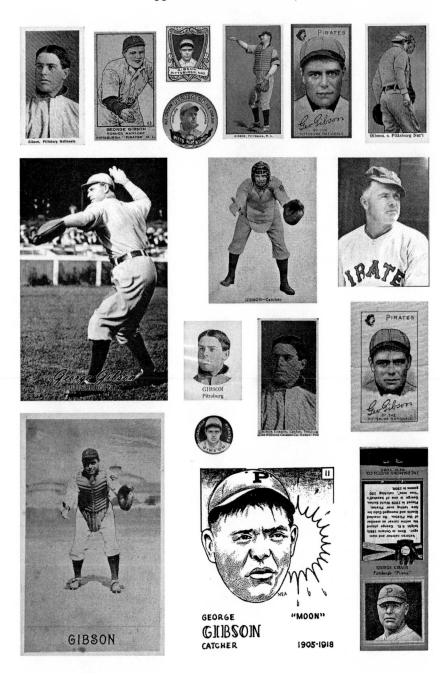

Above and opposite: During, and even after, George's playing career, he appeared on numerous collectible baseball cards. Shown here are just a few of the many cards featuring George Gibson (Armstrong and Healy Collections).

GIBSON

GIBSON, CATCHER PITTSBURGH
NATIONALS.

Chapter Notes

Introduction

1. Stephen V. Rice, "Bill Phillips," a Bio-Project of the Society for American Baseball Research, accessed April 2017, https://sabr.org/bioproj/person/e17af7a3.
2. "Players by birthplace: Canada Baseball Stats and Info," Baseball Reference, accessed April 2017, https://www.baseball-reference.com/bio/Canada_born.shtml.
3. "Tip O'Neill," Baseball Reference, accessed April 2017, https://www.baseball-reference.com/bullpen/Tip_O%27Neill.
4. Mike Lackey, "Larry McLean," a Bio-Project of the Society for American Baseball Research, accessed April 2017, https://sabr.org/bioproj/person/c2dad2dc.
5. *Ibid.*
6. "Tom Daly Stats," Baseball Reference, accessed April 2017, https://www.baseball-reference.com/players/d/dalyto02.shtml.
7. *Ibid.*
8. "Sports pioneers named to Hall of Fame (00/02/17)," Government of New Brunswick website, accessed April 2017, http://www.gnb.ca/cnb/news/misc/2000e0124mi.htm.
9. "Nig Clarke," Wikipedia, accessed April 2017, https://en.wikipedia.org/wiki/Nig_Clarke.
10. "Nig Clarke Enthuses Over Service In Marines," *Plain Cleveland Dealer*, December 16, 1917.
11. "Nig Clarke," Wikipedia, accessed April 2017, https://en.wikipedia.org/wiki/Nig_Clarke.
12. "Back of the Home Plate," *Sporting News*, April 16, 1925.
13. Bill Bishop, "Jimmy Archer," a Bio-Project of the Society for American Baseball Research, accessed April 2017, https://sabr.org/bioproj/person/c89dee76.
14. *Ibid.*

Chapter 1

1. "Untitled," *Pittsburgh Daily Post*, September 30, 1909.
2. "Gibson Greater Factor Than Wagner In Pittsburgh Team," *London Free Press*, October 8, 1909.
3. Lawrence Ritter Interview.
4. "Gibson Greater Factor Than Wagner In Pittsburgh Team," *London Free Press*, October 8, 1909.
5. *Ibid.*
6. "Pirate Pitcher Gives Much Credit To Gibson," *Pittsburgh Press*, October 9, 1909.
7. "Gibson's Good Work," *Pittsburgh Post-Gazette*, October 9, 1909.
8. Lawrence Ritter Interview.
9. *Ibid.*
10. *Ibid.*
11. *Ibid.*
12. "Cobb Really Showed How To Steal Home In '09 Series Here," *Pittsburgh Press*, July 21, 1961.
13. "Detroit Had Lead To Overcome Right At Start," *Detroit Free Press*, October 10, 1909.
14. "Pirates And Tigers Leave For Detroit," *Pittsburgh Press*, October 10, 1909.
15. *Ibid.*
16. "'Mooney' Gibson Given Big Ovation Yesterday," *London Advertiser*, October 12, 1909.
17. "Make A Rally In Seventh," *Detroit Free Press*, October 12, 1909.
18. "Told About The Tigers," *Detroit Free Press*, October 12, 1909.

19. "Pirates Shutout By Tigers," *Pittsburgh Daily Post*, October 13, 1909.
20. "I Only Wish I Had A Few Like Gibson," *London Free Press*, October 14, 1909.
21. "Pirates Take Fifth Game On Home Lot," *Pittsburgh Post-Gazette*, October 14, 1909.
22. "Adams In Fine Form, Score 8–4," *Pittsburgh Daily Post*, October 14, 1909.
23. "Buccaneers Likely To Clinch The World's Championship To-day," *Pittsburgh Daily Post*, October 14, 1909.
24. "Why Cobb Was Easy," *Pittsburgh Press*, October 21, 1909.
25. "Mullin Again Beats The Pittsburgh Team," *Pittsburgh Post-Gazette*, October 15, 1909.
26. "Teams Confident As They Prepare For Final Fight," *Pittsburgh Press*, October 15, 1909.
27. "'Babe' Adams May Pitch For Pirates Today," *Pittsburgh Post-Gazette*, October 16, 1909.
28. "Monster Crowd To See Pirates Play The Tigers," *Pittsburgh Press*, October 16, 1909.
29. "Pirates Are World Champions, 8–0," *Pittsburgh Daily Post*, October 17, 1909.
30. "Notes Jotted Down During Yesterday's Great Contest," *Pittsburgh Press*, October 17, 1909.
31. "Banquet For World Champs," *Pittsburgh Daily Post*, October 19, 1909.
32. "Glorious Greeting For Champion Pirates," *Pittsburgh Post-Gazette*, October 19, 1909.
33. "George Gibson's 1909 Pittsburgh Pirates World Championship Gold Pocketwatch," *Sotheby's*, accessed June 2017, http://www.sothebys.com/en/auctions/ecatalogue/2005/important-sports-memorabilia-and-cards-n08155/lot.120.html.
34. "Pirates Will Not Go On Barnstorming Trip," *Pittsburgh Post-Gazette*, October 19, 1909.
35. "Gibson Home Tuesday," *London Advertiser*, October 19, 1909.
36. "Tips and Thoughts," *Syracuse Journal*, January 31, 1907.
37. "National Is Better Than The American," *Pittsburgh Press*, October 19, 1909.
38. "The Real Mainstay Is Catcher Gibson," *Evening Chronicle*, September 8, 1910.
39. "Obey Orders And Keep Eyes Open, Says Adams," *Bismarck Tribune*, August 2, 1910.
40. *Ibid.*

41. "Niagara Falls Episode Told By Buc Pilot," *Pittsburgh Post-Gazette*, February 13, 1933.

Chapter 2

1. "All London Turns Out To Welcome 'Mooney' Home," *London Free Press*, October 27, 1909.
2. "West London Will Welcome Its Hero," *London Free Press*, October 26, 1909.
3. "All London Turns Out To Welcome 'Mooney' Home," *London Free Press*, October 27, 1909.
4. *Ibid.*
5. "London Catcher Presented With Silver Set," *London Advertiser*, October 27, 1909.
6. "All London Turns Out To Welcome 'Mooney' Home," *London Free Press*, October 27, 1909.
7. "Jennings Praises Gibson," *London Advertiser*, October 27, 1909.
8. "Gibson As A Catcher Is The Best In The Business," *London Free Press*, October 27, 1909.
9. "All London Turns Out To Welcome 'Mooney' Home," *London Free Press*, October 27, 1909.
10. "Jennings Praises Gibson," *London Advertiser*, October 27, 1909.
11. "London Catcher Presented With Silver Set," *London Advertiser*, October 27, 1909.
12. 1901 Canadian Census.
13. Multiple family tree sources on ancestry.com.
14. Frederick H. Armstrong, *The Forest City: An Illustrated History of London, Canada* (Burlington, ON: Windsor Publications, 1986), 81.
15. 1881 Canadian Census.
16. Brian Martin, *The Tecumsehs of the International Association: Canada's First Major League Baseball Champions* (Jefferson, NC: Mcfarland, 2015), 46.
17. *Ibid.*, 53.
18. *Ibid.*, 11.
19. Chip Martin, "Re: Tecumseh Book," email message to Martin Healy, February 6, 2018.
20. Lawrence Ritter Interview.
21. *Ibid.*
22. *Ibid.*
23. "Untitled, The Knox team…," *London Free Press*, July 26, 1898.

24. "Among The Amateurs," *London Free Press*, August 30, 1898.

25. "Need newspaper heading," *London Free Press*, June 6, 1903.

26. Multiple family tree sources on ancestry.com.

27. 1901 Canadian Census.

28. "Knox Vs. Woodstock," *London Free Press*, August 14, 1900.

29. 1901 Canadian Census.

30. "Vanquished An Old Enemy," *London Free Press*, May 2, 1901.

31. "London Bagged Both," *London Free Press*, May 25, 1901.

32. *Ibid.*

33. Lawrence Ritter Interview.

34. "Games From Various Diamonds," *Buffalo Morning Express (Illustrated Buffalo Express)*, July 5, 1901.

35. "Orients Look Formidable," *London Free Press*, May 5, 1902.

36. "Mooney Gibson's Pitching," *London Free Press*, September 1, 1902.

37. "McClary's Wins The Championship," *London Free Press*, October 17, 1902.

38. "Gibson Goes To Toronto," *London Free Press*, October 14, 1902.

39. "Baseball," *Globe*, January 17, 1903.

40. "The Afternoon Game," *London Free Press*, July 2, 1903.

41. "Each Contestant Has an Inning of Grace," *Buffalo Courier*, August 27, 1903.

42. "Rain Throughout Circuit; Standing Unchanged," *Buffalo Courier*, August 29, 1903.

43. "Great Stickwork of Birds Finally Prevails," *Buffalo Courier*, August 30, 1903.

44. *Ibid.*

45. *Ibid.*

46. *Ibid.*

47. Lawrence Ritter Interview.

48. "Nine Innings Without a Run Being Scored," *Buffalo Courier*, September 1, 1903.

49. *Ibid.*

50. "A Londoner For Buffalo," *London Free Press*, September 1, 1903.

51. Lawrence Ritter Interview.

52. "Snappy Game is Won by Jennings' Team," *Buffalo Courier*, September 3, 1903.

53. *Ibid.*

54. "Doing Fine Work," *London Free Press*, September 4, 1903.

55. "Bruce Was An Enigma To Downward Bisons," *Buffalo Courier*, September 5, 1903.

56. Lawrence Ritter Interview.

57. "Pitcher Hardy Did Good Twirling For The Bisons," *Buffalo Courier*, September 15, 1903.

58. "Milligan's Home Run Won Out In The Ninth," *Buffalo Courier*, September 16, 1903.

59. "Base Ball," *London Free Press*, September 19, 1903.

60. "Base Ball," *London Free Press*, August 21, 1903.

61. *Ibid.*

62. David Gibson's Family Tree, ancestry.com.

Chapter 3

1. "Stallings and his Buffalos," *Augusta Chronicle*, January 31, 1904.

2. "Untitled," *Democrat and Chronicle*, February 18, 1904.

3. "Buffalo Players to Train in the South," *Democrat and Chronicle*, March 14, 1904.

4. "Stallings' Bisons Have Begun Work," *Augusta Chronicle*, March 15, 1904.

5. *Ibid.*

6. "Kissinger Wore Green Over the Red," *Augusta Chronicle*, March 18, 1904.

7. Lawrence Ritter Interview.

8. "Augusta is Lauded by Stallings' Bisons," *Augusta Chronicle*, April 3, 1904.

9. "Buffaloes Left on Northern Trip," *Augusta Chronicle*, April 3, 1904.

10. "Shortal and Limrie Stars of the Game," *Buffalo Courier*, April 24, 1904.

11. "Buffalo Yarns About Many Subjects," *Augusta Chronicle*, March 28, 1904.

12. Lawrence Ritter Interview.

13. "The Team is Good," *Montreal Gazette*, May 10, 1904.

14. *Ibid.*

15. *Ibid.*

16. "Down the Line," *Montreal Gazette*, May 12, 1904.

17. Lawrence Ritter Interview.

18. "Best in the League," *Montreal Gazette*, May 16, 1904.

19. *Ibid.*

20. "Lost First Game," *Montreal Gazette*, May 18, 1904.

21. "Lost To Toronto," *Montreal Gazette*, June 8, 1904.

22. "Barrow's Reputation Travels Before Him," *Democrat and Chronicle*, August 9, 1904.

23. "Down the Line," *Montreal Gazette*, August 10, 1904.

24. "Barrow's Reputation Travels Before Him," *Democrat and Chronicle*, August 9, 1904.

25. "Down the Line," *Montreal Gazette*, August 15, 1904.

26. "Two Leagues At Baseball," *Ottawa Journal*, October 3, 1904.

27. "Condensed Jottings About The Magnates and Players," *Democrat and Chronicle*, December 25, 1904.

28. Daniel R. Levitt, *Ed Barrow: The Bulldog Who Built the Yankees' First Dynasty* (Lincoln: University of Nebraska Press, 2008), 68.

29. "Bannon Secured From Newark Club," *Montreal Gazette*, February 17, 1905.

30. "Lafayette Trims Montreal," *Philadelphia Inquirer*, April 9, 1905.

31. "Giants Shut Out Montrals, 8 to 0," *Evening World*, April 12, 1905.

32. "Kreitner Pleased," *Montreal Gazette*, April 14, 1905.

33. "Opening Tomorrow," *Montreal Gazette*, April 25, 1905.

34. "Bannon Is Pleased," *Montreal Gazette*, May 6, 1905.

35. "Baseball Opening," *Montreal Gazette*, May 8, 1905.

36. "Shut Out Bronchos," *Montreal Gazette*, May 12, 1905.

37. "Saturday's Dull Game," *Montreal Gazette*, May 15, 1905.

38. "Made A Hot Finish," *Montreal Gazette*, May 15, 1905.

39. *Ibid.*

40. "Leroy Invincible," *Montreal Gazette*, May 18, 1905.

41. "May Depose Bannon," *Montreal Gazette*, May 27, 1905.

42. "Diamond Gossip," *Montreal Gazette*, June 21, 1905.

43. Lawrence Ritter Interview.

44. "Baseball Notes," *Pittsburgh Press*, June 28, 1905.

45. "Diamond Gossip," *Montreal Gazette*, July 8, 1905.

46. "Diamond Gossip," *Montreal Gazette*, July 4, 1905.

47. *Ibid.*

48. "Took One of Three," *Montreal Gazette*, July 3, 1905.

49. "Beaten in Toronto," *Montreal Gazette*, July 6, 1905.

50. "New Catcher Signed," *Montreal Gazette*, July 8, 1905.

51. "Diamond Gossip," *Montreal Gazette*, August 9, 1905.

52. "Gibson Never Batted .300 In Professional Baseball But Caught Consistently," *Pittsburgh Daily Post*, December 13, 1919.

Chapter 4

1. "George Gibson," *Pittsburgh Daily Post*, July 1, 1905.

2. "St. Louis Team…," *Pittsburgh Press*, July 2, 1905.

3. Ring Lardner, *The Lost Journalism of Ring Lardner*, edited by Ron Rapoport (Lincoln: University of Nebraska Press, 2017), 544.

4. Lawrence Ritter Interview.

5. *Ibid.*

6. Lawrence S. Ritter, *The Glory of Their Times: The Story of the Early Days of Baseball Told by the Men Who Played It* (enlarged edition) (New York: Harper Perennial, 2010), 71.

7. "General Upheaval…," *Pittsburgh Press*, July 3, 1905.

8. "Ewings," *Cincinnati Enquirer*, July 3, 1905.

9. "General Upheaval…," *Pittsburgh Press*, July 3, 1905.

10. "Pirates Get An Easy Victory," *Pittsburgh Press*, July 12, 1905.

11. "Pirates Take Another Game," *Pittsburgh Press*, July 19, 1905.

12. *Ibid.*

13. "A Whitewash For Bostons," *Pittsburgh Press*, July 26, 1905.

14. "All Records Smashed…," *Pittsburgh Press*, August 6, 1905.

15. "Pirates Win By Forfeit," *Pittsburgh Daily Post*, August 6, 1905.

16. *Ibid.*

17. *Ibid.*

18. *Ibid.*

19. "Young Downs The Pirates," *Pittsburgh Press*, August 10, 1905.

20. "Umpires Watch Peitz…," *Pittsburgh Press*, August 15, 1905.

21. "Outhit and Outfielded," *Pittsburgh Press*, September 3, 1905.

22. "Reds Played Sleepily," *Pittsburgh Press*, September 10, 1905.

23. "Downpour Causes…," *Pittsburgh Daily Post*, October 3, 1905.

24. *Ibid.*

25. "Fittest Will Survive," *Buffalo Morning Express* (*Illustrated Buffalo Express*), December 23, 1905.

26. "Pittsburgh Club Is Not After Grady," *Pittsburgh Press*, November 12, 1905.

27. "Atlanta Signs Two More Men," *Atlanta Constitution*, March 2, 1905.

28. "Pruning Pirate Squad," *Pittsburgh Press*, December 10, 1905.

29. "Will Keep All Valuable Men," *Pittsburgh Press*, December 24, 1905.

30. *Ibid.*

31. "Home Run Drives," *Pittsburgh Press*, December 21, 1905.

32. "Other Gossip For Fans," *Courier-News*, November 18, 1905.

33. "Members of Pirate Crew," *Pittsburgh Daily Post*, February 4, 1906.

34. "Gossip of the World of Sports," *Scranton Truth*, January 11, 1906.

35. "Major League Spring Training in Hot Springs," CALS Encyclopedia of Arkansas, accessed April 2018, http://www.encyclopediaofarkansas.net/encyclopedia/entry-detail.aspx?entryID=6221.

36. "Pirate Plans Are Complete," *Pittsburgh Daily Post*, February 25, 1906.

37. "Peitz was Stabbed By Jealous Woman," *Pittsburgh Press*, March 5, 1906.

38. "James Archer," *Pittsburgh Press*, March 18, 1906.

39. "Harry Smith Leaves Camp," *Pittsburgh Press*, March 12, 1906.

40. "May Be Made Leach's Successor," *Pittsburgh Daily Post*, April 12, 1906.

41. "Pirates Win First…," *Pittsburgh Daily Post*, April 13, 1906.

42. "Pirates Win In Twelfth," *Pittsburgh Daily Post*, April 18, 1906.

43. "Terrific Slugging By The…," *Pittsburgh Press*, May 6, 1906.

44. "Phelps Will Soon Don The Pirate Uniform," *Pittsburgh Daily Post*, May 17, 1906.

45. "Pittsburgh Points," *Sporting Life*, June 9, 1906.

46. "Baseball Notes," *Pittsburgh Press*, July 18, 1906.

47. Daniel R. Levitt, *Ed Barrow: The Bulldog Who Built the Yankees' First Dynasty* (Lincoln: University of Nebraska Press, 2008), 71.

48. "Baseball Notes," *Pittsburgh Press*, July 18, 1906.

49. "Catcher Gibson Had an Off Year," *Brooklyn Daily Eagle*, June 5, 1910.

50. "Winter Plans Of Pirates," *Pittsburgh Daily Post*, October 18, 1906.

51. "Views of the Sporting Editor," *Pittsburgh Press*, October 28, 1906.

52. "Views of the Sporting Editor," *Pittsburgh Press*, November 18, 1906.

53. "Views of the Sporting Editor," *Pittsburgh Press*, December 16, 1906.

Chapter 5

1. "Financial Gain Is Not Thought Of," *Pittsburgh Press*, January 27, 1907.

2. "Plans of Pirates Are Now Complete," *Pittsburgh Daily Post*, February 3, 1907.

3. "Pirates Are Off For West Baden," *Pittsburgh Daily Post*, March 5, 1907.

4. "Pirates Steal March on Cubs at West Baden," *Pittsburgh Daily Post*, March 9, 1907.

5. "Sheehan To Play In Old Position," *Pittsburgh Daily Post*, March 26, 1907.

6. "Clarke Is Pleased With Pirate Team," *Pittsburgh Daily Post*, April 7, 1907.

7. *Ibid.*

8. "Kling Will Play For Local Club," *Chicago Tribune*, April 9, 1907.

9. "Clarke Is Pleased With Pirate Team," *Pittsburgh Daily Post*, April 7, 1907.

10. "Big Pennant Race Starts To-morrow," *Pittsburgh Daily Post*, April 10, 1907.

11. "Clarke to Run Club From Behind the Bench…," *Pittsburgh Daily Post*, April 13, 1907.

12. "Notes of the Game," *Pittsburgh Daily Post*, April 18, 1907.

13. "Cardinals Kindly Hand Victory Over," *Pittsburgh Daily Post*, May 3, 1907.

14. *Ibid.*

15. "Baseball Crowd Causes Forfeit," *New York Times*, April 12, 1907.

16. Peter Morris, *Catcher: How the Man Behind the Plate Became an American Folk Hero* (Chicago: Ivan R. Dee, 2009), 229.

17. "Sporting Notes," *Pittsburgh Daily Post*, May 14, 1907.

18. "Clarke Orders Armor," *Pittsburgh Daily Post*, May 22, 1907.

19. *Ibid.*

20. *Ibid.*

21. "Gibson Knows No Fear," *Pittsburgh Press*, June 21, 1907.

22. "Big Baseball Clubs Depart for Redland," *Pittsburgh Daily Post*, June 23, 1907.

23. "Wagner Fears Minors…," *Pittsburgh Daily Post*, September 10, 1907.

24. "Baseball Players In First Field Meet Hang Up Some Good Records," *Rock Island Argus and Daily Union*, September 12, 1907.

25. "No Hit Game For Maddox," *Pittsburgh Daily Post*, August 23, 1907.

26. "M'Closkey's Batsmen Mystified By Maddox," *Pittsburgh Daily Post*, September 14, 1907.

27. "Maddox Proves Bright Star...," *Pittsburgh Daily Post*, September 21, 1907.

28. *Ibid.*

29. "Pirate Barnstormers End Successful Trip," *Pittsburgh Daily Post*, October 23, 1907.

30. "The Value of a Good Catcher," *Pittsburgh Press*, October 27, 1907.

31. *Ibid.*

32. "The Pittsburgh Team," *Pittsburgh Press*, December 29, 1907.

33. "Pittsburgh Pirates Will Play Ball," *Pittsburgh Daily Post*, January 5, 1908.

34. *Ibid.*

35. "Why Leach Holds Out," *Pittsburgh Press*, February 9, 1908.

36. "Tips and Thoughts," *Syracuse Journal*, January 31, 1907.

37. "Baseball Gossip," *Montreal Gazette*, March 3, 1908.

38. "Baseball Notes," *Pittsburgh Press*, March 10, 1908.

39. "Gibson Not Heard From," *Pittsburgh Daily Post*, March 15, 1908.

40. "The Pirate Recruits," *Pittsburgh Press*, March 22, 1908.

41. "In Pittsburgh," *Sporting Life*, March 28, 1908.

42. *Ibid.*

43. "Wagner Goes West With Dreyfuss," *Pittsburgh Daily Post*, April 4, 1908.

44. "Rain Prevents Oklahoma City Game," *Pittsburgh Daily Post*, April 5, 1908.

45. "News In Brief About Pittsburgh Ball Team," *Pittsburgh Press*, April 12, 1908.

46. "Wagner Goes West With Dreyfuss," *Pittsburgh Daily Post*, April 4, 1908.

47. *Ibid.*

48. *Ibid.*

49. "Hans Wagner Dons Pirate Uniform," *Pittsburgh Daily Post*, April 8, 1908.

50. "Wagner and Smith Homeward Bound," *Pittsburgh Daily Post*, April 9, 1908.

51. "Pirates are Beaten at Kansas City," *Pittsburgh Daily Post*, April 12, 1908.

52. "Pittsburgh Conquers Cardinals," *Pittsburgh Daily Post*, April 26, 1908.

53. "Cubs Hand Goose-Egg To Pirates," *Pittsburgh Daily Post*, May 10, 1908.

54. *Ibid.*

55. "Brief Baseball Bits," *Pittsburgh Press*, July 5, 1908.

56. "Rowdy Tactics Used By Giants," *Pittsburgh Press*, July 28, 1908.

57. "A Better Grip...," *Pittsburgh Press*, July 28, 1908.

58. "Gibson On The Bench," *Pittsburgh Press*, August 1, 1908.

59. "Brief Baseball Bits," *Pittsburgh Press*, August 27, 1908.

60. "Gibson a Hard Worker," *Pittsburgh Press*, August 30, 1908.

61. "Buccaneers Kalsomine Quakers," *Pittsburgh Daily Post*, August 30, 1908.

62. "Vic Willis Likely to Face...," *Pittsburgh Press*, September 3, 1908.

63. "Cubs Protest Yesterday's Ball Game," *Pittsburgh Daily Post*, September 5, 1908.

64. *Ibid.*

65. Dennis Snelling, *Johnny Evers: A Baseball Life* (Jefferson, NC: McFarland, 2014), 71.

66. "Baseball Notes," *Pittsburgh Post-Gazette*, September 12, 1908.

67. "Gritty Boys Out for Flag," *Pittsburgh Press*, September 18, 1908.

68. "Story of the Second Game," *Pittsburgh Daily Post*, October 3, 1908.

69. Front-page headline, *Pittsburgh Post-Gazette*, October 4, 1908.

70. "Pirates Are Defeated By Chicago Champions," *Pittsburgh Daily Post*, October 5, 1908.

71. "Buccaneers are Welcomed Home," *Pittsburgh Daily Post*, October 6, 1908.

Chapter 6

1. "'Mooney' And His Phantom Rabbit," *London Free Press*, January 1909.

2. "Don't Be Without a Copy," *Pittsburgh Press*, April 30, 1910.

3. "Pirate Points," *Sporting News*, May 1, 1909.

4. "Phillippe Conquers Cardinals," *Pittsburgh Daily Post*, May 6, 1909.

5. "Baseball Notes," *Pittsburgh Press*, May 6, 1909.

6. "Great Finishes By Buccaneers...," *Pittsburgh Press*, June 9, 1909.

7. "Only Four Hits Off Vic Willis...," *Pittsburgh Daily Post*, June 24, 1909.

8. "Gibson Cuts Wide Swath," *Pittsburgh Daily Post*, June 29, 1909.

9. "Timely Sporting Comment," *Pittsburgh Post-Gazette*, June 29, 1909.

10. "Bugle Plays Good Night," *Pittsburgh Daily Post*, June 30, 1909.

11. "Bugle Sounds Good Bye Expo," *Pittsburgh Post-Gazette*, June 30, 1909.

12. "Forbes Field," ballparksofbaseball.com, accessed June 2018, http://www.ballparksofbaseball.com/forbes.

13. "How the Game Was Lost…," *Pittsburgh Daily Post*, July 1, 1909.

14. Brian J. Cudahy, *Rails Under the Mighty Hudson* (2nd ed.) (New York: Fordham University Press, 2002), 44, and Frank P. Donovan Jr., *Railroads of America* (Waukesha, WI: Kalmbach Publishing, 1949).

15. "New York Hopes To Beat Out Chicago," *Pittsburgh Press*, July 9, 1909.

16. "Buccaneers Meet Waterloo…," *Pittsburgh Daily Post*, July 9, 1909.

17. "Hard Task To Pick The Best Catcher," *Pittsburgh Press*, July 26, 1909.

18. "Diamond Dust," *Pittsburgh Press*, August 4, 1909.

19. "George Gibson Worth His Weight In Radium," *Pittsburgh Press*, August 4, 1909.

20. *Ibid.*

21. "Buccaneers Open In East," *Pittsburgh Daily Post*, August 21, 1909.

22. "Uphill Victories Are Most Pleasing," *Pittsburgh Press*, August 21, 1909.

23. "Clarke's Men Mean to Fight to Limit," *Pittsburgh Press*, August 26, 1909.

24. "World Record Within George Gibson's Grasp," *Pittsburgh Press*, September 5, 1909.

25. "Davis' Dope," *Pittsburgh Press*, September 8, 1909.

26. "Tribute To Gibson," *Pittsburgh Press*, September 11, 1909.

27. "Davis' Dope," *Pittsburgh Press*, October 11, 1909.

28. Lawrence Ritter Interview.

29. *Ibid.*

30. *Ibid.*

31. *Ibid.*

32. "Sports of the Day," *New York Times*, March 9, 1910.

33. Joseph Wancho, "Rube Marquard," a BioProject of the Society for American Baseball Research, accessed June 2018, https://sabr.org/bioproj/person/566fa007.

34. "Hero Worshipers Have Not…," *Pittsburgh Press*, December 5, 1909.

Chapter 7

1. "Pirates At Work At West Baden," *Pittsburgh Post-Gazette*, March 13, 1910.

2. "Pirate Battery Men Off For West Baden," *Pittsburgh Post-Gazette*, March 8, 1910.

3. "Pirates Are Concentrating…," *Pittsburgh Daily Post*, March 8, 1910.

4. "Pittsburgh Batteries Off for West Baden," *Pittsburgh Post-Gazette*, March 8, 1910.

5. "Advance Squad of Pirates…," *Pittsburgh Daily Post*, March 9, 1910.

6. "Several Pirates Missing…," *Pittsburgh Daily Post*, March 10, 1910.

7. "Cutting and Humphries…," *Pittsburgh Press*, March 11, 1910.

8. *Ibid.*

9. "Pirate Batteries Land in West Baden Mud," *Pittsburgh Post-Gazette*, March 10, 1910.

10. "Wilson Cannot Report…," *Pittsburgh Daily Post*, March 14, 1910.

11. "Cutting and Humphries…," *Pittsburgh Press*, March 11, 1910.

12. "Members of the Premier Battery…," *Pittsburgh Daily Post*, March 13, 1910.

13. "Pirates in Spring Quarters Doing Fine," *Pittsburgh Post-Gazette*, March 15, 1910.

14. "Clarke Rejoins Teammates…," *Pittsburgh Daily Post*, March 16, 1910.

15. "World Champion Scrubs…," *Pittsburgh Daily Post*, March 23, 1910.

16. "Gibson is World's Premier Catcher," *Pittsburgh Press*, April 30, 1910.

17. "Catcher George Gibson to Be Given Rest," *Pittsburgh Press*, June 3, 1910.

18. "Silly Story of Quarrel Is Vigorously Denied," *Pittsburgh Press*, June 5, 1910.

19. *Ibid.*

20. "How I Win," *Anaconda Standard*, July 10, 1910.

21. "Bits of Sports Gossip by Bal," *Pittsburgh Daily Post*, August 11, 1910.

22. "Other Managers Adopt Temperance Measure…," *Pittsburgh Press*, December 25, 1910.

23. "Gibson Looks Forward To Baseball Campaign," *Pittsburgh Daily Post*, December 22, 1910.

24. "First Squad of Pirates, Reach Headquarters," *Pittsburgh Press*, March 6, 1911.

25. "Gibson Fine Help To Young Heavers," *Pittsburgh Press*, March 22, 1911.

26. *Ibid.*

27. "Crisp Notes of the Game," *Pittsburgh Post-Gazette*, April 27, 1911.

28. "Some Scrappy Scenes," *Pittsburgh Daily Post*, April 29, 1911.

29. Larry Gerlach, "The History of Umpiring," Steve O's Baseball Umpire Resources, accessed November 2018, http://

www.stevetheump.com/umpiring_history.htm.

30. "Roast For Finneran," *Pittsburgh Post-Gazette*, May 12, 1911.

31. "Bal's Baseball Biffs," *Pittsburgh Daily Post*, May 13, 1911.

32. "Pirates Are Bristling With Indignation," *Pittsburgh Post-Gazette*, May 13, 1911.

33. "Simon Boosted By Backstop Gibson," *Pittsburgh Press*, May 15, 1911.

34. David W. Anderson, "Bonesetter Reese," a BioProject of the Society for American Baseball Research, accessed January 2018, https://sabr.org/bioproj/person/c067dc95.

35. "Gibson Steals a Base...," *Pittsburgh Post-Gazette*, June 14, 1911.

36. "Crisp Notes of the Game," *Pittsburgh Post-Gazette*, July 11, 1911.

37. "Honors Divided in Double Bill," *Pittsburgh Daily Post*, August 20, 1911.

38. "Bal's Baseball Biffs," *Pittsburgh Daily Post*, August 21, 1911.

39. "O'Toole is Given Workout by Gibson," *Pittsburgh Press*, August 18, 1911.

40. "By John Kling," *Pittsburgh Press*, August 31, 1911.

Chapter 8

1. "Baseball Gossip," *Pittsburgh Press*, January 3, 1912.

2. "Gibson Stars at Great Game of Canadians," *Pittsburgh Post-Gazette*, February 18, 1912.

3. "Pirate Points," *Sporting Life*, March 2, 1912.

4. "Gibson Conducts Baseball School," *Pittsburgh Press*, March 27, 1912.

5. "Regulars Beat the Yannigans," *Pittsburgh Daily Post*, March 17, 1912.

6. Lawrence Ritter Interview.

7. "On and Off the Field," *Pittsburgh Post-Gazette*, May 27, 1912.

8. Lawrence Ritter Interview.

9. *Ibid.*

10. "George Gibson is Owner of Big Farm," *Pittsburgh Press*, November 4, 1912.

11. Lawrence Ritter Interview.

12. *Ibid.*

13. "Notes From Pirate Camp," *Pittsburgh Post-Gazette*, March 9, 1913.

14. "Breezy Notes From Corsairs Camp...," *Pittsburgh Daily Post*, March 23, 1913.

15. "Baseball From Winter Angle," *Pittsburgh Post-Gazette*, January 14, 1913.

16. "Pirates Tackle Superbas Today," *Pittsburgh Post-Gazette*, May 20, 1913.

17. "Costly Plaster For George Gibson," *Pittsburgh Press*, June 20, 1913.

18. "If They Use Pound It Will Be Costly," *Syracuse Journal*, July 10, 1913.

19. "Will Locke," *Pittsburgh Press*, August 15, 1913.

20. "By George Gibson," *Pittsburgh Press*, August 15, 1913.

21. "Pirates Have Run-in with...," *Pittsburgh Daily Post*, August 25, 1913.

22. "Pirate-Nap Series Dates Are Named," *Pittsburgh Post-Gazette*, September 30, 1913.

23. "Ralph Davis Column," *Pittsburgh Press*, January 22, 1914.

24. "Exhibition Game Booked...," *Pittsburgh Daily Post*, February 15, 1914.

25. "Cop Pinches Fan...," *Pittsburgh Daily Post*, May 16, 1914.

26. "Double-Header Jottings," *Pittsburgh Press*, July 19, 1914.

27. "More New Players Report...," *Pittsburgh Press*, September 10, 1914.

28. "On and Off The Field," *Pittsburgh Post-Gazette*, September 20, 1914.

29. "O'Toole Marked Down...," *Pittsburgh Post-Gazette*, September 2, 1914.

30. "Ralph Davis Column," *Pittsburgh Press*, September 5, 1914.

31. "Ax to Fall Before Training Begins," *Pittsburgh Press*, December 11, 1914.

32. "Retirement of Pirate Leader...," *Pittsburgh Press*, September 8, 1915.

33. "1916 Manager is Matter of Doubt," *Pittsburgh Press*, September 8, 1915.

34. "Successor Not Named," *Pittsburgh Daily Post*, September 9, 1915.

35. "On and Off The Field," *Pittsburgh Post-Gazette*, September 21, 1915.

36. Lawrence Ritter Interview.

37. *Ibid.*

38. *Ibid.*

39. "First Off-Season Note From Gibson," *Pittsburgh Press*, November 9, 1915.

Chapter 9

1. James Elfers, "Nixey Callahan," a BioProject of the Society for American Baseball Research, accessed December 2017, https://sabr.org/bioproj/person/ee2e44fa.

2. "Callahan Will Pilot Corsairs," *Pittsburgh Press*, December 17, 1915.

3. *Ibid.*

4. "Pirates' New Leader To Be Here

Monday," *Pittsburgh Press*, December 19, 1915.

5. "Sinclair's Next Move is Awaited," *Pittsburgh Press*, January 4, 1916.

6. "Great Bare-hand Stop…," *Pittsburgh Post-Gazette*, April 30, 1916.

7. "Al Mamaux Hammered By M'Grawmen, 6–2," *Pittsburgh Post-Gazette*, August 3, 1916.

8. "Babe Adams is Let Out," *Pittsburgh Press*, August 3, 1916.

9. "Babe Adams Released By The Pirates," *Pittsburgh Post-Gazette*, August 4, 1916.

10. "Goes To New York Giants," *Pittsburgh Press*, August 15, 1916.

11. Lawrence Ritter Interview.

12. *Ibid.*

13. *Ibid.*

14. "Gibson Returns Home…," *Pittsburgh Daily Post*, August 21, 1916.

15. "Misses Battery Mate," *Pittsburgh Daily Post*, August 17, 1916.

16. "Bouquets Handed To Hack Gibson," *Pittsburgh Daily Post*, August 17, 1916.

17. Lawrence Ritter Interview.

18. *Ibid.*

19. Don Jensen, "John McGraw," a Bio-Project of the Society for American Baseball Research, accessed December 2017, https://sabr.org/bioproj/person/fef5035f.

20. Lawrence Ritter Interview.

21. *Ibid.*

22. *Ibid.*

23. *Ibid.*

24. *Ibid.*

25. *Ibid.*

26. "Herzog Only Giant Missing At Marlin," *New York Sun*, March 5, 1917.

27. "He's Showing up Youth," *Baltimore Sun*, March 21, 1917.

28. "McGraw Allowed His Men to Work Slower," *Houston Post*, March 20, 1917.

29. "Gibson Restored To Good Standing," *Pittsburgh Daily Post*, March 27, 1917.

30. "Cobb Sore At Way He Was Used," *Detroit Free Press*, April 1, 1917.

31. *Ibid.*

32. Lawrence Ritter Interview.

33. *Ibid.*

34. "Forbes Field Fannings," *Pittsburgh Daily Post*, June 14, 1917.

35. Lawrence Ritter Interview.

36. *Ibid.*

37. "Carelessness Costs Giants a Ball Game," *New York Tribune*, August 19, 1917.

38. Lawrence Ritter Interview.

39. *Ibid.*

40. "Few Players Last Ten Years In Major Leagues," *Reading Times*, January 9, 1918.

41. "New Man For The Colonels," *Courier-Journal*, March 10, 1918.

42. "Highlights and Shadows…," *New York Herald*, March 14, 1918.

43. "N.Y. Giants Work Out; Kauff Is Examined," *Houston Post*, March 17, 1918.

44. "Manager John McGraw to Escort 'Vets' of Giants to Hot Springs," *Evening World*, February 13, 1918.

45. "Two Squads Kept Busy," *New York Herald*, March 17, 1918.

46. "Giants Will Play Indians," *Courier-Journal*, November 22, 1918.

47. "Phils Fall Before Assault of Giants," *New York Times*, May 1, 1918.

48. "Baseball Season Will Close Sept. 1," *New York Times*, August 3, 1918.

49. "Praise For Gibby," *Pittsburgh Post-Gazette*, August 21, 1918.

Chapter 10

1. Kevin Plummer, "Historicist: The Unknown Impresario," accessed June 2017, https://torontoist.com/2013/09/historicist-the-unknown-impresario/.

2. Lawrence Ritter Interview.

3. *Ibid.*

4. "Toronto Supporters Elated…," *London Free Press*, January 22, 1919.

5. "Job For George Gibson," *Pittsburgh Daily Post*, January 22, 1919.

6. "Gibson Pleased," *Globe and Mail*, January 24, 1919.

7. "Gibson Has Charge Of Icemaking Job," *Globe and Mail*, January 24, 1919.

8. "Gibson Signs With Toronto," *Globe and Mail*, January 30, 1919.

9. "Leaf Pilot's Daughter is Winning Basketeer," *Globe and Mail*, February 4, 1919.

10. "Gibson Helps To Retain…," *Globe and Mail*, March 15, 1919.

11. Lawrence Ritter Interview.

12. "Indoor Work For Pitchers," *Globe and Mail*, April 17, 1919.

13. "First Glimpse Of High Speed," *Globe and Mail*, April 19, 1919.

14. "Toronto Gets Giant Pitcher," *Globe and Mail*, April 12, 1919.

15. "No Wonder Gibson Smiles," *Globe and Mail*, May 8, 1919.

16. "Karpe's Comment On Sport Topics," *Buffalo Evening News*, May 27, 1919.

17. "Bisons Lose Sixteen Inning Game...," *Buffalo Enquirer*, May 27, 1919.

18. "Leafs Angling For More Men," *Globe and Mail*, July 30, 1919.

19. "Wet Grounds Stops Leafs," *Globe and Mail*, August 22, 1919.

20. Lawrence Ritter Interview.

21. *Ibid.*

22. *Ibid.*

23. "Exhibition Games Are Not As Enticing...," *Hamilton Spectator*, September 13, 1919.

24. Lawrence Ritter Interview.

25. *Ibid.*

26. *Ibid.*

27. *Ibid.*

28. "Scramble For Job As Corsair Pilot...," *Pittsburgh Daily Post*, November 21, 1919.

29. "How George Gibson Keeps Self Posted...," *Pittsburgh Daily Post*, December 1, 1919.

30. "George Gibson Stands Well...," *Pittsburgh Daily Post*, December 6, 1919.

31. Lawrence Ritter Interview.

32. "Former Backstop Accepts Terms," *Pittsburgh Press*, December 8, 1919.

33. "Club Owner Makes Spa Reservations...," *Pittsburgh Daily Post*, December 12, 1919.

34. *Ibid.*

35. "New Manager Well Trained," *Pittsburgh Post*, December 14, 1919.

36. "New Pirate Pilot May Be Announced...," *Pittsburgh Daily Post*, December 7, 1919.

Chapter 11

1. "Corsair Helmsman Is Well Satisfied...," *Pittsburgh Daily Post*, February 22, 1920.

2. "Forty-Sixth Anniversary...," *Pittsburgh Post-Gazette*, February 29, 1920.

3. "Gibson's Proteges Wade Into Water...," *Pittsburgh Daily Post*, March 5, 1920.

4. *Ibid.*

5. "Hope For Schmidt," *Pittsburgh Daily Post*, March 11, 1920.

6. "Gibson's Men Snap Into First Days Workout," *Pittsburgh Post-Gazette*, March 9, 1920.

7. "Pirates Lectured By Klem...," *Pittsburgh Daily Post*, March 16, 1920.

8. "Hope For Schmidt," *Pittsburgh Daily Post*, March 11, 1920.

9. "Gibby And Barney Split," *Pittsburgh Daily Post*, April 3, 1920.

10. "Schmidt Given 8,000...," *Pittsburgh Press*, April 14, 1920.

11. "Gibby Confident On Eve Of Debut...," *Pittsburgh Post-Gazette*, April 14, 1920.

12. "Ralph Davis Column," *Pittsburgh Press*, April 24, 1920.

13. "Thousands Witness Opening Battle," *Pittsburgh Press*, April 23, 1920.

14. "Ralph Davis Column," *Pittsburgh Press*, April 24, 1920.

15. "Gibby Sure Club Will Hit Stride," *Pittsburgh Press*, June 7, 1920.

16. "Pirates Still Have Chance...," *Pittsburgh Post-Gazette*, July 12, 1920.

17. "Ralph Davis Column," *Pittsburgh Press*, August 10, 1920.

18. *Ibid.*

19. Lawrence Ritter Interview.

20. *Ibid.*

21. *Ibid.*

22. "Gibson Signs Up To Lead Pirates...," *Pittsburgh Daily Post*, September 8, 1920.

23. "Anticipated Break Dwindles...," *Pittsburgh Daily Post*, January 11, 1921.

24. *Ibid.*

25. "Maranville Trade Confab...," *Pittsburgh Post-Gazette*, January 12, 1921.

26. "Babe Adams To Pitch...," *Pittsburgh Post-Gazette*, April 13, 1921.

27. "Giants Must Beat Pirates...," *Pittsburgh Daily Post*, May 25, 1921.

28. *Ibid.*

29. "Ralph Davis Column," *Pittsburgh Press*, June 7, 1921.

30. "Ralph Davis Column," *Pittsburgh Press*, June 9, 1921.

31. "Gibson Praises Pirates," *Pittsburgh Press*, July 9, 1921.

32. *Ibid.*

33. "Gibson Full Of Ginger," *Pittsburgh Press*, August 31, 1921.

34. "I Do Not Claim To Have A Sabbath...," *Pittsburgh Daily Post*, September 20, 1921.

35. *Ibid.*

36. "Thorough Shakeup In Corsair Ranks...," *Pittsburgh Daily Post*, October 2, 1921.

37. "Corsairs Get Hard Workout," *Pittsburgh Press*, March 5, 1922.

38. Lawrence Ritter Interview.

39. *Ibid.*

40. *Ibid.*

41. *Ibid.*

42. "Gibson Quits As Pirates Chief," *Pittsburgh Post-Gazette*, July 1, 1922.
43. "Ralph Davis Column," *Pittsburgh Press*, July 24, 1922.
44. *Ibid.*
45. "Gibson's Passing," *Pittsburgh Press*, July 7, 1922.
46. "Ralph Davis Column," *Pittsburgh Press*, July 24, 1922.

Chapter 12

1. "Ed Onslow May Join The Birds," *Reading Times*, August 4, 1922.
2. "Geo. Gibson May Get Back Into Game," *Pittsburgh Daily Post*, November 8, 1922.
3. "'Mooney' Gibson Not for Reading," *Toronto Daily Star*, November 17, 1922.
4. "'Gibby' At Meeting," *Pittsburgh Daily Post*, December 13, 1922.
5. "Spencer Abbot is Reading's New Manager...," *Reading Times*, November 23, 1922.
6. "Five Chiefs In Four Years At Reading," *Press and Sun-Bulletin*, December 13, 1922.
7. "Eat It Up!," *Courier-News*, December 13, 1922.
8. Lawrence Ritter Interview.
9. *Ibid.*
10. "Sport Salad," *Evening Leader*, January 9, 1923.
11. "Griffith Will Rebuild Ball Club...," *Washington Times*, December 15, 1922.
12. Henry W. Thomas, *Walter Johnson: Baseball's Big Train* (Lincoln: University of Nebraska Press, 1998), 182.
13. "Remainder Of Team Now Florida-Bound," *Washington Post*, March 8, 1923.
14. Lawrence Ritter Interview.
15. *Ibid.*
16. Henry W. Thomas, *Walter Johnson: Baseball's Big Train* (Lincoln: University of Nebraska Press, 1998), 184.
17. "Washington Wins Game; Nick Altrock Is Funny," *London Free Press*, May 24, 1923.
18. Lawrence Ritter Interview.
19. Henry W. Thomas, *Walter Johnson: Baseball's Big Train* (Lincoln: University of Nebraska Press, 1998), 184.
20. Lawrence Ritter Interview.
21. "Send Hubbell To Showers In Third," *Washington Post*, August 1, 1923.
22. Lawrence Ritter Interview.
23. "George Gibson Picked As Handy Man...," *Chicago Tribune*, January 13, 1925.
24. "Warwick Says He Is Now...," *Shreveport Times*, April 4, 1926.
25. Lawrence Ritter Interview.
26. "Coach Gibson May Lead Chicago Cubs," *Montreal Gazette*, September 3, 1925.
27. "Gehringer Leads Toronto To Eleven-Inning Victory," *Globe*, September 3, 1925.
28. "Coach Gibson To Be Cubs Scout," *Chicago Tribune*, December 7, 1925.
29. "Cubs win Chicago City...," *Alton Evening Telegraph*, October 14, 1925.
30. "Gibson To Be New Manager Of Bucs...," *Pittsburgh Press*, September 22, 1931.
31. Lawrence Ritter Interview.
32. "Gibson Named New Buc Pilot," *Pittsburgh Press*, November 30, 1931.
33. "Baseball Gossip," *Pittsburgh Post-Gazette*, December 3, 1931.
34. "Baseball Leaders, Friends Pay Tribute To Dreyfuss," *Pittsburgh Post-Gazette*, February 6, 1932.
35. Sam Bernstein, "Barney Dreyfuss," a BioProject of the Society for American Baseball Research, accessed June 2018, https://sabr.org/bioproj/person/29ceb9e0.
36. Lawrence Ritter Interview.
37. "Details Of Camp...," *Pittsburgh Post-Gazette*, January 28, 1932.
38. "Team Work, Hitting, Baserunning...," *Pittsburgh Press*, March 24, 1932.
39. "Swetonic Shuts Out Cards...," *Pittsburgh Post-Gazette*, April 21, 1932.
40. "Baseball Gossip," *Pittsburgh Post-Gazette*, October 13, 1932.
41. "Pirate Manager Given One-Year Contract...," *Pittsburgh Post-Gazette*, October 20, 1932.
42. Lawrence Ritter Interview.
43. "National League Has Hard Hitters...," *Pittsburgh Press*, February 5, 1933.
44. "The Village Smithy," *Pittsburgh Press*, February 12, 1933.
45. "Honus Wagner Happy...," *Pittsburgh Press*, February 3, 1933.
46. "Gibson Gets Fan Letter From India," *Pittsburgh Post-Gazette*, March 21, 1933.
47. "Three Pilots Lose Jobs...," *Pittsburgh Press*, July 25, 1933.
48. "Won't Stand For That Kind Of Stuff...," *Pittsburgh Post-Gazette*, August 3, 1933.
49. "He Accepts Terms For '34...," *Pittsburgh Press*, October 21, 1933.

50. "The Village Smithy," *Pittsburgh Press,* January 25, 1934.

51. "Buc Players...," *Pittsburgh Post-Gazette,* November 28, 1933.

52. "Lively Ball Seen As Boon...," *Pittsburgh Press,* December 28, 1933.

53. "Ace Southpaw...," *Pittsburgh Press,* March 3, 1934.

54. Lawrence Ritter Interview.

55. "'Pie' Assumes New Duties...," *Pittsburgh Press,* June 19, 1934.

56. Lawrence Ritter Interview.

Chapter 13

1. Friends of Labatt Park.com/ Timeline,1937: "Changing Face."

2. "The Flood of April 1937," Upper Thames River Conservation Authority website, accessed March 2019, http://thamesriver.on.ca/water-management/flooding-on-the-thames-river/1937-flood/.

3. "Ex-Major League Pilot To Be Guest Tonight," *London Free Press,* July 9, 1955.

4. "Buc Farm May Be Transferred," *Pittsburgh Post-Gazette,* January 18, 1940.

5. "Pirates Will Transfer Farm," *Pittsburgh Post-Gazette,* February 1, 1940.

6. "Frisch Here, Goes Over Official Plans For Trip With Buc Officials," *Pittsburgh Post-Gazette,* February 17, 1940.

7. "Bucs Drop London, Move To Hornell," *Pittsburgh Press,* November 19, 1941.

8. "The Blitz—World War II," *Encyclopedia Britannica,* accessed March 2019, https://www.britannica.com/event/the-Blitz.

9. "Honus And Mooney...," *London Free Press,* August 5, 1943.

10. "Over 300 At Thamesville Ball School," *London Free Press,* August 23, 1947.

11. "The Essence of Obligation," *Forbes Health System Review* 8, no. 2 (June 1983).

12. "The Scoreboard," *Pittsburgh Press,* September 5, 1953.

13. Jeffery Reed, *EBBA: 40 Years of Baseball* (London: Jeffery Reed Reporting, 1994).

14. "Eager Beaver Parade...," *London Free Press,* June 4, 1955.

15. "Durable Catcher," *Wilkes-Barre Record,* July 4, 1955.

16. Lawrence Ritter Interview.

17. "Run Over By Dray...," *Republican and Herald* (Pottsville), December 27, 1943.

18. John J. Evers and Hugh S. Fullerton, *Touching Second* (Jefferson, NC: McFarland, 2005), 73.

19. "Letter from George Gibson to Ford Frick, 1936 April 17," National Baseball Hall of Fame website, accessed March 2019, https://collection.baseballhall.org/PASTIME/letter-george-gibson-ford-frick-1936-april-17-0.

20. Bucky Smith, telephone conversation with Richard Armstrong, January 23, 2019.

21. Julie Anne Baskette, "Re: Thank You," email message to Richard Armstrong, November 5, 2018.

22. Bill James, "The Top Ten Catchers of Whenever," Bill James Online, accessed March 2019, https://www.billjamesonline.com/the_top_ten_catchers_of_whenever/.

23. "Local Lines," *Pittsburgh Press,* August 5, 1982.

24. "George 'Mooney' Gibson, 1880–1967 (plaque no. 33)," London Public Library website, accessed March 2019, http://www.londonpubliclibrary.ca/research/local-history/historic-sites-committee/george-mooney-gibson-1880-1967-plaque-no-33.

25. "My Greatest Thrill," *Pittsburgh Post-Gazette,* February 22, 1919.

Epilogue

1. "Homer Made Decision Tough For Robinson," *San Diego Union-Tribune,* July 15, 2014.

Bibliography

Articles

"Baseball At the Forks" (London Baseball Pamphlet). Museum London.
Bronson, Les. "London Baseball." London-Middlesex Historical Society, Feb. 15, 1972.
"The Essence of Obligation." *Forbes Health System Review* 8, no. 2 (June 1983).
Macht, Norman L. "When Texas Was Baseball's Spring Kingdom." *Texas Co-op Power,* March 2008.
Plummer, Kevin. "Historicist: The Unknown Impresario." *Torontoist,* Sept. 21, 2013.
Smith, Anne. "One of a Kind." *London CityLine Magazine,* Aug./Sept. 2003.
Thomson, Andrew. "John McClary, Biography." Biographi.ca.

Books

Armstrong, Frederick H. *The Forest City: An Illustrated History of London, Canada.* Burlington, ON: Windsor Publications, 1986.
Bogen, Gil. *Johnny Kling: A Baseball Biography.* Jefferson, NC: McFarland, 2006.
Brown, William. *Baseball's Fabulous Montreal Royals.* Montreal, QC: Robert Davies Publishing, 1996.
Cauz, Luis. *Baseball's Back in Town: From the Don to the Blue Jays, A History of Baseball in Toronto.* Toronto: CMC, 1977.
Cudahy, Brian J. *Rails Under the Mighty Hudson* (2nd ed.). New York: Fordham University Press, 2002.
Culbert, Terry. *Terry Culbert's Lucan, Home of the Donnellys.* Renfrew, ON: General Store Publishing House, 2005.
Evers, John J., and Fullerton, Hugh S. *Touching* Second. Jefferson, NC: McFarland, 2005.
Finoli, David, and Ranier, Bill. *The Pittsburgh Pirates Encyclopedia: Second Edition.* New York: Sports Publishing, 2015.
Finoli, David, and Ranier, Bill. *When Cobb Met Wagner: The Seven-Game World Series of 1909.* Jefferson, NC: McFarland, 2011.
Forr, James, and Proctor, David. *Pie Taynor: A Baseball Biography.* Jefferson, NC: McFarland, 2010.
Hittner, Arthur D. *Honus Wagner: The Life of Baseball's "Flying Dutchman."* Jefferson, NC: McFarland, 1996.
Lardner, Ring. *The Lost Journalism of Ring Lardner.* Edited by Ron Rapoport. Lincoln: University of Nebraska Press, 2017.
Leehrsen, Charles. *Ty Cobb: A Terrible Beauty.* New York: Simon & Schuster, 2015.

Levitt, Daniel R. *Ed Barrow: The Bulldog Who Built the Yankees' First Dynasty*. Lincoln: University of Nebraska Press, 2008.

Lieb, Fred. *The Pittsburgh Pirates*. New York: GP Putnam & Sons, 1948.

Martin, Brian. *The Tecumsehs of the International Association, Canada's First Major League Baseball Champions*. Jefferson, NC: Mcfarland, 2015.

Morris, Peter. *Catcher: How the Man Behind the Plate Became an American Folk Hero*. Chicago: Ivan R. Dee, 2009.

Murphy, Cait. *Crazy '08: How a Cast of Cranks, Rogues, Boneheads, and Magnates Created the Greatest Year in Baseball History*. New York: HarperCollins, 2008.

Okkonen, Marc. *Baseball Uniforms of the 20th Century*. New York: Sterling Publishing, 1991.

Reed, Jeffery. *EBBA: 40 Years of Baseball*. London: Jeffery Reed Reporting, 1994.

Ritter, Lawrence S. *The Glory of Their Times: The Story of the Early Days of Baseball Told by the Men Who Played It* (enlarged edition). New York: Harper Perennial, 2010.

Shearon, Jim. *Canada's Baseball Legends: True Stories, Records, and Photos of Canadian-born Players in Baseball's Major Leagues Since 1879*. Kanata, ON: Malin Head Press, 1994.

Shearon, Jim. *Over the Fence is Out! The Larry Walker Story and More of Canada's Baseball Legends*. Kanata, ON: Malin Head Press, 2009.

Smiles, Jack. *"EE-YAH": The Life and Times of Hughie Jennings, Baseball Hall of Famer*. Jefferson, NC: McFarland, 2005.

Snelling, Dennis. *Johnny Evers: A Baseball Life*. Jefferson, NC: McFarland, 2014.

Spink, Alfred H. *The National Game, Second Edition* (Writing Baseball Series Edition). Carbondale: Southern Illinois University Press, 2010.

Stinson, Mitchell Conrad. *Deacon Bill McKechnie: A Baseball Biography*. Jefferson, NC: McFarland, 2012.

Thomas, Henry W. *Walter Johnson: Baseball's Big Train*. Lincoln: University of Nebraska Press, 1998.

Waldo, Ronald T. *Fred Clarke: A Biography of the Baseball Hall of Fame Player-Manager*. Jefferson, NC: McFarland, 2011.

Young, William A. *John Tortes "Chief" Meyers: A Baseball Biography*. Jefferson, NC: McFarland, 2012.

Canadian Census

1881 Canadian Census   1901 Canadian Census
1891 Canadian Census   1911 Canadian Census

Interviews

Ritter, Lawrence S. Interview Recording. August 20, 1963, and January 29, 1965. George Gibson Players File. National Baseball Hall of Fame Library. Cooperstown, New York.

Newspapers

Alton Evening Telegraph   *Bismarck Tribune*
Anaconda Standard   *Brooklyn Daily Eagle*
Atlanta Constitution   *Buffalo Courier*
Augusta Chronicle   *Buffalo Enquirer*
Baltimore Sun   *Buffalo Evening News*

Buffalo Morning Express (Illustrated Buffalo
    Express)
Buffalo Times
Chicago Tribune
Cincinnati Enquirer
Cleveland Plain Dealer
Courier-Journal
Courier-News
Democrat and Chronicle (Rochester)
Detroit Free Press
Evening Chronicle
Evening Leader
Globe
Globe and Mail
Hamilton Spectator
Harrisburg Daily Independent
Houston Post
Ithaca Daily News
Kingston Daily Freeman
London Advertiser
London Free Press
Montreal Gazette
Montrose Democrat
New York Evening Sun
New York Herald
New York Sun
New York Times
New York Tribune
New York World
Ottawa Journal
Philadelphia Enquirer
Pittsburgh Daily Post
Pittsburgh Post-Gazette
Pittsburgh Press
Post Standard
Press & Sun-Bulletin
Reading Times
Republican Herald (Pottsville)
Rock Island Argus and Daily Union
San Diego Union-Tribune
Scranton Truth
Shreveport Times
Sporting Life
Sporting News
Sun New York
Syracuse Herald
Syracuse Journal
Toronto Daily Star
Toronto Star
Vancouver Daily World
Washington Post
Washington Times
Wilkes-Barre Record
York Daily

Websites

american-rails.com
ancestry.com
ballparksofbaseball.com
baseball-almanac.com
baseball-reference.com
baseballhall.org
billjamesonline.com
biographi.ca
britannica.com
encyclopediaofarkansas.net
gnb.ca
labattpark.wordpress.com

londonpubliclibrary.ca
mlb.com
newspapers.com
ontariotown.blogspot.ca
sabr.org
sothebys.com
stevetheump.com
thamesriver.on.ca
thebaseballgauge.com
torontohistory.org
torontoist.com
wikipedia.org

Index